Utopian Nights

Newell and Sorrell

Utopian Nights

A unique collection of inspirational talks at Newell and Sorrell

Introduced by **John Sorrell**

Edited by Katherine Sorrell

Acknowledgements
We are enormously grateful to our speakers, for their inspirational talks and for their vital assistance with the text and illustrations in this book; also to the numerous individuals and organisations who have kindly given us their help along the way. Without them all, this book would not have been possible. We would also like to give a very special thanks to *Caroline Wilson*, and to everyone at Newell and Sorrell who has been involved in our Utopian Nights evenings and in producing this book.

Printed by BAS Printers Ltd
Text set in Franklin Gothin (Adobe) and Sabon (Adobe)
Designed by Newell and Sorrell

Newell and Sorrell UK
4 Utopia Village, Chalcot Road, London NW1 8LH, United Kingdom
Telephone +44 (0)171 722 1113
Facsimile +44 (0)171 722 0259
ISDN +44 (0)171 722 6988
E mail n+s-utop@online.rednet.co.uk

Newell and Sorrell Nederland
MGR Van de Weteringstraat 132E, 3581, En Utrecht, Nederland
Telefoon +31 (0)30 2302 802
Facsimile +31 (0)30 2367 501
ISDN +31 (0)30 300 2864

CONTENTS

INTRODUCTION **John Sorrell**

"A pint? Have you gone raving mad? I don't mind giving a reasonable amount, but a pint... why, that's very nearly an armful. I'm sorry, I'm not walking around with an empty arm for anybody."

Do you remember Tony Hancock's "Blood Donor" sketch? I've always loved that sketch, partly because it makes me laugh so much and partly because the idea of empty arms sums up the way I feel when I've been working flat out. I know other people often feel drained in the same way. At Newell and Sorrell we spend most of our lives solving problems, realising new opportunities and exploring inspirational ideas. It can be all too easy to find yourself with at least one "empty arm". As Frances Newell says, there's no output without input. It's impossible to be creative and innovative, to work effectively, to have great ideas – to run any successful business – without inspiration from other sources. And you can never get too much inspiration; it's what makes the difference between the ordinary and the extraordinary.

So, we created our UTOPIAN NIGHTS seminar programme to provide a new kind of input – *a transfusion of inspiration.*

The programme has been running for six years now and this book is a collection of nearly all the talks given by our speakers over that time.

As you will see, it is an eclectic mix, open-minded, forward-looking, funny, exciting and, often, surprising. We have just two rules. First, our speakers have to be passionate about their subject. Second, they can talk about anything they like... except design. I have to admit that the second rule has been broken a couple of times, but the first one, never.

There is not meant to be any central theme to the talks but, on reflection, some have emerged – the environment, the arts, exploration, sport – all linked by the common idea of achievement. Mountaineering has been another theme – both literally and metaphorically. "All my life is Everest," declared Brian Blessed, whose vivid talks took us from his childhood dreams of following in the footsteps of Mallory and Irvine to the reality of his gruelling ascents of the world's highest mountain. And all our speakers, in their own ways, brilliantly described how they had reached the summits of their own Everests – and encouraged us to head for ours.

At every seminar we are joined by around two hundred guests, some of whom have been coming ever since we started the programme. And, as one of them once said to me: "These seminars are a great excuse for a party every other month." Well, yes, they are. Each seminar is an event in its own right, with its own atmosphere, and there is always a party mood.

The evenings begin when people gather in our café for food and drinks which our hospitality team brilliantly themes to the evening's subject. There is usually an exhibition in our gallery – Robert Swan's Antarctic tents and equipment, John Stephenson's Turtle suits, the amazing pictures by Boyle Family. After the talk we end with more food, drink and conversation in our café. This can go on into the small hours for those who have the energy. Inspiration comes from the speakers but also from the evening itself.

So far, our seminars have covered subjects as diverse as fashion and football, sales and sport and animatronics and the environment. What's next?

As Brian Blessed said: "The possibilities are endless." And, as Chris Woodhams told us, it's all very well knowing things, knowing that you don't know other things, and even forgetting that you ever knew yet more things – the great exploration in life is finding out *what you don't know you don't know.*

I have always been hungry for new knowledge and new insights. I am enormously grateful when someone inspires me with an idea or an act of courage, or opens my mind to new possibilities. That's happened so many times during our seminar programme. When I introduce our speakers at Utopia Village I always say that our aim is to inform, entertain and, especially, to *inspire* our guests. This book is designed to do the same thing for its readers. I hope you find some inspiration in its pages.

John Sorrell January 1996

PAUL SMITH dropped out of school at 15 and had no formal training in fashion, but is now one of Britain's most successful designers and entrepreneurs. He began selling clothes two days a week from a back street in Nottingham; today, he sells to stores in 34 countries and trades from his own distinctive shops in London, Nottingham, New York, Paris, Hong Kong, Singapore, Bangkok, Korea, Taiwan – and 147 outlets in Japan. His label is now famous throughout the world and he is a passionate advocate of the contribution design can make to any business. In 1992 Paul was made a Royal Designer for Industry, and two years later he was awarded the CBE. In 1995 Paul Smith Ltd won the Queen's Award for Export.

We had a great evening with Paul in June 1989, when he told us about his life and his business and gave us an insight into why he is so successful. Paul showed dozens of slides to illustrate his witty and honest talk and, at the end, he surprised us all with his unique approach to question-and-answer: he said that, in his experience, you need an incentive to get the questions going. So, from a large, black bag he produced a collection of Paul Smith products which he offered as prizes for questions. We have never seen so many hands shoot up.

When I was very young I wanted to be a racing cyclist,

I didn't want to be a designer at all. I left school at 15 and got a job as a gofer in a clothing warehouse in Nottingham. I wasn't bothered about work – all I wanted to do was to wear the yellow jersey in the Tour de France. One day, though, a car and I had a bit of a meeting and I ended up in hospital for six months. That was when I realised that there was more to life than riding a bike: things like wine, women and song; art, fashion… and beer.

I hadn't had much of a social life before, but I started to go to the Bell Inn in Nottingham. It was the pub where all the fashion and art students from the college went, and a whole new world was opened up to me – major influences like the Bauhaus, Kandinsky, Warhol. I was fascinated by all of it. I left my warehouse job and went to work as a shop assistant in a clothes shop (I think they called them "boutiques" in those days!).

Then I met a designer who wanted to open a shop. She knew nothing about how to run a business, and neither did I, but she asked me to help. I talked to estate agents, got the lease for her, and I learnt about management. I ran the shop for six years.

Then I met this delicious lady called Pauline, who I still live with. She was teaching at the college in Nottingham and we ended up together. She gave me the encouragement and confidence to think about opening my own shop. So every Monday, on my day off, I used to do any work that came along, mostly production such as getting shirts made – anything to get some money. I even did alterations on my mum's sewing machine.

Until 9 October 1970, when I had managed to save £600. I pleaded with my tailor, who had a spare back room at 10 Byard Lane in Nottingham, and eventually he rented it to me for ten shillings a week. It was 12 feet square and I called it "Vestes Pour Hommes". I took £35 on my first day, and somehow just kept going.

By this time I had Pauline, two dogs, two cats and two kids. It was a bit different to living on £12 a week with your mum and dad. Quite a responsibility. And I realised that we wouldn't survive on the income from my shop. I was selling – or attempting to sell – everything that no-one wanted. Everyone had wide trousers; I had narrow trousers. Everyone had narrow shirts; I had wide shirts. So we only opened on a Friday and

Saturday, while on a Monday to Thursday I was trying to earn a living doing other things, as well as going to night school to learn pattern-cutting.

This period was all about learning, doing anything to do with fashion that came along. I was learning by doing. In the beginning I bought things in from other designers, but eventually I had loads of my own ideas and began to make them up, always helped by Pauline, who taught me about the construction of clothes.

A few years later I was invited to work as a designer for Browns in London, a job I did two or three days a week for three years. I was also working for a big shirt maker in Rome, and as a colourist for the International Wool Secretariat. The reason I was offered so much work was because I had lots of energy and I didn't let people down.

In 1976 I thought I would start my own collection – the Paul Smith collection – which was just a small group of shirts. Gene Pressman, who is now the president of Barneys, the New York department store, was in London, and I managed to get to see him. When I went into his hotel room he was doing sit-ups; I showed him my shirts as he went up and down – and sold him 450.

Then I did a tiny collection of jackets, which we showed in a hotel room. All my own clothes were on the floor in the bathroom, while the collection was in the wardrobe with the door open and a spotlight from Habitat tastefully focused on it. I sat there for a week, and then someone from Texas came and bought something. Then someone from a French company bought something. I was there for another six days and I sold £17,000 worth of clothes.

The first show I did was in a friend's flat in Paris. There were about 35 in the audience (including Charlotte Rampling), the hi-fi had come straight from my house, the lighting was garage inspection lamps, the models were all pals, the dressers were all pals, and the champagne came from the supermarket. But it seemed terribly grand to us at the time.

It was great, but at the same time it's sad that we have to hear stories like this about the British fashion industry time and time again. Design is not taken seriously enough at the moment. We have to make it better known and more important. We lose most of our designers because it is

very difficult for them to find jobs in this country. The attitude is all wrong: there is no awareness and no investment.

Fortunately, I managed to move on from my meagre beginnings. I was learning all the time. I think one of the reasons why I do okay (and unfortunately, a lot of English designers are not doing so), is because I am okay at design and okay at business. It's very important to be able to do both.

I was based in Nottingham until 1976, by which time I had a shop on the main street and was opening full time. I had a nice car and everyone knew me, but I wanted to go out into the big world, which was good, because change is very challenging.

I wanted to get a London shop, not realising how much they cost. I thought I would get one in Bond Street or the King's Road, but we couldn't afford them, so we ended up looking for a place in Covent Garden – which turned out to be brilliant anyway, although we didn't know that at the time.

I loved the Bauhaus, the Twenties German art school which promoted minimalism and new ideas, and I wanted to have a shop which had that feeling. I spent six months looking through letterboxes with a torch for a shop that had a concrete floor and eventually found one at 44 Floral Street, which is where we are now. I knew I had to have it. It took eight months to find out who owned it – a retired baker from Gloucester. I rang him up and he eventually said he would rent it to me. But then I remembered my dad saying it was good to buy things, so I rang the baker up and asked if he would sell it.

Eventually he said he would – for £35,000. I managed to rake up £15,000. I rang him up again and said: "I've got a problem: I really want this place, it's great, but I haven't got enough money." He said: "How much have you got?" And I said: "£25,000." He said: "All right." Then I said: "Actually, I was fibbing. I really only have £15,000." He said: "I can't let you have it for £15,000, but I'll lend you the other £10,000 and you can pay it back over ten years." And that was it.

The shop took ages to do because I couldn't afford it – it took me from 1976 to 1979 to get back onto my feet and to get the finesse we wanted in the shop. And then we opened.

There are too many designers in the world, too many shops, too many

Paul Smith Changed Clive's image, Audrey changed his life...

airlines, too many manufacturers. There's still a marvellous opportunity out there, but the secret is to work out what you have to offer. So, on a very small budget, I tried to work out how to sell clothes in a very small market. My four secret ingredients were colour, coordination, cloth and cut.

I am not a trained designer, so I tend to work with simple shapes, using little surprises like a bright lining. The success of the clothes is very much to do with how they are worn. Take Jean Paul Gaultier or Coco Chanel – I like both of them, but they are very identifiable. When you put on a Jean Paul Gaultier suit you are saying either: "I am very fashionable," or: "I am very rich." I try to put clothes on people that let the person say: "I am me." They are clothes for individuals. You needn't worry about wearing a Paul Smith suit with a pair of your dad's old shoes.

When you are building a collection it's not just about clothes, it's also about business. You design them, but you also have to sell them. If you only do clothes that are very classic it can be seen as a bit boring. And if you only do clothes that are very avant-garde it's interesting – but also very hard to sell. You need a balance of things that pay the rent and things that pull people in; that are good window pieces and good for publicity.

I try to mix the fashionable with the classic, so I always have classic colours in a collection: navy, white, grey and black. And then there are colours I call the "new classics", which are very acceptable and which are new each season: it might be dusty burgundy or a dusty charcoal. Then there are the highlights, which are used for stripes, for decoration in ties, for patterns in socks. They can be more punchy. But the combination of colours is important. If you put together navy and white it says "I am smart," or "I am nautical," or "I am clean and fresh." The colours you choose are vital and the use of colour is very important. You can even put clashing colours together where they don't quite work, because design is not just about good taste, it's also about bad taste. People think design has some strange formula about it, where you have to have an intellectual thought and put it down on a plain white piece of paper. But in fact it's just observation, looking and enjoying life, seeing things and taking them in – inspiration can come from anywhere, from graffiti, from tapestry yarns in John Lewis, from Matisse's paintings, anywhere at all.

Something else I do quite a lot is to make things in the wrong colours. Instead of doing a duffle coat in camel or navy, I do it in red. Instead of doing a Harris tweed jacket in ginger or grey, I do it in yellow. And I do a traditional cashmere overcoat, which should be in navy, in purple. Of course I also make them in their "proper" colours as well, because that's what pays the rent. My work is all about tradition, but given a new twist.

We work a lot with exclusive prints. All our designs come from observation. It's amazing what you can find if you look: pictures in the back of a fish tank, fruit and veg, guitars, pieces of rope (very Hermès!), old books, or travel – tiles in the Alhambra Palace in Spain, tomatoes drying in Greece, terracotta jugs in Italy.

I also do a lot of playing around with coordinates. For example, you could take a striped shirt with a classic tie, but instead of wearing it with a blue blazer you would wear it with a jeans-jacket. When I started out that was considered pioneering.

I have always insisted on very good quality. I was fortunate enough to visit Coco Chanel's studio just before she died, when couture was still very important. I visited St Laurent when he did his first totally black collection in honour of Vietnam, and also when he did his first see-through collection. And I visited Pierre Cardin (that guy can *cut* – his full skirts are brilliant) where I saw suits with pad stitching that made the seams roll beautifully, and sleeves with rope shoulders that were put in perfectly. I came back and tried to do it in England, and it was very hard; I met with a lot of resistance. But I worked on it, I went to the factories and stuck it out, and at the end of the day I got what I wanted.

There is no mystery about fashion, it's all about looking, taking it in, observing, not being scared to break the rules and get out there and do it.

In 1982 the shop next door came up for sale. It was a banana warehouse built in 1850, and it had lovely floors, beams and brickwork. It seemed a shame to cover it with plaster and do a minimal interior, so we decided to use shop fittings. But rather than using normal fittings, we found old tailors' and chemists' interiors, made of worn out mahogany. This new look turned out to be really important. It went on to become the big Paul Smith look, the blueprint for the Paul Smith interiors of the future.

That same year I went to Japan and opened a shop there – its interior was a chocolate shop from Newcastle. Japan has been absolutely fantastic for us. People say that it's difficult to get into Japan, but it's not if you work hard at it, respect the people and pay attention to their culture. There's a lot that our country can learn from the Japanese – their attitude and their management skills are absolutely fantastic, they are willing to learn and they pay attention to detail.

In the Tokyo shop, as in all our shops around the world, we don't just sell clothes. We sell old Sixties vinyl, Beatles memorabilia, Stones memorabilia, photographic books, cameras, all sorts of things to make the shop feel special and interesting. I even had a £20 note trompe l'oeiled on the stairs. (I did the same in Paris but I felt so guilty about making all these smart French people bend down to try to pick it up that I painted a nail through it. They still try, though!)

I think it's very important to make my shops more than just a shop. I hate shops where you feel as though you need a stiff drink and a new hairdo before you go in. So I try to soften them up by putting in things other than clothes. My shops are like an Aladdin's cave. Because I travel so much I am always finding things, like wonderful penknives or crazy watches. When I started doing this, everything used to sell out in a day, and I realised that people like to discover things. Believe it or not, we have even sold vacuum cleaners in London – 50 pink and lilac vacuum cleaners in a men's clothes shop! We try to make our windows humorous as well, so you feel good before you even go in. When you walk into one of my shops you might think: "This is really stupid," or: "This is really wonderful." But at least you have a reaction.

The chore of fashion is that you never stop developing ideas. And you are only as good as today and tomorrow. As soon as you sit back and say: "Oh, yeah, I've been on TV and in Vogue, I'm great," someone will come along in the fast lane and overtake you. You can't rest on your laurels; you always have to change.

Thinking about design and business – that's how I have progressed. And, of course, it's all about imagination and making people smile.

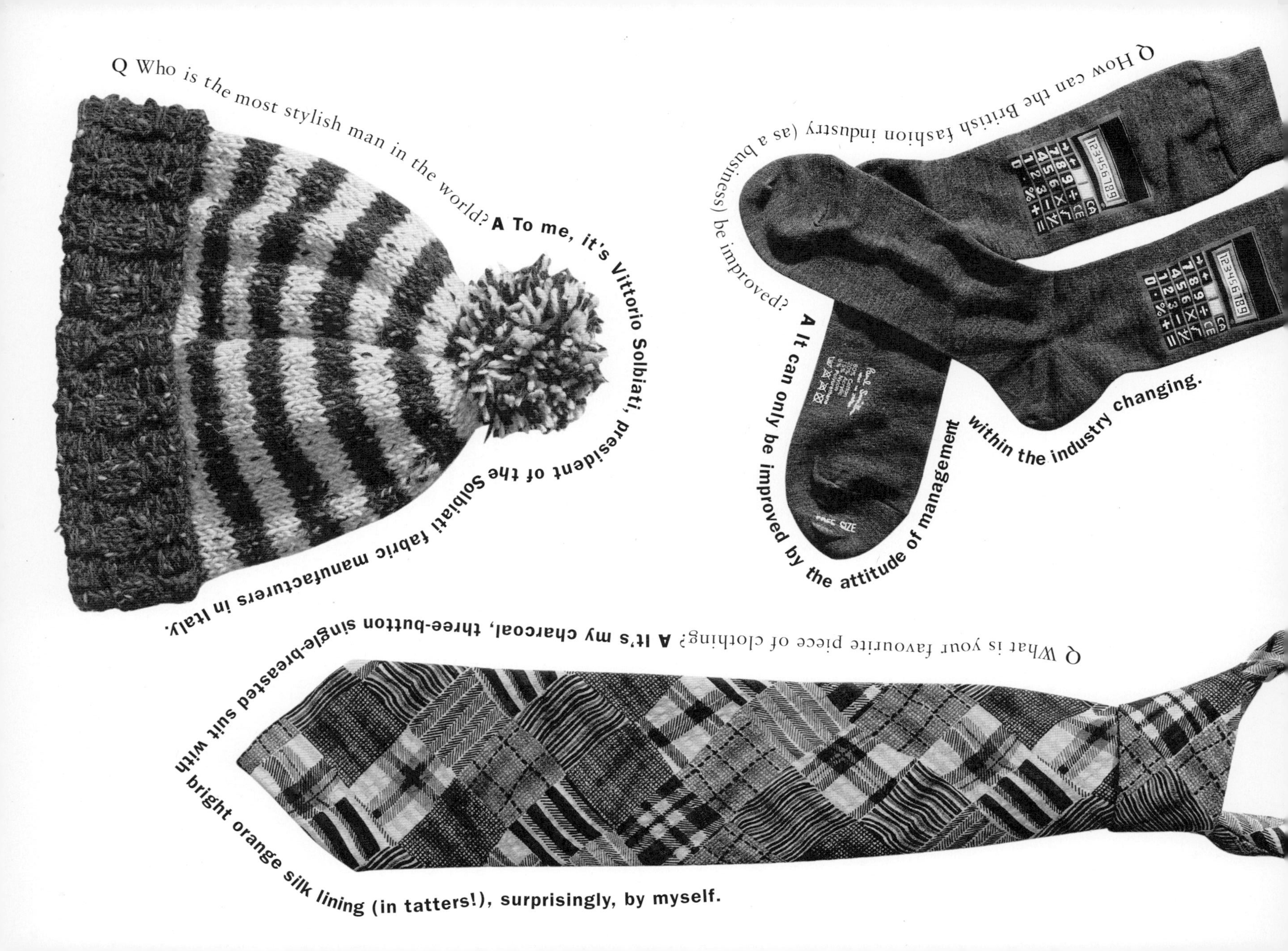
Q Who is the most stylish man in the world? A To me, it's Vittorio Solbiati, president of the Solbiati fabric manufacturers in Italy.
Q How can the British fashion industry (as a business) be improved?
A It can only be improved by the attitude of management within the industry changing.
Q What is your favourite piece of clothing? A It's my charcoal, three-button single-breasted suit with bright orange silk lining (in tatters!), surprisingly, by myself.

Q What business skills have you found most useful?

A Diplomacy and endless enthusiasm.

Q What advice would you give to people starting their own fashion business now?

A It's not just about clothes; it's about much, much more. As a designer in Britain you have to have a broad understanding of business as well as being a good designer.

ERIK REES was born in Prague, Czechoslovakia, the son of an expert in deciphering handwriting. He is one of Europe's few full-time graphologists, and a founding member of the British Institute of Graphologists, where he was instrumental in developing a three-year course and an accredited examination. He works for many major companies, in particular helping them with recruitment and team-building.

On a very hot evening in July 1989 Erik fascinated our audience with his description of the way the graphologist works, showing us intriguing examples of famous people's handwriting to illustrate his points. However, at the end of Erik's talk there were still some people who were not convinced and the discussion continued in the bar, where Erik was surrounded by people requesting analysis of their own handwriting. His insight into their backgrounds and personalities was absolutely extraordinary, confounding all the sceptics.

Handwriting is a very delicate movement of the fingers operated by a motor activity of the left side of the brain.

The brain transmits impulses through the spinal cord to the arms and hands, so that the wrists, hands and fingers are merely instruments of muscular expansion and contraction controlled by the nervous system. Writing is, therefore, a dynamic process portraying the characteristics of the writer to anyone who is versed in its analysis.

The name graphology comes from the Greek "*grapho*" – "I write", and "*logos*" – "logic". Analysing handwriting takes time, skill and a few basic necessities, and anyone who uses a graphologist should first of all make absolutely sure that they are bona fide – if in doubt contact The British Institute of Graphologists. To be certain of being accurate, a graphologist would need at least a full sheet of unlined A4 paper, written with a fountain pen or biro, and a signature. It is also helpful to know the subject's sex and age, whether they are right- or left-handed, and in what country they learned to write.

Then, using a magnifying glass, a protractor and a ruler, a graphologist could study the basic elements of handwriting.

Richard Nixon's signature when he was Vice President in 1959

As newly-elected President in 1968

As the Watergate net tightened

Just before his resignation

Size

This represents the writer's stature (or claimed stature) among fellow men. It can be either absolute or relative to others.

Zones

These represent the writer's psyche. The upper zone is the conscious area, representing intellect, imagination and ideas. The middle zone represents daily routine, social life, relationships, likes and dislikes, and habits. The lower zone is the subconscious, emotional and survival area.

Slant

This measures the influence the writer's parents have over him. It represents opposition and assent, regression and progress, and some emotions, and is assessed on the basis of whether it is upright or slants to the left or the right.

Pressure

Visible pressure – the pen on the paper – is a measure of the writer's vitality. Invisible pressure – the fingers on the pen – is a measure of persistence and precision.

Speed

This is the yardstick for spontaneity.

Connectedness

This shows the extent to which the writer relies on others or on his own intuition. It shows his logical and lateral thought processes.

Form of connection

The four ways of connecting letters demonstrate the writer's attitude towards cooperation with other people. "Garlands" are the most practical and easy form; "arcades" are the least practical and natural, but most artistic; "angles" are the most difficult and precise, requiring self-discipline and persistence; and "threads" are unconventional and require great

is not to reason, so sufficient
to say, glad that you are
settling in the 'Big Apple'

A warm, passionate and generous woman.
Introverted, with the covering image of a "party bombshell"

Space! Unless something is forthcoming
the earth Planets are in peril. The War
of The Worlds, is just not a movie, but

A mentally disturbed man.
Note the periodic changes in form and slant. The excellent line spacing indicates that he is intelligent, motivated and striving for perfection

P.S. In the case of candidates I and K it would
probably be of more interest to examine their personal
characteristics as well.

Assessed by a graphologist as untrustworthy.
The man was later fired for attempted embezzlement

mental speed, showing very positive or negative personality traits, depending on legibility and execution.

Direction of lines

This shows the way in which the writer pursues his or her aims.

Spacing

Line spacing is a measure of the organisation of the writer's mind, word spacing shows the extent of any introversion, and letter spacing is an indication of the writer's ability to communicate.

Regularity and rhythm

These indicate the writer's state of mind and, again, some emotions.

Layout

This shows the position the writer wishes to occupy among his fellow men and the true reality of where he actually stands.

Degree of attention

This shows the writer's capacity for accuracy and attention to detail, as well as pinpointing certain aspects of character. It is measured in terms of the beginnings and endings of letter formation, and in i-dots and t-crossings.

Form standard

This is how close the writer comes to recreating the standard forms of each letter. It is one of the most important guides to a person's character, and is what makes graphology extremely accurate. It is an indication of intelligence, integrity and sensibility, showing where the sufficiency of any attribute within a person becomes an excess. In graphology terms, it can be "neglected", "enriched", "simplified" or "original".

I once conducted a student graphology seminar where we gave out samples of writing by Kim Philby and Winston Churchill. We asked, without revealing the names of the writers, various questions, including whether the students would appoint Philby as a chief security officer and what they would give Churchill as a present. Every one of them said Philby should never be employed in security because he was too secretive and, of the 15, 11 said Churchill should be given works of English literature, while four said he should be given paints. Reading and painting were his favourite hobbies.

Know, according to the
in your department,
dates on which all

Winston Churchill

Would you drop me a line
to let me know what the Xmas
closing plans will be this year

Kim Philby

CHAPTER 3 **Architecture for the Layman**

VICTORIA THORNTON

spent five years organising exhibitions and lecture programmes at the Royal Institute of British Architects, where her eyes were opened to the delights of architecture – and particularly 20th-century buildings. In 1980 she founded Architectural Dialogue, which specialises in taking small groups of people to study architecture around the world, as well as producing publications, mounting exhibitions and undertaking research. Victoria describes her work as "P R for architecture" and, appropriately, she is the linchpin of Open House, an annual event which promotes London's buildings by opening them up to the general public.

In her illustrated talk at Utopia in August 1989, Victoria discussed some examples of excellent modern buildings and demonstrated how – with an open mind and open eyes – it's possible to find good architectural design all around us.

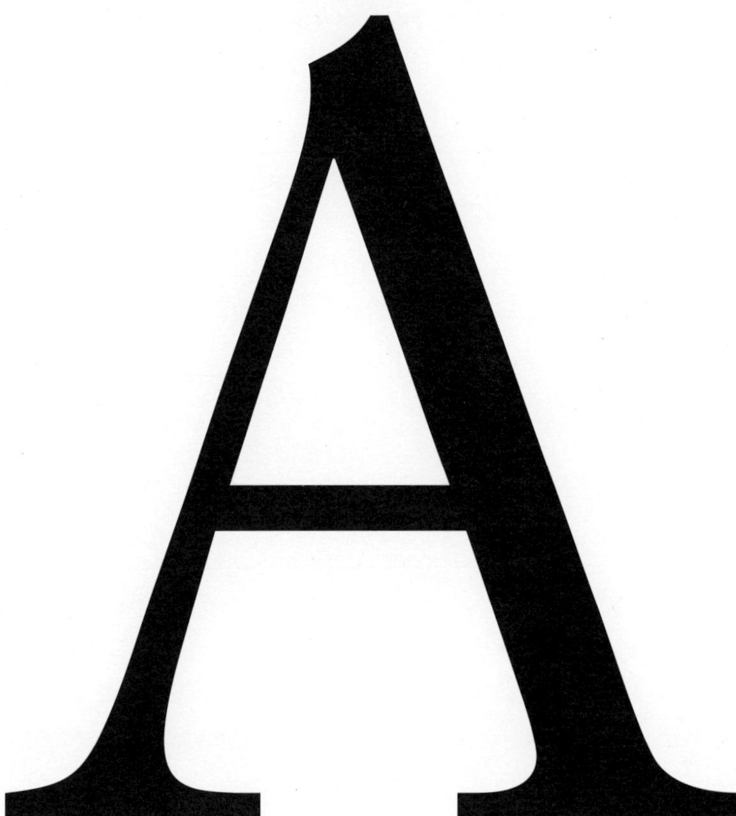

rchitecture is not widely appreciated in Britain. One difficulty is that it is actually quite unlike its more popular – and so-called "sister arts" – painting and sculpture. Architecture is not a discrete, portable object which adorns a wall while maintaining an essential indifference to it. A building's design is rarely divorced from its function, from its site, and from a huge number of socio-economic circumstances. Its aesthetic qualities are almost invariably wedded to a mundane use at odds with that rarefied atmosphere enjoyed by fine art. Also, many people, often hundreds, are involved in the design and construction of a building. If there are parallels with other disciplines, then they are probably with the making of movies, not fine art or sculpture.

The philosopher Walter Benjamin commented that a key difference between a painting and architecture is that you can stand in front of a painting and appreciate it simply and directly; architecture, however, has to be dealt with in a tactile way – it has to be experienced in time and learned. This is a marvellous idea: that you learn architecture! Encouraging the general public to enter through architectural doors, however, can be exasperating, especially when the building in question is contemporary.

You can dislike an old building without anything more being at issue than good taste, and there is usually an abundance of markers to guide the way. But admitting to an enjoyment of contemporary architecture is to enter more dangerous territory; it is to expose yourself to all kinds of uncertainty – as anyone familiar with the politics of taste will attest. The patina of age is not just a delight to the eye – it signals all kinds of reassurance which, legitimately, we all enjoy. Modern architecture appears to be a difficult, inaccessible subject of dubious aesthetic credentials.

I once hosted a group of prestigious English art enthusiasts visiting art collections in Houston and Dallas. Few members of the group were willing to entertain my contention that some of the buildings we could see could be enjoyed as a legitimate art form. Certainly, the idea that Texan architecture might compete with the fruits of oil wealth which adorn the walls of Texan galleries and homes seemed, at best, unlikely. Unlikely, that is, until we entered the Kimball Museum in Houston: jaws dropped collectively and the fine art was clearly in danger of being upstaged by Louis Kahn's impressive architectural achievement.

The orchestration of dropped jaws, however, is only one dimension of promoting architectural appreciation. Excellent architecture isn't always a building which seeks to compete on some scale of global wonders. It doesn't have to be foreign, grand, spectacular or novel to be a worthy building which can provide uplift and a feeling of wellbeing. There is more to the enjoyment of architecture than a celebration of baroque gigantism in Rome, incongruous pyramids in Paris, skyscrapers in New York, exotic monuments in India or acrobatic opera houses in Sydney. There is much more, and it is often modest and just around the corner.

Good architectural design can be found all around us, including the "almost alright" (as Robert Venturi called it) which didn't quite make it;

Overleaf: (Left) The Sackler Gallery by Norman Foster;
(Right) The National Gallery's Sainsbury Wing by Robert Venturi

the small gem, whose diminutiveness disguises its worth; the building which is difficult to photograph and transform into a strong media image; the changed buildings betraying a history of uses and alterations which don't always harmonise or enhance; and those buildings now out of fashion or belonging to some uncelebrated era. Contemporary excellence is as likely to be found in the small retail outlet as the large opera house. In Camden Town alone there are significant pieces of excellent architectural design which include a supermarket, TV and radio studios, and private houses and showrooms; there is Cedric Price's aviary in London Zoo; Denys Lasdun's College of Physicians; Nash's superb work in Regents Park; Terry Farrell's marvellous (but now, sadly, repainted) former TVAM building; the adjacent structural heroics of his former partner Nicholas Grimshaw for Sainsbury; some excellent low-cost housing by Jestico Whiles; a fine jazz bar by Chaik Chassay; Stanton and Williams' superb Classic FM studios; and much more to interest and delight the enthusiast.

There is much to be said in favour of a catholic taste, and good architecture comes in many guises. On the street, you have to be ready to directly experience a heady mix which can then be informed with background information.

You can easily experience how varied architecture is by spending a day visiting recent art galleries in central London – for example, the National Gallery's Sainsbury Wing, the Clore Gallery at the Tate, the Royal Academy's Sackler Gallery, the Saatchi Gallery in St John's Wood and – if you are feeling energetic – the Whitechapel Gallery in the East End and the Lisson Gallery in Marylebone. They all address different concerns and demonstrate disparate aesthetic values. Your personal preference might favour one against another, but I would argue that each can be enjoyed and all demonstrate architectural excellence. With an open mind – and open eyes – you can make marvellous comparisons.

Consider, for example, the ways in which both Bob Venturi at the Sainsbury and Jim Stirling at the Clore have handled new work as an addition to an existing building – the former with a profound erudition, a weighty intellect and a poker-faced sense of humour; the latter with equal learning and intelligence, but with a mischievousness which, I suspect, sets out to irritate as well as humour. Both designs play games by providing reference to other contexts – but how different are their kinds of excellence!

The Sainsbury Wing offers distortions of perspective, clever alignments and views through rooms, and a variety of arcane references. The grand staircase in the foyer has a precedent in a stair designed by Finland's great architectural hero, Alvar Aalto (the only architect I know of besides Wren to have got his head onto a banknote). Its curious, look-no-hands, suspended arches hover overhead and, upon close examination, appear to defy gravity and contradict the initial assumption that they must be structural steel. The designs for the gallery rooms refer to John Soane's work at the Dulwich Gallery some 150 years ago, letting only a minute amount of harmful daylight penetrate, while avoiding claustrophobia. The exterior changes radically as you move around the building – the south front acknowledging William Wilkin's rather weak original building of the 1830s, and the large sign cut into the north face bizarrely acknowledging Las Vegas and a well-known book written by Venturi on that subject some years ago.

In contrast, the Clore features an underplayed, landscaped, entry court set calmly to one side of the original building's portico and stair, acidic green window frames (Stirling's trademark) and a flow of internal spaces punctuated by considerate gestures such as the oriel window, allowing a respite from those wonderful Turners and a view back to the outer court. And in that court – tucked away in a corner – is a jokey reference to one of Stirling's most famous buildings: the celebrated Staatsgalerie in Stuttgart, where stones from the car parking podium have "fallen out" and lie in the grass.

Both these designs are entirely different from Sir Norman Foster's unlikely Sackler Gallery commission for the Royal Academy. Here, a mansion house with more than 330 years of almost continuous alterations, additions and accretions has been surgically operated upon to provide a new heart and make sense of the circulation. The conceptual clarity and high technology so beloved by Foster's team is used to revitalise the old beast and introduce a harmonious juxtaposition between old and new which is comparatively rare in this country.

The Clore Gallery by Jim Stirling

What the Sackler shares with the Clore and the Sainsbury is obsessiveness – invariably an aspect of good architecture. But all three of them also share problems – and these, too, are an absorbing dimension of architectural appreciation: a crucial part of that tactile learning experience. I confess that the Sainsbury doesn't provide me with any emotional uplift (despite my admiration for its intellectual content), and I find many of its features and spaces unpleasant or disappointing (for example, the entry foyer and the failure to address Trafalgar Square). The Clore suffers from its low budget and doesn't entirely work as the pavilion in the garden that it pretends to be. And the minimalist-designed Sackler suffers the indignation of having to accommodate the usual pile of catalogues, postcards, posters and so on found in all museums these days. Such is life! And such is architecture, too – this comparing and contrasting is an essential part of its enjoyment.

The dramatic contrast with all three of these galleries is in St John's Wood: the private Saatchi Gallery designed by the late Max Gordon. This gallery is a former dairy, its prosaic structure countered by an internal "wrap" of simple plasterboard on studs which can be read as separate from the existing structure, creating spaces for toilets, stores and the like. It is all utterly simple: the floors are grey-painted concrete; the rest of the toplit exterior is white. Everything is low-tech and characterised by an ascetic quality. But what spaces! Nothing delights me more than to sit there in these huge volumes – among half a dozen or so works of art languishing on their acres of white wall – watching bodies glide through the spaces, beautifully realising the fundamental empathy all architecture must achieve between itself and the human body. On the right day, in the right mood, this is my favourite space in London.

The Sainsbury Wing, the Clore, the Sackler and the Saatchi are all contemporary. Stepping back just slightly in time – to the early 1800s – we find another London example of splendid architecture which still speaks clearly to us: John Soane's remarkable museum in Lincoln's Inn. This astounding complex of domestic spaces was once Soane's family home, his office, a place to indulge in architectural experimentation and somewhere to house his amazing collection of classical souvenirs. The place still speaks to us, denying its status as frozen cultural heritage, and it remains one of the most delightful architectural experiences in London.

In fact, Soane and his enthusiasms make an appropriate note on which to finish: an acknowledgement both of how absorbing architectural appreciation can be, and how good architecture remains timeless. Architects – such a frustrated breed – sometimes have the possibility and potential to become true alchemists, turning ordinary dross into gold. Perhaps, at the end of the day, there is too much fool's gold and not enough of the real thing; perhaps there are too many buildings in the "almost alright" category; but it is this scene of challenges presented and met which marks out the worthwhile building. It may be a Taj Mahal or how your front door has been handled, but the "right stuff" – as Tom Wolfe called it in another context – is all over the place and worth finding.

CHAPTER 4 **Cinema**

IAIN JOHNSTONE has an extensive and authoritative knowledge of the film industry. Chief film critic for the *Sunday Times* from 1983 to 1993, and the person responsible for devising Barry Norman's famous BBC TV film criticism programme, he has written books on Clint Eastwood and Dustin Hoffman and directed documentaries on Muhammad Ali, Ted Turner, the *Superman* films, *Batman* and *A Fish called Wanda*. He co-wrote *Fierce Creatures*, the sequel to *A Fish called Wanda*, with John Cleese; it's due out next summer.

Iain's wide-ranging talk in September 1989 featured video clips and lots of juicy (but unrepeatable!) gossip about the movie industry, including anecdotes about stars, films and off-camera goings-on. Our extract covers his view of the Oscars and Cannes.

IAIN JOHNSTONE

The Oscars

began in 1929, when the film mogul Louis B Mayer, trying to break the power of the unions, formed an all-industry association to set pay and conditions. The association decided to give out prizes, and in the first year 270 people got together at the Roosevelt Hotel to watch 12 awards being given out. A librarian at the Academy called Margaret Herrick commented that the prize, a gold statuette, looked like her uncle Oscar – and the name stuck. As is frequently the case with the Oscars, the film that was a hot favourite that year didn't win – *The Jazz Singer* got nowhere, in spite of being the first "talkie", because the judges felt it had an unfair advantage. By the following year, all the shortlisted films were talkies, and the Oscars as we know them had truly begun.

And so they went on, going from strength to strength, with marvellous winners such as *Broadway Melody*, *It Happened One Night*, *Gone with the Wind*, *Casablanca*, *Hamlet* and *All About Eve*. It wasn't all plain sailing, though. In 1952 there was another notorious non-winner, *High Noon*, an avowedly anti-witch-hunt film which was prevented from winning by the crackdown of the House UnAmerican Activities Committee.

1952 was also the first year that the Oscars were televised. Everyone in the movie industry felt in danger of being undermined by television, which was becoming ever more popular, and that year's Oscars compere, Bob Hope, caused a sensation by calling the new medium "the place where movies go when they die", and the television set "furniture that stares back at you". MGM executives were even forbidden to have TVs in their offices, and mentioning television in films was out of the question. Now, of course, TV is an essential part of the industry – as the machine on which you play a video which makes huge returns for the studios.

Criticism, of course, is not something that has a major influence over a prize-giving ceremony such as the Oscars. A lot of it is to do with marketing. There is great pressure from the studios for people to vote for their films. The 5,000 members of the Academy – the only people eligible to vote – are sent videos of the contending films, sometimes before they are even released, to try to influence their decision. Such campaigns can be quite effective. Take a film like *The Field*, which no-one in America saw: the members were all sent video cassettes and it was nominated anyway, almost certainly as a result of the intensive marketing campaign.

The Oscars always take place on a Monday night, and a rehearsal is held the Sunday before. The venue is filled with actors who are paid to sit behind photographs of the stars who will be there in person the following day – Paul Newman, Warren Beatty, Barbra Streisand. They rehearse the whole ceremony, with winners chosen at random. Nobody knows who has won except for two people from Price Waterhouse, the company that does the counting, and even then the votes are split up between different members of staff before they are counted so that no-one would be able to make even an educated guess as to the result – betting is fierce and someone could make a small fortune if they received inside information.

It takes an occurrence of enormous significance to shake a major cinema event from its schedule. The only time that the Oscars have been postponed from their Monday night slot was in 1981, when Ronald Reagan – who did the voice-over for the first broadcast 29 years earlier – was almost assassinated. It was felt to be in poor taste to go ahead when the life of the President was in danger, and the ceremony eventually took place on the following day.

It took a war to delay that other great essential of the film critic's year:

Cannes

Planned as a riposte to Mussolini's gaudy Venice Film Festival (from which Hitler had banned Jean Renoir's film *La Grande Illusion* because it showed a German guard refusing to shoot a French prisoner), the first Cannes Film Festival began on 1 September 1939 – the same day Hitler invaded Poland. It closed the following morning.

Cannes got going again properly when the war ended, and what had started out comparatively modestly, as a serious film festival, soon turned into the multi-ringed circus that it is today. It is perfectly possible – in fact, all too easy – for someone to come to Cannes and never watch a film at all. Running parallel to the artistic competition is an enormously powerful and influential commercial market, where having dinner with Arnold Schwarzenegger or swapping anecdotes with Dustin Hoffman over lunch on a 40-foot yacht is as important as watching screenings of the 20 or so selected films, most of which will not go on to have success in the Oscars because they are too "arty".

If you do take the option of actually trying to report on the films at Cannes it can be a pretty tricky business. In order to get in, you need accreditation. But to get your accreditation, you need different, additional accreditation. Hotel rooms are heavily oversubscribed, and unless you bribe the receptionists heavily they will only write in your booking in pencil – which is as good as not writing it in at all. The Festival keeps all the articles written by those of us who write regularly about Cannes and underlines all the relevant parts in red pen – and if your comments are too adverse your privileges can be severely reduced.

There is a hierarchy of passes, and a standard pass only allows you in to screenings at 8am and 9pm. When an intrepid London critic, Victoria Mather, pointed out that if one had been enjoying the delights of the local restaurants the previous evening, 8am was a little early for a morning movie, the formidable controller of the press, Mme Fargette, replied (with watertight rationality) that if one had taken an early dinner, attended the 9pm screening and gone sensibly to bed, the system worked perfectly!

Some members of the press are, however, accorded more comfortable credentials, with a gold dot that admits them to a wider choice of screenings; some are even made *Soiristes,* which means they can get into the nightly premieres at which evening dress, or *le smoking,* as the French call it, is *de rigueur* – even though smoking itself is rigorously prohibited.

Hard though it is to believe, Cannes was not always the extravaganza of glitz and glamour that it is today. What started out as a canny way of filling the local hotels with movie buffs two weeks before the start of the tourist season was only thrown into the world spotlight by a widely reported act of immodesty that took place in 1954. A French actress, Simone Silva (who wanted to be France's answer to Marilyn Monroe but managed to match her only in her subsequent suicide), threw off the top of her bikini and embraced Robert Mitchum. This was way before women ever sunbathed topless, and even though the resulting photos – which travelled round the globe – were airbrushed to remove any trace of indecency, Cannes' reputation as rather a racy place was made. And, as with all such myths, reality was more than happy to live up to it...

CHAPTER 5 **Icetalk**

ROBERT SWAN is the first person ever to have walked to both the North and South Poles. His adventures started as a dream while he was at Durham University – to walk in the footsteps of Scott to the South Pole. In 1986 he led an expedition which did just that, hauling supplies 883 miles without radios or assistance. The success of that expedition, coupled with his growing concern about man's treatment of the environment, motivated Robert to walk to the North Pole in May 1989. Just six months after his successful journey, he came to talk at Newell and Sorrell.

Robert's tale of bravery in the face of one of the harshest climates in the world was unbelievably powerful, and his description of the destruction of the polar environment shocked our audience. At the end of the talk, his plea for the future and his expression of hope through young people left us emotionally drained – but inspired. Robert has since been awarded the Queen's Polar Medal and the OBE, and is the UNESCO Special Envoy for the Environment and UNEP Goodwill Ambassador For Youth.

Here, Robert's talk is set against extracts from the diary he kept on his journey to the Pole.

I'm not one of those people who do 400 press-ups before breakfast and drink orange juice all the time. I smoke a pack of cigarettes a day and drink like a fish. The question is: why the hell did I bother to walk all this way - twice - when, frankly, I don't like walking very much? I also don't enjoy being cold - only somebody very strange would actually enjoy having ice in their underpants.

The answer is this: Antarctica is twice the size of Australia and no-one owns it. The last wilderness on earth – it's all we've got left that we haven't destroyed yet. Somewhere in the history of mankind we must draw the line, and Antarctica is a place where we can do just that and show the future that we actually did care. I think it's important that we have at least one place left.

I went to Antarctica in 1986; when we were there we touched the future and it hurt. We walked underneath this hole in the ozone layer without even knowing about it. We couldn't understand why we were getting sunburnt when we were surrounded by ice and, when the skin took three months to stop rotting off our faces, I began to take a little more interest in what was happening to the environment. It was time for a second expedition: to head North, and to find a new team.

My style is not to choose people just because I like them: you're choosing people to take to a place that wants you dead, and if you make a mistake in my business you don't lose money, you don't lose your job; you die. There's no desk to hide behind. You can't sack these people, because it's 3,000 miles to civilisation. You can't stop their pay, because you've never paid them. Basically, they can turn round to you and say: "No, we won't." And short of beating them up there's really nothing you can do. What I learned from being so close to the rest of the teams on the two expeditions is that, on average, people are not psychic. You know that somebody picks their nose and you want to kill them, but you sit there stewing. Under these circumstances there is no escape. You can't go out of the hut. The temperature outside is minus 55 degrees C, the wind is blowing in excess of 150 miles an hour. So we overcame our problems by sitting down once a week and telling each other how we really felt about each other – and it worked.

We set out Monday afternoon, March 20. It was minus 55 degrees C – as cold as it ever became down South. Our departure from Advance Base at Cape Aldrich was inauspicious. We were just eight red dots traipsing North. The journey had begun. Ahead lay who knows what. Physically we felt small, but in our hearts strong…

A noisy lunch in the humid – and at times putrid – Polar Haven served as our last supper. I stood up and could think of little else to say except: "Well, gentlemen, I'm going to the North Pole; is anybody coming?"

I realised again that this was not going to be the gut-wrenching slog of the South but something far tougher. Here we clamber, climb and claw our way up vast walls of ice, passing sleds from one man to the other. Then in a tangle of equipment we tumble down the other side. We edge sideways up sheer slopes, vast icescrapers towering 30 or 40 feet above us. Encumbered with 150lbs of sleds and backpacks, we face at least a further 70 miles of this...

In the first nine hours we covered one-and-a-half miles. I was a very popular person that evening, saying: "Don't worry chaps, it'll only take 600 days at this rate." The temperature was minus 56 degrees Celsius. How cold is that? Cold enough to freeze the water in your eyes. If you inhale through your nose or mouth you end up with ice all the way up inside your nose, so that it feels like it's up to your brain. If you take your gloves off for more than 30 seconds your fingers turn white, then if you don't warm them up they turn black after a week, green after another week, and the week after that they drop off.

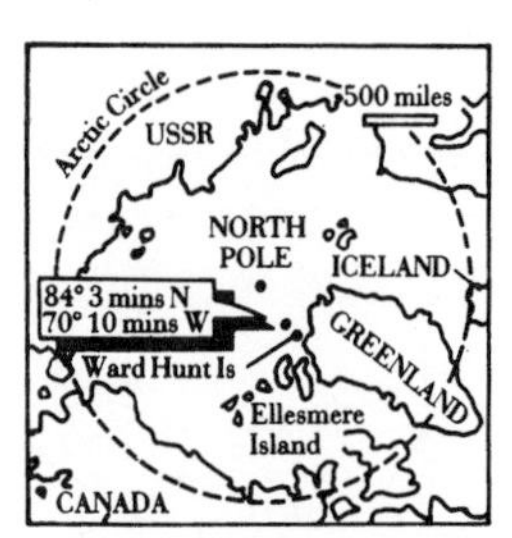

April 1st

The cold envelopes us. It is the toughest opponent of all. Buried beneath layers of clothing, the sweat freezes, like armour against your skin. It's an eternal struggle to ensure the cold doesn't turn to frostbite. When I can no longer feel the cold, I know it will have won. We must all feel that cold, always...

The other problem was that we were entering the living room of the polar bear. Polar bears don't like visitors much. A polar bear has forearms the size of Daley Thompson's thigh, and they're not something to argue with – one swipe of their paw can take your head off. Now, being a very democratic, full of cooperation type, I put the Russian at the front so he could bite them back.

> *Misha is a brilliant companion. He's been to the Pole; he knows it. And he is a dedicated doctor. Very dedicated. Very Soviet. We live in dread of the morning group pee. It heralds yet another phase of his ongoing medical programme. On Tuesday Rupert was wired up to a portable ECG; at least Rupert will know when he's on his last legs...*

We would eat 8,100 calories a day. This consisted of three-quarters of a pound of butter on its own, like a chocolate bar. We ate buckwheat from the Soviet Union that was disgusting. We had ten-year-old dried meat from some Inuit village that was highly suspicious, and we had these special chocolate bars made by our sponsors in America that had 1,000 calories in each bar. When I saw Rupert eat five for breakfast one morning I knew I'd seen everything.

> *The snow is a lot softer than expected; it's thick and sticks like glue. But we are encountering a hell of a lot of broken ice. I think God must have hurled a giant iceberg from the sky, watched it shatter and then refreeze into millions of ice blue fragments...*

One of the most suicidal things you can ever attempt is to have a bath in the Arctic at minus 60. It's something you shouldn't do. But when it warmed up to minus 30, we would attempt to bathe, because we had straps on our bodies, pulling these sledges, and if you get a sore which then gets infected, you might have to quit going to the Pole. The procedure was as follows. Save two chocolate bars over two days. Bribe Soviet doctor to turn up stove in tent. Soviet doctor takes bars, says: "Capitalist system," eats them and turns up the stoves. Strip stark naked except for your boots. Exit at high speed reminding people that if they did up the tent door and you could not get back in, someone was going to die. Roll vigorously in the nearest snowdrift. Rub soap all over your body. Dive back into the snowdrift again. Rub all the soap off. Re-enter tent at very high speed. No more relief can be explained than by this moment of getting back inside the tent.

> *Respect for this place is the key to survival; it so very much wants one dead...*

As usual, I made some pretty bad mistakes. My biggest, probably of my life, was when Darryl fell down in between two blocks of ice. I thought he was going to get squashed, so I stupidly went over, got hold of the guy and lifted him up. Darryl weighs 200lbs and his pack weighed 100lbs. My back registered a sort of elastic feeling and for the rest of the journey it was highly painful – I wore out a whole disc in the bottom of my spine. Carrying on wasn't a question of being heroic, but of covering one's marketplaces. So I continued to walk.

After 100 miles people were relatively exhausted. But Misha and I, who were the only people stupid enough to have done this more than once, realised that this would be halcyon days compared to what lay ahead.

> *One hundred miles down; three hundred to go. Six feet below, the ocean – a dark, still menace – groans, slowly shifting and cracking the ice... The horizon spread before us like a rumpled white sheet and I thought again of Antarctica. Conditions are appalling. We had expected the pressure ridges to ease off at this latitude but instead we battle ten to 12 hours a day sometimes making only five miles. We should be averaging at least ten...*

Every 20 days an aeroplane would arrive and every time we would hope that somebody might have some imagination at base camp and send something other than just butter and buckwheat and those foul chocolate bars, but they never sent us much. And then some idiot came on this aeroplane with flu. Aaagh! To give people on a polar journey flu is like trying to kill them quick. The Arctic Ocean is a very, very lonely place when things go wrong. Hiro got that flu. He's tiny, he weighs 120lbs and he was carrying 200lbs of equipment. And he went down like a brick. If

you can't eat in the Arctic, you'll die in three days. Every time he ate, he was sick. Every time he drank, he was sick. He was dehydrating; in a dreadful condition. One morning, when he had made a bit of a recovery, I told him we had to carry on, because we were drifting backwards on a moving ice floe, and he turned to me and said: "We've got to get there. And we're going to do it together – if you help me now." I took a bigger sled so I could take some of his gear, and he and I walked along at the back of the group for ten hours a day with him wobbling all over the place, collapsing, throwing up, but always apologising. And gradually he made a recovery.

> *I had lost my spoon, Misha his balaclava. Minor incidents in the explorer's almanac of calamities, but inconvenient nevertheless. Misha found the balaclava on his head and, at the end of a day's uncomfortable travel, I found the spoon in my boot. I knew then we were exhausted...*

Then Darryl blew it.

> *Frostbite is all about. Darryl's feet are frostbitten and blistered; he is limping now. Arved's face is peeling off in great chunks while Hiro's cheek is scorched. Gus is an excellent, hard man; a true Inuit in his element at long last...*

The reality of polar exploration is that, if you make a mistake, you pay for it. Darryl got a blister, got frostbite on the blister and his heel fell off. And I made one of the better decisions that I ever made, realising that the only way he'd get there would be never to see his foot. So I said: "Darryl, you are ordered not to look at your foot," and he was rather angry, but every night we would cover his eyes and tell him it looked much better.

> *So the race for the Pole gathers momentum. Having hit flatter ice last week we continue to slog 12 hours a day, marching at least ten. We camp and attempt to locate some smooth ice for the resupply aircraft, delayed once again by bad weather. Our radios are down*

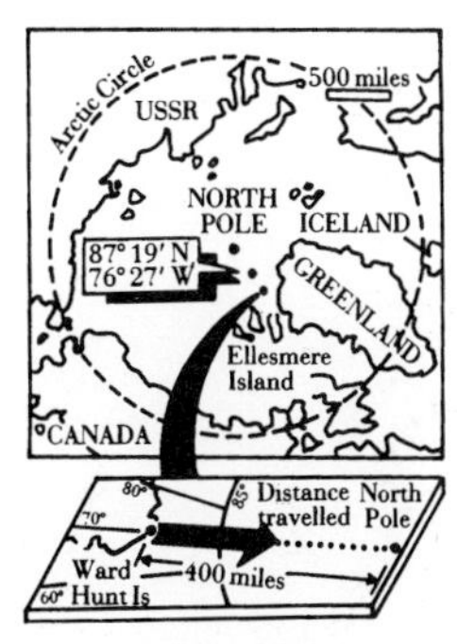

April 28th

and we have had only scant contact with Advance Base Camp at Cape Aldrich these last few days... Misha and I surge ahead at the close of each day's march and watch the men "finish". There ain't nothing or nobody who could stop the men at this point. They are grimly determined; their bodies frozen but for the mechanical movements of their arms and legs. Ice coats their faces; they stop, unable to move for a moment; comically bedraggled...

The Arctic Ocean didn't want us to get to the North Pole, because suddenly, without warning, the temperature went up from minus 30 to minus 15, to minus ten, to minus five. Never in living memory or records had the Arctic Ocean ever been this warm, and under our feet it just smashed up completely. All around us ice was smashing up, opening up; behind us, in front of us, all around us. And somehow we had to weave our way through huge holes and open water. And suddenly, out of nowhere, the team came together. We just said: "OK, Arctic Ocean, give it to us, pal. Do what you can. We ain't gonna quit." We marched for 18 or 20 hours a day as we moved in towards the North Pole. Walking on thin ice, with currents underneath that can take you under the ice itself. And we stuck to it, day in, day out.

We march around the clock setting out at 2am, not halting to camp until 4pm. At least ten of these 14 hours are spent moving; that's 600 long minutes each day. A further six hours disappear sorting the camp morning and evening, leaving only four hours in which to sleep. We need rest so have adopted a 26-hour day; a practical solution for us but somewhat confusing for the support team at base camp...

Open leads of water grow and flourish beneath the warm spring sun. We continue to attempt quite dangerous crossings. Misha, Gus and Graeme scout ahead for likely locations; on their advice we crawl like insects across thin ice – our skis laid out like rafts...

> *Overcome with weariness, men fall asleep on their packs. Graeme continues to struggle on the radio, tackling the worst ionospheric disturbances in recent memory...*
>
> *Our sealskin kamiks, which proved so useful in those halcyon days of towering pressure ridges and minus 40 degree temperatures, have lost their edge in this heat – it's like skiing in bedroom slippers...*
>
> *Temperatures are unpleasantly warm, sapping energy. Fresh snow, sometimes as deep as one-and-a-half metres, makes travelling slow and arduous, particularly on rough ice...*

When we were about 100 miles from the Pole, 22 students from 15 countries arrived at our base camp. They weren't there for the fresh air; they were there to do a job. They did their own experiments and they saw with their own eyes the pollution of the Arctic. They visited Inuit villages to speak to pregnant ladies who were suffering. Mothers who were nursing their children had polluted milk because they'd eaten the animals that had eaten the snow that's full of our blasted chemicals. To a certain extent the students experienced what we were going through, working together, side by side, from all those different countries. They saw clear evidence, even on the surface, of how the Arctic is being trashed, just like the Antarctic.

> *We know that while we march the Icewalk Student Expedition is winging its way North to the 80th Parallel to get cold, to monitor our progress and to make its own statement about the shit the industrialised world is heaping on this remote and fragile place...*

We were also doing experiments of our own. Because pollutant levels over the Poles are lower than anywhere else, they give you a baseline figure to use as a yardstick when measuring pollution over the rest of the globe. We measured the levels of mercury, chlorides, sulphates, nitrates and graphite particles from Ellesmere Island to the North Pole. Every time the supply plane left we would load onto it our experiments and air samples. We found pesticides in the snow of the Arctic Ocean that are only used in Moscow. We would often see smog on the horizon, like in Los Angeles – but in the middle of the Arctic Ocean, thousands of miles away from civilisation. And it was frightening; it was a shock.

May 13th

Tomorrow we arrive at the Pole – a small, tattered, battle-weary troop. Soon we must all part and return home. I won't do anything like this again...

Fifty miles to go. We were in full flight to the Pole, there was no stopping us now. Up to 20 hours a day, still moving on the ice pack. Often going to sleep for a few hours and finding that the ice had drifted back seven miles in the night towards where we'd come from. It was like one step forward, two steps back; not very pleasant. But eventually the navigators Rupert and Arved got rather excited – we were homing in on the Pole.

Suddenly Misha just stopped. We were there. The North Pole...

We embraced each other; sat down; it was over... I was humbled. It was a feeling of not being big but rather incredibly small. The Arctic suddenly felt so immense it belittled all else. Eight men from seven countries were silenced. Now all that was left to us was the journey home...

That's my story. I think that it's important always to place yourself in the right spot, and I know that my spot's with young people. I get on well with them and they like me, because they think I'm crazy and also because they realise they've met a person who followed their dream. If you were 16 now you'd be rather angry, because young people have been completely excluded from their own future. When we went to the South Pole we suffered badly through our lack of care for the world; and when we went to the North Pole we suffered again. I speak to kids and I say: "OK, the grown-ups have blown it. What are you going to do about it?" My concern now is the fact that there are a billion Chinese about to go crazy in an industrial revolution. There are places like Indonesia that have got three times the population of the British Isles, and they don't even know the word "environment". Sometimes I look at the world and I think: "Why bother?" But when I see young people, that inspires me to continue the struggle. I'm not an explorer, because everywhere on this planet has been explored, but I'm exploring the idea of inspiring youngsters to hit back and do something.

> *People ask me why I do it. Wally Herbert once said: "And of what value is this journey? It is well for those who ask such a question that there are others who feel the answer and never need to ask..."*

I beseech you as individuals to think what you and your company are actually doing. How much recycled material one is actually using. Does one just recycle a couple of milk bottles and feel fabulous? What am I doing? That's a question you must always ask yourselves. I sincerely believe the American Indians had it right. Whenever they made a decision of any type, they made that decision bearing in mind what it would mean for people in seven generations' time. We've forgotten it. And if we don't wake up, we're going to blow it, because I've been there, I've seen the future, and it hurts. But I've also seen the future of young people doing something, and I reckon it works.

PS Despite Robert's resolution "never to do this again" he has, in fact, mounted another, two-stage, expedition to the South Pole: One Step Beyond – The Antarctic Challenge. This time he will take with him up to eight young people from different countries and, while the walkers are making their way on foot to the South Pole, two ships will leave from South America, the continent where the first Earth Summit was held, their destination the Arctic continent. On board the ships will be approximately 50 young people from 50 different nations. They will undertake an extensive educational programme, based on the Earth Summit's Agenda 21, and will join the walkers, after their successful journey to the South Pole, at the edge of Antarctica in celebration of the 50th anniversary of UNESCO. Afterwards, all the youngsters will be made Special Envoys to UNESCO, with the task of raising public and government awareness throughout the world. GOOD LUCK EVERYONE!

CHAPTER 6 **Breaking the Sales Barrier**

ALAN WHERRY started his first business at the tender age of ten in his home town of Belfast, selling imported American comics. Selling has always been Alan's forté, and in his time he has sold pinball machines, one-arm bandits and jukeboxes. He spent 12 years working for Procter & Gamble in sales and advertising then, in the early 1980s, became sales director of Penguin Books, where he helped turn the company around. When he became a founder of the new publishing company, Bloomsbury, it was a gamble – which, as we now know, paid off gloriously.

In a wonderful, funny talk in January 1990, Alan gave us his secrets for breaking the sales barrier, explained why you should love the word "no" and recounted the unforgettable tale of the enthusiastic terrier...

ALAN WHERRY

Do you remember the first time you sat on an aeroplane and it was about to take off?

It's a pretty terrifying experience – most people who are in that position for the first time are really rather nervous. And when the cabin staff came over and explained the emergency procedures, you really listened, didn't you? "The emergency exits are over here and over here, and your lifebelt is tied like this, in a bow at the back." You listened as if your life depended on it.

I'd like to make an invitation for you to listen to me tonight as though it was your first time on an aeroplane; as if what I said could really make a difference for you, could help you in your work, or in your family life – or just life in general – to be more successful. And the promise that I make you is this: you won't like all that I have to say, I guarantee it, but it's simple, and it works.

Most people haven't got a clue what selling is all about. If we were going to hire a sales person, what sort of qualities would we be looking for? Credibility? Personality? Fluency? A tough skin? Understanding what the customer needs? When you ask this question, on average, about 80 per cent of people will talk about techniques and about 20 per cent will mention attitudes. Most training is about the technical aspects of jobs, how to do things, not about attitudes. But attitudes are what is most important.

Every Saturday morning, my wife and I go to our local supermarket. There's one woman who's happy and friendly, who always comes over and says hello. She's helpful, points out where things are, helps you pack your bag. The other staff are well trained. They look nice, they're efficient, courteous and so on. But there's only one like her. How come? All the rest have had the training. The interesting thing about attitudes is that, essentially, they're not about what's right and wrong, or what's good or bad – they're about what empowers you in your job and what stops you.

So I'd like first to talk for a moment about what stops us all. It's obvious as you go about your daily life that most people you meet are stuck in a rut. And, very largely, it's the things they say about themselves that put them in that position. "My parents screwed me up..."; "I went to boarding school and..."; "I was born working class..."; "I didn't really have the right qualifications for what I wanted to do..." Those stories are actually what hold people up. They're interesting and often true. But the people who are really successful are the ones who are able to carry on regardless.

It's not that they're geniuses, that in every area they're much better than the rest of us. The main thing is, they're not stopped by themselves.

My father, a joiner by trade, was good with people and good at talking in front of an audience. But he was stopped by himself. He had a story that life was such that "they" were out to get you, and so you should never really trust people too far, because as soon as you opened up you'd get a knife in the back. Needless to say, with that story he didn't get very far.

I read this some time ago. It's about being stopped by yourself, and I'd like to share it with you: "For a long time it seemed to me that life was about to begin. Real life. But there was always some obstacle in the way to be got through first. Time still to be served, a debt to be paid and then life to begin. At last, it dawned on me that these obstacles were my life."

So, if successful people aren't stopped by themselves, what tricks do they use? The first is to recognise the characteristics that we all have as human beings – and not allow them to stop them.

If we look at the nature of what being human is, there are a number of things that I'd like to draw to your attention.

There is, for example, looking good. Most of us would do anything to look good – as we see it. Like those guys on the plane who are sitting reading the paper while you're listening to the emergency procedures. If there was an emergency they'd be in deep trouble, yet they're still into looking good.

Another one is this: "I know how life is. Don't tell me about it." Very much like my father.

Another one is being right. When I have an argument with my 20-year-old, I know I'm right and he knows he's right, so there's nowhere to go. We all like being right, but it's better to look wrong and win than insist you're right and lose.

Another is: "That's not it." No matter how successful you are right now, now matter how great you're doing, you always feel: "That's not really it – if only... and then it would be great..." But it almost never is. When you get to that point there's always something else: it's human nature.

Another is this notion of minimising risk. We all like to create a cocoon around ourselves where we're not exposed to risk, where we've got nothing at stake.

And yet another thing is that we're stuck with our beliefs. If we put a rat in a maze with four tunnels and always put the cheese in the fourth tunnel, after a while the rat always learns to go to the fourth tunnel to get the cheese. A human will learn to do that too. You want the cheese? Go down the fourth tunnel. Now, after a while, the great god in the white suit moves the cheese to another tunnel. The rat goes to the fourth tunnel. No cheese. Comes out, looks around, back down the fourth tunnel. After a few attempts the rat will stop looking in the fourth tunnel and look elsewhere. But the difference between humans and rats is simple: humans will go down that tunnel for ever. Rats don't believe in anything; humans come to believe in that fourth tunnel, whether there's cheese in it or not. And the human would rather be right than get the cheese.

Do you know the first law of holes? If you're in a hole, stop digging. Most of us don't. When I got the job as sales director of Penguin, I was really thrilled. The only problem was, the company was losing two million quid a year and the sales force wasn't up to much. For three months it was OK, and then I had a terrible shock. I went into the Vice Chairman's office (and I must say here that of all the techniques a sales person should have, being able to read upside down is often very useful) and I saw a list of all the non-main board directors. Next to my name was only one comment: "Overpaid". Every month, for about a year, I was terrified, scared stiff. But at the next sales conference I stood up and said to the reps: "Do you know what the real problem is here? You lot think you're the best in the industry, but you're not in the top five. I'm making a commitment here and now that within two years you will be the best in the industry, whether you want to be or not – and I hope a lot of you will want to."

At that stage, I'd taken on board that I'd rather get fired for trying to make it work than please everybody else and get fired anyway. And it worked. Four or five years followed where I enjoyed being the sales director of Penguin, going around Europe, meeting nice people, talking about books, and it was really good. But the trouble was that I was bored, and there was no risk in my life. Starting Bloomsbury was an enormous risk, because in order to get the company going we had to resign our existing jobs before the full investment in Bloomsbury was agreed. I had a wife, three kids, a bloody great mortgage, I was scared and, you know what – it was great fun! Taking a risk is not always pleasant, but what I'm saying is that we minimise risk too much and don't often enough put ourselves in the position where we have something at stake.

The next point is the distinction between goals and intentions. Normally, I've got lots of intentions and very few goals. For example: I intend to stop smoking, I intend to get fit. I've got an exercise video and I really intend to do it. In fact I did do it – once. Diet books feed off people's intentions. You could write a diet book in one page: eat less, eat healthy, exercise. One page. The trouble is, books that are one page long don't sell. But diet books sell by the cartload, usually all to the same people. So how do you distinguish goals from intentions? Because intentions are all up here in our heads – they're not worth anything.

The first thing about a goal is that it must be in writing. If it's not written down, it's not a goal. The second thing is that it must be specific. I remember a manager saying to me: "Your objective is to maximise sales in your territory." What does this mean? How would you know when you got there? So, I like the mnemonic BOMM. BASE: Say you get four displays in a sales cycle. OBJECTIVE: The objective is to get ten. MEASUREMENT: How are you going to measure your achievements? (In this case, it's fairly straightforward.) METHOD: How are you going to go about it? If you haven't got BOMM, or something like it, it's not a goal. A goal has to be believable; you must be able to adjust to new information as and when it appears; and goals must be daily, short-term and long-term, otherwise you can forget about them. One of the most important things about a goal is that you have to share it with others. Have you noticed that none of us are very good at doing things on our own? And yet we try to. We say: "I'm all right, I know how to do this." You must share your goals with others. It is also important to review goals regularly and to base your review on activities rather than results. The other thing is, if it's valid, start today. Don't wait. If the goals are that important, start right now. Most people say: "In three months time, I'm going to…" You've heard it all before.

Another technique that successful people use is to bring down the barriers. Most sales people tell customers things which make the sales rep look good. But when you ask customers questions you give *them* the opportunity to look good. When we started Bloomsbury, most of our reps had no experience. I was in this little independent bookstore in the Midlands with a new rep and she was really nervous. She said: "I really find this one difficult." "Why is that?" "Because every time I ask the manager to buy ten copies, I never get them. If I ask for six copies, I don't even get them." So I started talking to the manager, and I asked: "How do you do your buying here?" And he said: "Basically, with new books, I buy either one, two or three copies." Once she'd understood the context in which this guy did his buying her life became a little easier and, if she'd wanted to ask him to buy ten, she could acknowledge his usual buying policy, and say: "Now, I know you only normally buy one, two or three new books, but this time I'm asking you to buy ten because..." And the barriers come down.

There's a story that really moved me recently.

> *A friend of mine has a family business in Northern Ireland. They make exercise books; if you go into a shop and buy an exercise book, there's a fifty-fifty chance it's one of theirs. And they opened up a telecommunications company, selling telephone systems for small companies. But it was a disaster. In their fourth year they were still losing money, and the sales people were making a thousand calls for every order they got. They were losing them in droves, as you can imagine. So they headhunted for an individual to run the business. One of the questions they asked applicants was: "Are you enthusiastic?" And one guy came along and said: "Let me tell you about enthusiasm. I've got a little terrier, it's 12 years old, and every night we like to sit by the fire and watch TV, with the dog lying beside us. Every time the doorbell rings, the terrier's up and out to the door to see who's there. I'm like that terrier, I'm that enthusiastic. And do you know what? Never in 12 years has the person knocking on the door been calling for the terrier."*

This applicant was sharing his experience of life in a way that everyone can understand. He didn't just answer the question. Most people would have said: "Yeah, I'm enthusiastic." But in answering the way he did, he brought the barriers down – and got the job.

Another technique. Have you ever noticed how few people seek help to develop their skills? When I was first a salesman, I was terrified of the manager of the Birkenhead Co-op in Heswall, Cheshire. Everybody was terrified of him; he was an animal, and I used to dread going in to see him. He used to make mincemeat of me. I said to my boss: "Every time I go to see this guy it's appalling, he just wipes the floor with me. What can I do?" And he replied: "Try this – go in and just ask him why he behaves the way he does with you." So I went in and I said: "Do you mind if I ask you something? How long have you been doing your job?" He said: "Thirty-two years." I said: "I've only been doing this job three months." And he said: "I know, it shows." So I said: "Look, I've got about 80 customers and I get on pretty well with most of them, but for some reason whatever I say seems to really upset you. What am I doing wrong? I am prepared to change." The guy just looked at me and said: "It's nothing son, don't worry about it. I'm just a crotchety old geezer." The next time I called, he took me to one side and said: "Do you know what? Most people think the best display sites in my supermarket are just inside the door, but on my busiest days I open the glass doors and you can't get at those sites. In fact, the best sites are at the checkout, because that's where the queues are." He was prepared to share, but first I had to do my bit, to admit that I wasn't all that brilliant, and to ask for his help.

Have you noticed that when other people – your wife, husband, friends, colleagues – describe you, their description of you is usually a lot better than the one that you would apply to yourself? So, that being the case, think of what would be possible if we could live our lives in that description, rather than the one we apply to ourselves.

You know, for most people, you can cross out the word "commitment" and write in "burden". That's me. Have you noticed how a lot of sales people dislike targets? It's fear of failure. But have you heard the John F Kennedy story? When JFK became president, he got a group of people around him and said that he wanted a man on the moon in ten years. Everybody said it wasn't possible; or that it might be possible by the end of the century, but that it would cost a fortune. However, in an area where there had been no possibility, just one man's commitment meant that in ten years the Americans did put a man on the moon.

Another very important strategy is this little word "No". A couple of weeks ago a man from a courier company phoned me up and said: "I sent you our brochure last week, Mr Wherry, did you get it?" I said: "No," because I had thrown it in the bin and didn't want to admit that I hadn't read it. So he said: "Do you use couriers?" I said: "No." He said: "Why not?" "Too expensive." "Did you ever use couriers?" "Well, we did at one time, but it was costing us a fortune to send the books to Hong Kong, Japan and Australia." "Why did you stop?" "Too expensive, I've already said that." So he said: "Well, if you ever want anything, give me a bell." Now, you can see what's going on there. That guy writes down: "One call," but it wasn't, was it? What could he have done? He could have started to clarify, to use "No" as the start point and to say: "Where do you most often send overseas parcels? What method do you use? Would you look at it if I came back with a quote? The cost of airmail is such and such, and this is what we could do it for – could we talk about it?" But he didn't. And the thing is that the average sales person doesn't recognise "No" for what it is: an opportunity to ask another question, to clarify and to open the doors. What they usually do is what he did, withdraw and lose the sale, or get hostile and lose the sale. So, although it sounds a terrible cliché, you just have to learn to love the word "No".

Another thing I've noticed really successful people do is to operate the GOYA principle. Have you come across it? Get Off Your Arse. And stop procrastinating. Part of the principle is to take each day at a time, so that if you had a rotten day yesterday, it doesn't mean that you're going to have a rotten day today. You've got to plan your future instead of worrying about it. You have to stop looking for fairness in life; life's not fair. A lot of people think it should be, but it's not. So you shouldn't feel guilty when you fail and you should always commit to high performance. And develop your sense of humour.

The final technique is the most important – you should *enjoy* yourself. Have you noticed that successful people enjoy themselves at work? There's a funny thing about enjoying yourself. Sometimes when you're doing something really well and enjoying it, you're not really conscious of what you're doing. For example, I'm a terrible dancer because I'm always aware of what I'm doing, how gauche I probably look. But on the rare occasions when I'm having a really good time nobody notices what a terrible dancer I am. When Cantona scores, he's not aware – he's just doing. Enjoy yourself; it's really important.

If you're in doubt about the things I'm saying, don't worry about whether you believe me or not: try them and see if they work, because if they do you're quids in. What I promise you, if you do try them, is this:

a) The techniques work;
b) You'll be at least twice as effective in your job as you are at the moment;
c) Your life and your job will be a lot easier;
d) You'll definitely enjoy yourself – and you'll be successful.

MALCOLM POYNTER

grew up in south east London and left school at 15 with no qualifications. In six years he was employed in more than 30 different jobs, from puff pastry chef to hairdresser, before deciding to study vocational graphics at Goldsmiths' College of Art. He also spent three years at the Royal College of Art studying sculpture. Since then his achievements include 35 major international sculpture exhibitions, the concept and design of two restaurants in Japan, an experimental video project with Peter Gabriel, album covers, jewellery design and recording a 12-inch single. He has also worked on theatre projects and opened a museum of his work in a Tokyo superstore.

Malcolm's passion for his subject was obvious as he gave us his forthright views about the art establishment when he visited Utopia in March 1990. Our gallery was filled with an exhibition of his figures and other works which typified his approach – described by the *Observer* as being "as subtle as a kick in the crotch".

When I was at school the only thing I was good at was

From the age of about ten years old I knew what I wanted to do. But my parents thought of education as something you had the minimum of before going and getting a job as quickly as possible – it was a class thing. So it never occurred to me to go to college, and I spent six or seven years working in so many jobs you wouldn't believe it, some of the time doing little drawings and things like that at home. I always wanted to make "stuff" (I didn't even know the word sculpture), and one day I met a guy in a pub who told me you could get a grant to go to college – and that was it. I was 21, and I had the major problem of not having any qualifications, so I ended up at Goldsmiths' doing vocational graphics.

After about the first year I was totally convinced I couldn't do it, so I went back to doing bits of painting and things, but far more seriously; it felt like something I ought to be doing. Then the painting started to go three-dimensional, and I spent a lot of time at the ceramics school learning about moulding and casting. In fact, I spent most of my time there, and I was also working back at home.

When I got to the third year they asked me what I was going to do afterwards, and since everyone else was applying to the Royal College I thought I would, too. I couldn't believe it when I got in. We then had to put on our final-year show: vocational graphics. Of course I had all this work at home, stacks and stacks of it, and for the show we had one little cubicle. One of my pieces would have taken up the whole cubicle, so I asked if I could have more space. They couldn't understand it because I hadn't done any graphics work all year, but eventually I managed to secure one of the small halls they used for dancing, and I filled it with photographs, information, lots of deformed babies that I had been investigating. It was quite good. It certainly made people respond.

When I started at the RCA I met some guys in the Students' Union who got me interested in politics. I started to find out why I was making what I was. At this time I was concentrating on references to the family, and this idea of how, as a culture, we treated each other. I used to go down to Bexley Mental Hospital with a video camera and interview the consultant psychiatrist. Almost every hospital I went to had a psycho-geriatric ward to which people were condemned. This fascinated me, and I still make a point of going into hospital museums around the world, to get into the nub of what drives "us". That's where my work always comes from.

I was producing tableaux of elderly people in pyjamas, and I liked the confrontation with brutality combined with the fact that you could almost sit down with these people. It produced a certain amount of disturbance; you would walk into the room not quite knowing who was who.

After my final show I set off for New York and did some exhibitions there, and then I did some teaching back in England. My work at the time – the late Seventies and early Eighties – involved figures looking into mirrors, conflicting with each other, abusing each other. Sometimes they were installation pieces involving ten or 12 figures. I also started what is now an ongoing theme, *The Horsemen of the Apocalypse*. It's a "piece" that is continually running through my work.

I was working on the same themes as before: observation and the way we behave with each other. So *Having and Being* is about the fact that there are two sorts of people: the "having" people who want everything – all the money, everything; and the "being" people, who want to interact with other people and to give to people. *Threatened by the Big I* is all about gays being hounded. These intrinsic interests that we all have never leave you, they just get transmuted and changed into new ideas. Following the hospital research, I was getting into behavioural psychology, reading as much as possible. I found a book on the First World War called *The Atrocities of Man*, which had a profound influence on me.

I am not interested in horror. I am interested in our darker side, but also in our marvellous side. I try to imbue my work with a conscious sense of beauty which, because it is disturbing, might not necessarily be easily seen – but to me it has a certain aesthetic. I used to go out of my way to upset people, but nowadays I don't seem to have to bother. Ever since I started, people have said: "Why can't you make something that's nice?" My answer is that there should be a spectrum of work, and there's enough "nice" English, middle-class work.

If I were a woman I would be tempted to be a feminist separatist – I wouldn't have much to do with men. I did quite a lot of work in the mid-Eighties concerning my attitude and responses to women. I had been brought up to believe that women and black people were meant to know their place, and this period was like a revelation to me. This process of creating and exploring was very much about finding out where I was coming from. You have to sort these things out within yourself before you can go out and create "your work".

Then I moved on to work that was concerned with stripping away all the layers that are not essential: clothes and hair and the things we disguise ourselves with culturally. I have always felt that the male of the species is very destructive, and I tried to show this by using shaved, bald people: whatever I do, my work always comes back to life-sized figures. Life-sized can be indeterminate, from four-foot to seven-foot people, but one can respond to a life-sized figure in certain ways and it's that response I'm after.

Then I started to use my work as more of an overview, looking at us as a species in an analytical way. I started to try and use smaller and more symbolic images within my work, making figures that were constructed of guns and toy soldiers – multiples, in other words – building up a comment on culturally specific facts, such as males being given guns to play with as children. Then I went on to use fish or vegetables – suggesting eco-themes like how marvellous fish are – and making pieces from pebbles. It's a question of selecting things and rearranging them. The work which is currently absorbing me is making multiples using faces and bones.

The most recent piece I have done is a giant wheel, called *One Step Forward*. I am very much a pessimist when I look at the way we develop, and the piece is all about how we don't seem to learn very much in terms of our various cultures. At the moment there are more wars going on than

"Untitled" (1992)

at any time in history. War, interpersonal relationships, sexuality, are the things that fascinate me about people. These experiences are vital to us all – but we rarely talk about them and are not educated to deal with them.

One Step Forward took about a year to make, and the way I work is to have, say, five different pieces going at the same time. I get fed up doing certain pieces because it takes so long – weeks and months – so I like to switch over to other work. My first sculptures were papier-mâché, like we all made at school – I do believe that "making" is innate in us all; we all like doodling in the sand. As my knowledge of different materials grew I started to use other materials, and as my money grew I could sometimes give something to a technician to work on – although I like to have as much control as possible over what I make. The textures of the materials and the aesthetic have all been incredibly important to me.

I work primarily for myself. The amount of "competition" all over the world is something I don't like: it's all about money. I am very old-fashioned – I never accept commissions; I never do anything unless I wish to do it. At the same time I agree with what Duchamp said, that art doesn't exist unless it's in the public arena. But the public arena is so boring. That's why, when people who know my work have asked me to get involved in collaborations, I have often done it – I see these projects as an absolute liberation; I can fashion ideas that don't seem to work in terms of sculpture and use them in terms of theatre, jewellery, sounds, publications and so on.

I use restaurants, record covers, jewellery, anything I can, because I know that most people can't afford to buy my work, so I want to get these images and the ideas associated with them out in as many ways as possible. I know that if I do a Peter Gabriel record cover it's going to reach hundreds of thousands of people.

I would just like to conclude with a Goethe couplet which continues to inspire me:

> "*Whatever you can do,*
> *Or dream you can*
> *Begin it.*
> *Boldness has genius,*
> *Power, and magic in it.*"

"Ecology 41" (1988) ➤

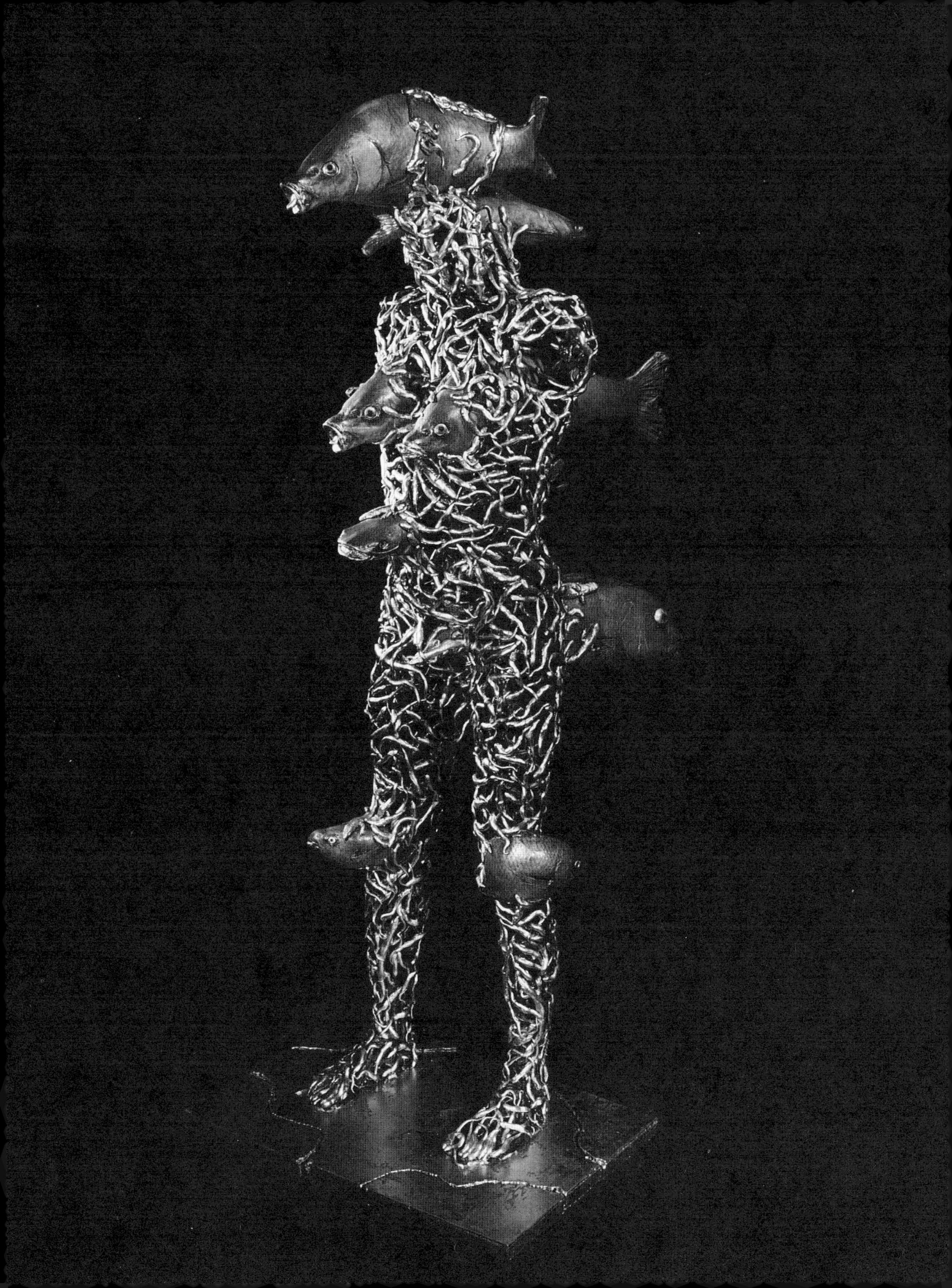

HN HEGARTY was fired his job with ad agency Benton and Bowles in and almost packed in his new career. Luckily advertising industry he didn't, and went on Cramer Saatchi (later to become Saatchi and i) and then to found TBWA as creative director. 2 John set up Bartle Bogle Hegarty, the agency ible for Audi's *Vorsprung durch Technik*, for ng sex as a selling point for Häagen-Dazs ice nd for making people want to buy Levi 501s the commercials had to be taken off air while tocked. John himself has won many awards, wo D&AD golds and six silvers, *Campaign* silvers for press campaigns and a British gold and several silvers.

When John came to Newell and Sorrell in April 1990 he brought with him a selection of show-reels which took us right back to the advent of TV advertising 40 years ago. His talk, combined with classic commercials from Gibbs SR to Hamlet, Heineken to Hovis, gave us an insight into the ways in which advertising has become an accurate mirror of society – and an essential part of our vocabulary.

Commercial television started transmitting in this country in 1955, during an era in which technology ruled supreme. A belief in science and the wonders that it would bring went almost unquestioned. We were on the threshold of a world of plenty–plenty for all.

British advertising at that time looked to America for its influences. America was, after all, not only fuelling this era of change, but also driving the engine. It was the source of inspiration and development – what America experienced today, we felt tomorrow.

At that time advertising in the States was under the influence of a man called Rosser Reeves, who, in the Forties, had coined a phrase: "The Unique Selling Proposition". In doing so, he had developed a framework within which to create and develop advertising. It was, and still is, a strong and very simple formula. It worked by highlighting a product difference and presented that difference as the product's advantage over its competitors. It also neatly fitted the attitude of mind at that time, the belief in the supremacy of technology and science.

British advertising, by and large, adopted this philosophy. Whatever you were selling, from toothpaste to women's underwear, the USP was presented as the product's reason to be.

It's tingling fresh. It's fresh as ice. It's Gibbs SR toothpaste. Tingling fresh toothpaste that does your gums good too. The tingle you get when you brush with SR is much more than a nice taste, it's a tingle of health. It tells you something very important, that you're doing your gums good and toughening them to resist infection. And as this chart shows, gum infection is the cause of more tooth losses than decay itself. The tingle in SR comes from Sodium Ricinoleate, a substance which both dental research and years of use in dental practice have shown to be good for the gums. So, to keep your teeth white as snow, your gums really healthy and your breath really fresh, see your dentist regularly and brush with SR, the tingling fresh toothpaste for teeth and gums. Gibbs SR.

GIBBS SR

The first advertisement shown on British television, in 1955

As we now look at these commercials, they are wonderfully naive – repetitive and crudely made. There was no attempt to entertain or to flatter the consumer's intelligence. A mindless repetition of the product's USP was seen as sufficient to persuade the viewer. Commercials often became more akin to short lectures, with bar charts and detailed drawings showing the product's effects or advantages. The viewer was expected to sit still and pay attention.

In the mid Fifties and early Sixties advertisers began to use music in an attempt to entertain. It was often specially written for advertising, and referred to as "jingles". It was given this name because it took some product difference or advantage and endlessly repeated, with a very simple tune, the product's USP – and jingled round your brain driving you insane.

Murray Mints, Murray Mints, too good to hurry mints,
Why make haste when you can taste
The hint of mint in Murray Mints?
Murray Mints, Murray Mints, too good to hurry mints.
Murray Mints, Murray Mints, too good to hurry mints.

Of course, television itself was still in its infancy. The growth in television ownership only really took off in the late Fifties, reaching something like 90 per cent of households by the late Sixties. As the medium itself began to develop, so did advertising. It had, after all, to compete with the programmes it was sandwiched between – and they were becoming better and better. So to stop viewers using the commercial break as the opportunity to make tea or visit the loo, advertising began to address the problem of entertainment.

How could commercials be made more involving, more enjoyable to watch, less banal and insulting to the ordinary viewer's intelligence? It also occurred to some people within the industry that if you were enjoying what you were watching there was a good chance you might be more receptive to the message being transmitted.

By the late Sixties British advertising had begun to distance itself from America and to develop a character of its own. It was often still wedded to the USP as a philosophy, but attempted to be British in character, to use a British sense of humour, to employ understatement and charm, in an attempt to compete with the growing quality of the programmes. It began to cast its actors more imaginatively, to use music in a more entertaining way and to accept that it didn't have to repeat the product name over and over again to get people to understand the point that was being made and to remember the message. Advertisers began to realise that they had to entertain before they could inform. So began the development of the British commercial as, almost, mini-programmes. We called it the 30-second theatre.

Happiness is a cigar called Hamlet.

By now the general public were becoming quite sophisticated in their knowledge and understanding of the advertising commercial, and along with that sophistication began the first glimmers of a disenchantment with the USP as a sole motivator. This change, of course, was being driven by events beyond the world of advertising.

All of a sudden, progress and technology were not so desirable. You began to hear words like "pollution" and "carcinogenic". Artificial additives in foods began to take on sinister overtones. Our love affair with progress as the answer to all our problems was starting to falter.

By the 1970s British advertising, in its growing maturity, reflected those changes. We realised that we could extol a product's virtues as being "unchanged". Nostalgia, the fact that a product was old-fashioned, became a potent marketing tool. Also, the desire for more stimulating advertising resulted in commercials rooted not just in advertising fantasy but also in how people perceived the real world.

Advertising realised that if it was going to be more entertaining the storylines could be more current and more stimulating.

Last on my round would be old Ma Peggotty's place. 'Twas like taking bread to the top of the world. 'Twas a grand ride back, though. And I knew 't baker'd have t'kettle on and doorsteps of hot Hovis ready. "There's wheatgerm in them loaves," he'd say. "Get it inside you, boy..." (Voiceover) Hovis still has many times more wheatgerm than ordinary bread. It's as good for you today as it's always been.

As technological developments and innovation gathered pace, and marketing departments of companies became increasingly sophisticated, the ability of products to remain technologically superior in any meaningful way became a thing of the past. Parity became the norm, not superiority. Products were separated by their emotional differences. In the 1980s we moved from advertising a product's USPs to its ESPs – the Emotional Selling Propositions.

Increasingly, today's society measures the value of something not only by its function and performance: does it do the job properly? is it reliable? is it competitively priced? – but also by a wider set of values: does it relate to my lifestyle? is it in keeping with my beliefs? do I sympathise with the company's corporate objectives?

Advertising's task has therefore grown more complex over the years. But so have its opportunities. If it effectively reflects the outside world's changes and concerns, it becomes more stimulating and involving. Part of the success of the industry has been to do just that and produce creative work, not rooted in inanity, but in the real world of aspiration and desire. It is this ability that has brought the industry so much publicity and stimulated the comment that sometimes the ads are better than the programmes.

By responding to change and social pressure, we have seen advertising emerge from a clichéd ghetto into a format that is stimulating, entertaining and stylish, and that has captured the public's attention. It has, in fact, joined the real world. It has become part of society's vocabulary. It does still plumb the depths, but as someone wisely said: "Without the bad, you can't have the good." It's just a shame that bad ads are also, so often, banal as well.

The best commercials today succeed not just because they are witty, clever or dramatically filmed, but because they capture a moment in time, they reflect the society they are in and are not afraid to do so in a way that will make people stand up and talk.

"The water in Mayorca doesn't taste like what it ought to."
"No, no. The wa'er in Majorka don't taste like wot i' ough'er."
"The water in Mayorca doesn't taste quite how it should?"
"Majorka!"
"Mayorca."
"MAJORKA!"
"Mayorca!"
"Hoi, Tel, looks like we need something fresh round 'ere."
"Get your laughing gear round that."
"Ooh! Fine – The wa'er in Majorka don't taste like wot i' ough'er.
Oh, gosh! The wa'er in Majorka don't taste like wot i' ough'er."
"She's cracked it! She's only cracked it!"
"Ya, absolutely Ron."

Heineken refreshes the parts wot other beers cannot reach.

FRED ATKINSON studied economics at Oxford University and lectured at Jesus and Trinity Colleges before taking up Government service in 1949. He worked in the Cabinet Office, the British Embassy in Washington, the Treasury, the Department of Trade and Industry, the OECD in Paris and the Department of Energy. From 1977 to 1979 he advised first Denis Healey as Chancellor of the Exchequer and then Sir Geoffrey Howe. He received a knighthood in 1979.

BRYAN QUILTER, who chaired our evening of economics questions and answers, held a number of influential posts with large business organisations, including managing director of Rank Leisure Services and director of the Rank Organisation, director of Granada Group Plc and, from 1985 until his retirement in 1988, industrial director and then non-executive director of the National Economic Development Office – where he worked with the Government, the CBI and the TUC. Bryan was awarded the CBE in 1985.

Very sadly, Bryan died in December 1993, and this chapter – based on the Question Time held in July 1990 – is published with the permission of his widow, Diana. We would like it to be a tribute to him.

Bryan *Fred is going to answer questions, and we'd like some comments from you on the answers he gives. Mark him quite severely. Artistic interpretation and technical excellence are two of the areas we will cover. So let's get going.*

Question

How accurate is economic forecasting?

I used to go by forecasts, and most of them were wrong.

Bryan *Fred, where would we stand in the international league of forecasters? Every time a league of any sort is published, we seem to be at the bottom of it, and I just wonder if all the other countries go around saying: "Well, we're not very good at this, but at least the British are worse."*

Fred Obviously, you can't get these things exactly right, any more than you can get weather forecasting or some diagnoses in medicine right all the time. Forecasting is far from accurate, as is not surprising when outcomes depend on the moods and decisions of 50 million people – not to mention the rest of the world, which may suddenly produce a doubling of the price of oil or a collapse in Wall Street. But I think most experience in the last ten or 15 years shows that, most of the time, forecasts get within a reasonable margin. The same is true in other countries. Every year, the Treasury publishes a table comparing forecasts with results. It shows many mistakes – but enough near misses to make forecasts worth taking note of.

> **Q** What's the realistic optimum rate of inflation? Is zero inflation ever possible?

Fred It would be desirable – money would retain its value, as it did from 1815 to 1914. This would simplify calculation and forward planning. However, no major country has achieved zero inflation during the last 50 years, and the costs of aiming seriously at it would be very high in terms of unemployment and bankruptcies, because economic policy would have to enforce a low level of demand – a long-lasting slump. So, most governments today aim at a low rate of inflation, about two to four per cent a year, rather than a zero rate.

> **Q** At the end of the day, if it's wages that drive underlying price inflation, is there some mechanism by which any government can begin to influence that fundamental problem?

Fred There have been a number of attempts, of course. Sometimes they've even worked for a while, and there have been several periods when the rate of inflation was drastically reduced. The last time it was done in a dramatic way was in 1975. Inflation had reached about 25 per cent and when some of the TUC were brought to accept a limit it came down to around ten per cent. It probably could not have been done without that kind of direct intervention. There are disadvantages, though, even while this measure is succeeding, because employers aren't really free to pay what they want for labour, which creates a bit of a blockage. These things also tend not to last very well, because eventually the unions or workers feel that they have made terrific sacrifices and the policy tends to weaken, followed by an outburst of wage inflation which some people say gets you back to where you started. Personally, I think wage controls have a part to play, but they are very much outside Conservative Party thinking, as they believe in a free-for-all (so to speak), subject only to general monetary policy.

Q I've always felt that the Government, of whichever colour, has a conceited view of being able to control interest rates, and that at the end of the day they are controlled by supply and demand. Do you agree?

Fred Yes, I mainly agree. But it depends so much on people's expectations. If a signal is given by the Bank of England or the Government, interest rates can suddenly be altered by that, rather than by the market.

Q Is it ever possible to have a booming economy which is not followed by a recession a few years later?

Fred Alternation between boom and slump has always been a feature of capitalist economies. However, in the last 50 years this "trade cycle" has been much milder than before. It is probably impossible to even it out completely, but governments nowadays are well aware of the need to check booms before they become too violent. Booms have usually been moderated by measures such as tax increases and rising interest rates. Recessions have often been alleviated by cheap credit and tax reductions, although sometimes the "recessions" have meant only a pause in growth.

Bryan *What is "short-termism", and is it a threat to a healthy economy?*

Fred The "short-termism" that one reads about in the press is a critical phrase suggesting that companies in this country actively watch their share price the whole time, making sure their dividends are going up, and so are not able to rely on finance remaining stable on a long-term basis. It's alleged that poor performance is punished, because the more profitable company can swallow up the less profitable one, even if the less profitable one is several times its size. I suppose short-termism is a good thing, within limits.

Q What level should personal taxation be set at to produce the most healthy economy?

Fred There is no proven answer to this question. It is noticeable that most major European economies have a rate of tax return to total national income of around 40 per cent, including taxes on goods and services such as VAT, as well as income tax and corporate taxation. Nor is there any great difference in the rates of personal income tax, so it might be concluded that current rates of taxation are bearable and do not interfere with economic growth.

Bryan *We are constantly told that a high pound inhibits exports, but given the rise in the D-mark and the yen in the last 30 years relative to other major currencies, how is it that their export performance is so good? We're supposed to have a weak pound to help our exports, but these two countries have strong currencies and they've done nothing but win all the prizes going.*

Fred I think the explanation is that the Germans and the Japanese have put up the most terrific economic performances. Quite irrespective of the exchange rate, they have increased their efficiency at an amazing pace in the post-war decades. The German currency started at a pretty low value, but their tremendous export activity tended naturally to push it up, because they started building up big surpluses. Its current high value has been a consequence of their efficiency.

The Consultant

"If I had been in charge what would I have done differently? Fair question. For starters, I would have had this line representing profits move up instead of down"

Q Why are we, as a nation, so keen on possessing our own homes? What effect does the growing number of home-owners have on the economy?

Fred Most countries with a high standard of living, such as the USA and Australia, are like us in having a high level of home ownership. It is, after all, a very natural thing, but was beyond the reach of many people in the past. I don't know why this is not as common on the Continent. The effect of this phenomenon on the economy is to absorb large quantities of savings which might otherwise be available to industrial investment. It may also reduce the mobility of labour, unless there is a very effective housing market and easy finance.

Q Have we still got a skills shortage? If so, what can we do about it?

Fred We do still have a skills shortage, though it is less apparent during and after a recession which has reduced demand for labour of all types. Many studies have shown that our provision for education and training falls short of that in some other European countries, especially Germany, and also in Japan. Many more young people in those countries acquire qualifications than in this country. The Government has just published plans to improve the situation, but as well as much more Government money to increase supply, industry must learn to demand and to use more skilled workers.

Q But won't increasing computerisation and improvements in all areas of technology carry on reducing the number of people in the workforce?

Fred Technology has been improving productivity for several centuries now; it is a fallacy to suppose it must reduce employment. As long as there are unsatisfied wants the market will expand – as it tends to do year by year. We have suffered a stretch of high unemployment over the last decade or so, but this results from the way the economy has been managed (in the fight against inflation) rather than from any remarkable technical progress. In fact, output per head has grown no faster than in the early post-war period. And although numbers in the manufacturing industry have fallen, in the service industry they have risen.

Bryan *Is our manufacturing base adequate? Is it important, or should we move away from manufacture into service industries?*

Fred Manufacturing does matter, because although insurance, banking, tourism and so on are important, most of our export earnings come from manufactured goods. With our oil resources, we have not needed them so much, but the oil earnings are getting run down. We can't go on borrowing, borrowing, borrowing, building up an enormous debt, because it will eventually swamp our overseas assets. So, at some time, we will have to have a revival. We will have to have a much faster rate of increase of exports than imports, because we've got quite a differential to get right. That will require manufacturers.

Bryan *We're getting towards the end. Is there one last question?*

> **Q** Sir Fred, if you were a few years younger, would you emigrate?

Fred I think this is a nice country to live in – especially if you've got an above-average income.

CHAPTER 10 **The Nice Company**

TOM LLOYD read economics at Liverpool University, then took up journalism. In 1982 he negotiated the purchase of *Financial Weekly* from Robert Maxwell, and was appointed editor a year later. In 1985 he led a management buyout of the magazine from the Maxwell Organisation. Five years later he became a freelance writer and consultant, and now writes regularly for the *Financial Times* and edits the journal *Transformation*. He has written five books – *Dinosaur & Co*, *Managing Knowhow* (with Karl Erik Sveiby), *The Nice Company*, *Entrepreneur!* and *The Charity Business*.

We've always believed that "nice" companies are the best companies. But when Tom visited Utopia in September 1990 he opened everyone's eyes to the business potential and measurable success of this theory, at the same time introducing us to a new game: "The Prisoner's Dilemma".

TOM LLOYD

Companies are alive. Not just metaphorically, but literally.

I can't prove it, but there's no definition of life that I know of that excludes the company. I've been watching and writing about companies for 20 years, and they seem alive to me. They're born, they grow, they get old and sometimes they die.

One of the ideas in evolutionary theory – for companies as well as animals – is that one needs to have a pool of genetic variation. And I see "nice" genes like philanthropic Quaker economics and the common-ownership tradition as being part of the company's genetic pool. Quaker economics is still very much alive – Barclays Bank comes from that tradition, as do J Walter Thompson and Rowntree. And there are other forms of genesis within the phylum: the building societies and the mutual insurance companies, which in their very structure are nice, non-exploitative, non-profit-making. So you can see where some of the ideas for the nice company come from. It's just been hanging around for a while, waiting for the appropriate combination of circumstances, which I think is here now.

Let's suppose that I am right and companies are alive in a meaningful sense. If so, they must be evolving. It's the fate of all life forms to adapt constantly to changes in their environment. As businesses interact with their environment, they play a whole series of multi-play games, or tournaments, with customers, suppliers, competitors, employees, banks, the City, the Government and the public at large. Each company, whether it knows it or not, is using a general strategy – what I call a meta-strategy – for playing its games. And I believe it's meta-strategy that evolves.

Depending on how profitable each meta-strategy turns out to be, natural selection will either allow the company to thrive or cause it to become extinct. An essential theme for the nice company argument is that a company's meta-strategy is reflected in what we might call its culture and values. In a nice company model, these qualities, or styles, are the corporate equivalent of meta-strategy.

The theoretical part of the argument for how a nice company behaves is based on the theory of games. The game I use, because I think it models businesses very well, is called "The Prisoner's Dilemma".

Games theorists and evolutionists have done a lot of work on "The Prisoner's Dilemma". An American, Robert Axelrod, tried to discover the best strategy – which he defined as the strategy that accumulated the highest overall score – by inviting games theorists to enter their strategies in a computer tournament. There was one particular kind of strategy, that Axelrod christened as "nice", because it was never the first to make an aggressive move (or to "defect", as he called it), which did surprisingly well in the tournament. It was a surprise because the conventional wisdom was that the best move was always to defect. The reason why the conventional solution does badly in our game is that we are playing the repeated version. Players meet each other frequently, as they do in business, and soon establish reputations. A nasty player does well at first, but then gets a reputation for being nasty and finds that no-one wants to play with him any more.

One of the reasons why I like this game as a model of business is that it exposes what seems to me to be a fundamental mistake in business outlook that has prevailed over the last 20 years or so. Business success is

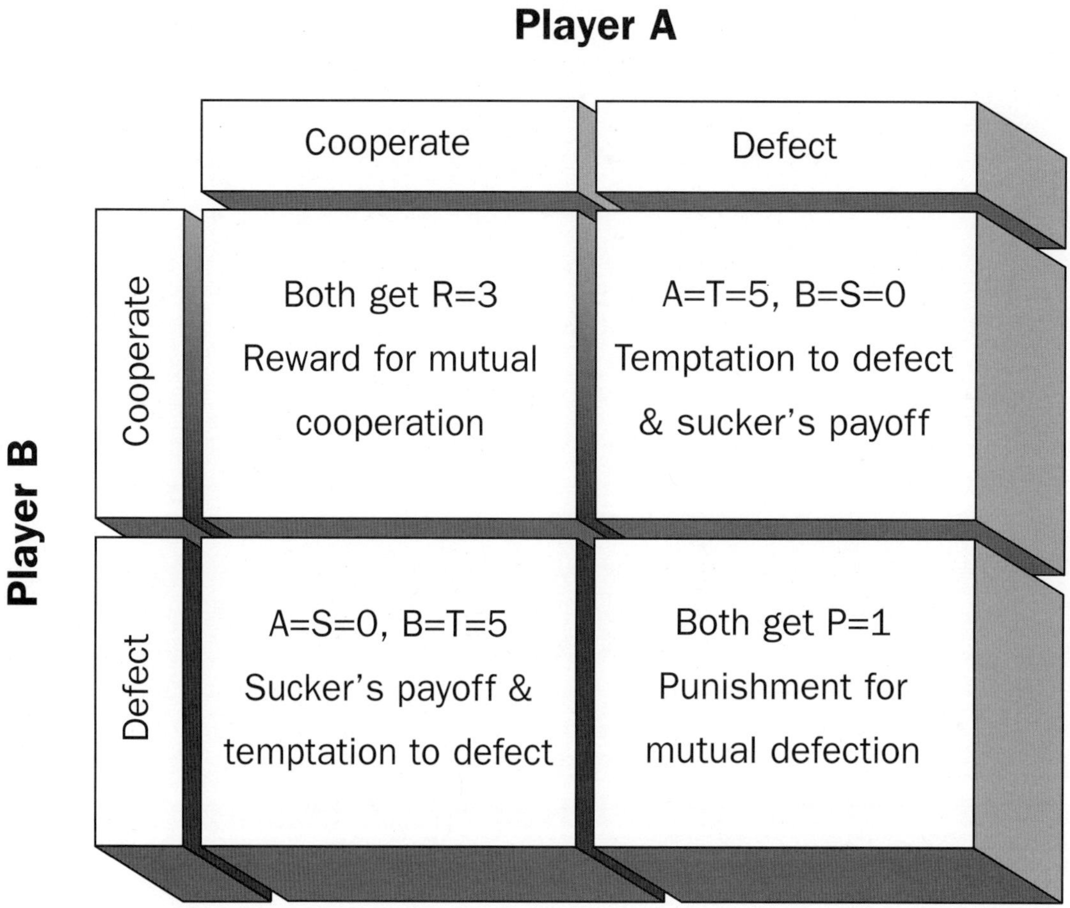

Player A

Player B	Cooperate	Defect
Cooperate	Both get R=3 Reward for mutual cooperation	A=T=5, B=S=0 Temptation to defect & sucker's payoff
Defect	A=S=0, B=T=5 Sucker's payoff & temptation to defect	Both get P=1 Punishment for mutual defection

"The Prisoner's Dilemma"

not measured ultimately, as many company leaders and strategy consultants in the Seventies and Eighties supposed it to be, by how many business battles are won; it's measured by how profitable the company is. And that depends on how many profitable business encounters the company becomes engaged in. Which company would you prefer to have your money in: one that had a reputation for winning takeovers or market-share battles, or one that had a reputation for being profitable? Put like that, it seems pretty obvious, but the importance of profitability was forgotten somehow; probably because, somewhere along the line, the maximisation of market share ceased to be seen as a means to an end and became an end in itself.

The reason why nice companies do well is that by playing the game their way, they establish attractive reputations. Companies that have reputations for being good employers find it easier to recruit and keep good people. Companies that have reputations for being good citizens find it easier to get planning permission for new projects. These days, companies that use non-toxic chemicals in their processing, that give to charity and refuse to trade with countries which have oppressive regimes tend to attract more customers. Companies that have reputations for paying their bills on time and for caring about their suppliers and customers give to their products and to their shares (which are just another kind of product) an additional, and rather special, kind of value. Company leaders are getting very interested in this "reputation" value. They're beginning to see it as an asset on what I call their "invisible balance sheets". Those are the balance sheets accountants can't see, but which contain the really crucial things like brand values, intellectual property and the know-how of employees.

The returns of the nice strategy can be very material, as investors in Anita Roddick's Body Shop have learned to their profit. And when another nice company, the transport group NFC, announced its financial results they showed the benefits of a "nice" strategy. In this company, employees have effective control, and the figures showed that, although operating profits had fallen, pre-tax profits had increased because the amount paid out to employees had fallen even more. The perceptive institutional investors were very interested in NFC's figures, because they showed that NFC's nice treatment of its employees made them willing to share some of the burden of a downturn in demand. This is true of very few large companies. The City has had to assume, up until now, that wage costs can only go up. Companies where wage costs can also go down are obviously more capable of sustaining their profits in a recession. That makes them very attractive investments.

Returning to games theory, Axelrod defined the nice type of strategy as one that was never the first to make an aggressive move – the "defecting" move in "The Prisoner's Dilemma". But there are all sorts of strategies that fall into this category: companies can choose never to defect at all, can choose not to defect unless their opponent defects twice in a row, or three times, or ten times, or can switch between various sequences. The strategy that won both of Axelrod's main tournaments, and almost all the variations with which he tried to beat it, was called "Tit for Tat".

It works just like it sounds. It always cooperates on the first move and then always repeats what the other player does. Its simplicity is its strength. Other players recognise it; they know that if they're aggressive it will be aggressive back. They also know that if they're nice, it will be nice back, and that a long and mutually profitable relationship will begin.

It is this very particular kind of niceness that I mean when I talk about the nice strategy. It's a very clear, deliberate and disciplined kind of niceness. It's not a woolly, soft, weak kind of niceness. It's not a Christian niceness – Tit for Tat never slaps first, but if it gets slapped it does not turn the other cheek, but slaps back straight away and keeps trading slaps until the other guy stops. Axelrod attributes Tit for Tat's success to four qualities: it's nice, it's retaliatory, it's forgiving and it's clear. I think all these qualities are desirable in a business strategy.

Niceness is a quality that has to infuse the whole organisation, particularly the way it behaves. However, sincerity is not necessary at all. It can be quite useful, because if you want to appear to be a type of person, the best way is actually to *be* that type of person. However, a company may simply wish to *select* a nice personality and then carry out that role. Once an organisation gets saturated in a strategy, it's very difficult to distinguish whether it's like that because it thinks it's smarter to be like that, or because it really is like that. In fact, the distinction doesn't matter.

If we agree that a company's reputation is its most valuable asset, and if we recognise that reputation consists not of reality, but of perceptions, then it is essential for a company to market a strategy. Reputation building and reputation maintenance are going to be key management tasks. It will become routine to try to acquire reputational assets at every opportunity. Until now, the big question for companies has been: "What shall we do?" In the future, the big question will be: "What am I?"

Today, the "nasty" paradigm for companies is, probably, still dominant. A nasty company can, of course, become a nice company, but it would be very hard because companies have so much inertia – their current personalities are creatures of a very long history. And I don't think the nasty strategy will ever become extinct. There will always be a place for a few Hansons and BTRs, and they're probably very healthy presences. They keep other companies on their toes. But, as I said at the start, companies must evolve if they are not to become extinct and, thanks to environmental issues, changes in public perceptions and development in government strategy, soft assets like reputation and know-how are becoming the nucleus of competitive advantage. Skill shortages, coupled with a more fastidious consuming and investing public, make it necessary for companies to take note of the human values that they could, in the past, afford to ignore. The end result is that the dominant business strategy of the future will be nothing other than to behave as a nice company.

WARNING

CHAPTER 11 **Pigeonholing Objects and People**

TIM HUNKIN doesn't like being called an inventor, an engineer or a designer; his work involves all these skills and more. After leaving Cambridge with a degree in engineering, he accepted many strange commissions – firework displays, *The Rudiments of Wisdom* cartoons for the *Observer*, water, wind and steam clocks, mechanical sculptures and a variety of TV programmes, including *The Secret Life of Machines* for Channel 4. His most recent project was creating the Science Museum's new gallery, *The Secret Life of the Home*.

In December 1990 Tim navigated us through the curious world of pigeonholing, telling us he chose this theme because he felt it was a subject both he and Newell and Sorrell were involved with. In a very personal, wry and witty talk, he used his own experiences and examples of his work to demonstrate why – no matter how hard we try – there's no escaping labelling and hype.

I hate being pigeonholed as a mad inventor –

or as anything else. I have had a large variety of temporary professions – cartoonist, journalist, furniture maker, pyrotechnician, teacher, sculptor, aid worker, clock maker, writer, illustrator, TV presenter, museum designer and others. When asked to describe what I do, I use different labels for different occasions: artist for tax forms (creating the impression of penury); cartoonist for passport (a harmless occupation so as not to alarm officials); engineer for insurance forms (safe and steady). Engineer is also useful at parties if I don't feel like getting into conversation. No single description means much; in reality I thrive on variety and change.

Pigeonholing People

Despite my own dislike of being pigeonholed, I can't explain why I have sideboards and wire-rimmed spectacles, the classic mad inventor stereotypes. The military general with the red face, puffed-out chest and beady eye; the world-weary, alcoholic barman with huge bags under the eyes; the pert, bossy hospital sister; the sharp, tough builder with a twinkle in his eye; categorising people like this can be an uncomfortable activity. Not only because people are more interesting and complicated, but also because it is potentially close to racism and fascism.

PIGEONHOLING

OBJECTS & PEOPLE

My own caricatures are mostly based on personal experiences – the General was based on my unhappy memories of the Combined Cadet Force at school; the barman on someone who I worked at the Fitzroy Tavern, next door to where I lived after leaving college; the sister on a hospital visit after dropping an enormous lump of metal on my foot; the

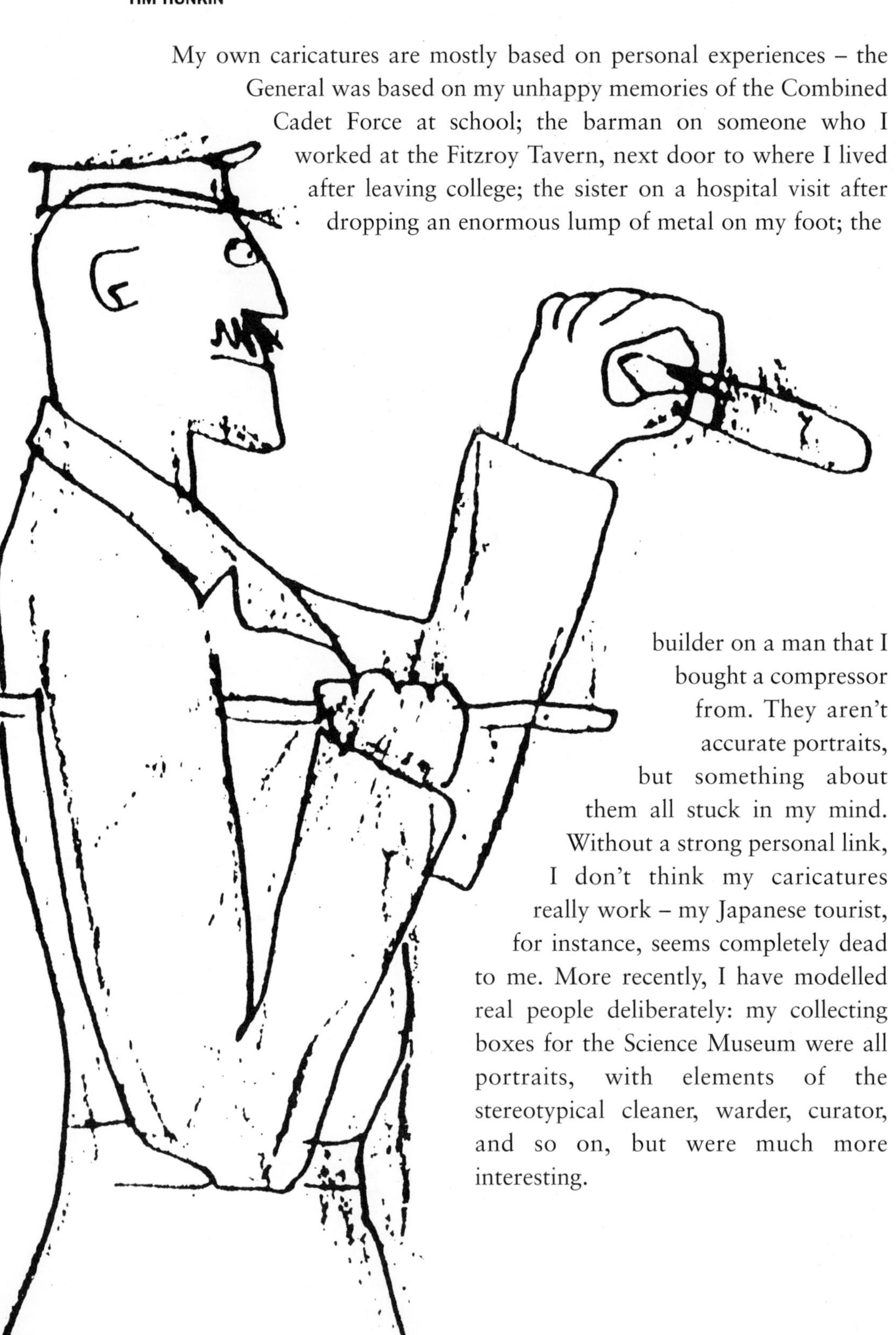

builder on a man that I bought a compressor from. They aren't accurate portraits, but something about them all stuck in my mind. Without a strong personal link, I don't think my caricatures really work – my Japanese tourist, for instance, seems completely dead to me. More recently, I have modelled real people deliberately: my collecting boxes for the Science Museum were all portraits, with elements of the stereotypical cleaner, warder, curator, and so on, but were much more interesting.

Pigeonholing Art

Any object in an art gallery is pigeonholed as "art". My parents often took me to galleries when I was a child. When I grew up I had an ambition to have an exhibition of my own, to see stuff I had made looking like real art. I pestered all sorts of galleries, and eventually persuaded the ICA to let me make them a collecting box (an artist pondering the existential void, who pauses to thank you for your donation). This was a sort of back way in, so when, a few months later, an exhibition fell through, I was allowed to have mine in its place: a series of coin-operated machines, called *The Disgusting Spectacle* after one figure that picked his nose. By exhibiting at the ICA, I gained instant credibility as an artist, and was besieged with requests for other exhibitions and lectures.

I persevered for a few years, producing a whole exhibition called *The Art Gallery*, a series of coin-operated, papier maché figures who looked at imaginary paintings with stereotypical reactions – baffled, shocked, bored, intellectual, reading the guide book, taking a photo. (Taken to art galleries as a child, I found the visitors more interesting than the art on the walls.) Gradually the art world invented a category, an "ism" for my slot machines, labelling them "modern automata" so they could be safely pigeonholed. Disillusionment started to set in. The reverential attitude of the real spectators started to irritate me (I found I much preferred the noisy chaos of the country fairs where I had previously been taking my slot machines). I was appalled by the jargon and snobbery of many of the art professionals and surprised at the importance they seemed to attach to the mysteriousness of art. Clarity and straightforwardness did not seem to be considered desirable virtues. I was also surprised at their difficulty with humour: it somehow didn't fit with their perception of "art".

At about the same time I did a commission for a local solicitor. I mechanised a large portrait of the founder of the firm so his eyes rolled round and his wig shot up. The solicitor originally intended to have the portrait behind his desk, reacting to dubious confidences from his clients, but had second thoughts and put it in the waiting room. Here, it was highly effective in entertaining his often nervous and fraught clients. I found the combination of unexpectedness and usefulness very attractive. Almost any space started to seem more interesting than the bland white walls and reverential atmosphere of the art gallery. Since the solicitor's commission, in 1984, I have not made anything to be exhibited in an art gallery.

Pigeonholing Commerce

Away from the quiet backwater of fine art, making things is not without its problems. Many of my favourite proposals have been rejected – like the plumber's sign: a suspended toilet with two feet sticking out of the cistern. The chain came down to pavement level and when you pulled it the feet disappeared and a head popped out of the bowl; this didn't get planning permission. Other good ideas have been nearly completed before being rejected. At the height of the Thatcher boom, together with a group of friends, I embarked on a £1 million Disney-style ride for a shopping centre, called *The Ride of Life*. We all finished our work and got paid, but the boom came to an end and the developer lost confidence, so the ride was never installed.

Most ideas require a considerable amount of compromise. The cover of *Almost Everything There is to Know*, my book of *The Rudiments of Wisdom* cartoon strips, is a good example. When deciding what to do, I realised that the covers of children's books are almost all bright primary colours – the children's section of a bookshop always stands out. I felt the colours were ugly and patronising (there is no evidence that children prefer bright colours, except possibly two-year-olds), so I tried to do a cover that was mainly black. The publishers didn't like it – it didn't fit the pigeonhole of what a children's book should look like. Eventually, after at least five versions, I don't think anybody was really happy with the final compromise.

Conservative Pigeonholes

My main problem working in the commercial world is that companies usually see themselves as being highly distinctive, and often say they want to commission something really bold and unusual, but are, in fact, terrified of looking different from their competitors. This is sad, because it tends to make everything very dull, bland and predictable. Supermarkets, for example, all have detail differences, but to an untrained eye appear almost indistinguishable. I could easily draw a cartoon of a supermarket from memory, but I couldn't specifically draw a Tesco or a Safeway. The pigeonhole is the category, not the individual. The same is true of banks, fast food outlets, interiors of offices and countless other familiar institutions. It is not just architecture and design. When I visit a company it is always the same standard foyer, security staff, receptionist, PR person – it is often quite a triumph to finally reach a real engineer. Every large company nowadays seems to have mission statements, and they all seem to be exactly the same, mentioning the word "quality" as many times as possible.

Pigeonholes and Hype

The pigeonholes which people, art and commerce use are often highly dependent on hype. Mission statements, for example, are not only all basically the same – they all fit in one pigeonhole – but the contents are also all basically hot air, or hype. Publishers have such well-defined pigeonholes for their products that book fairs consist largely of selling "dummies", books with full-colour covers but blank pages inside; potential books sold entirely on hype.

Personally, as with pigeonholes, I suspect the whole idea of corporate identity is basically hype. The problem is that companies rarely want to project what they are, but what they would like to be. And while this may be done with the best of intentions, from the outside it often just looks ridiculous. All the wispy figure logos of BT, the Prudential and the Conservative Party are almost indistinguishable. The silver birds on InterCity trains didn't obviously make the trains more punctual or reliable. With privatisation, an enormous amount is bound to be spent on this sort of thing, with equally little point or effect. On a broader perspective, the rise in awareness of corporate identity in the last 20 years has been mirrored by the collapse of Britain's manufacturing industries.

As with pigeonholes, hype is equally rife in the art world, though in a

INSIDE A SUPERMARKET
THE FIRST SELF-SERVICE GROCERIES, CALLED HUMPTY DUMPTY STORES, WERE OPENED IN AMERICA IN 1912. GOODS WERE STILL PAID FOR AT A COUNTER. THE FIRST GROCERY WITH A CHECK-OUT AT THE EXIT WAS THE PIGGLY WIGGLY, OPENED IN MEMPHIS IN 1916. THE IDEA WAS A SUCCESS & WITHIN 7 YEARS THERE WERE 2800 PIGGLY WIGGLYS IN THE US. THE FIRST BRITISH SUPERMARKET WAS THE CO-OP, MANOR PARK, LONDON (1948).
BAKERY
FRESHLY KILLED SANDWICHES
SMELLS FROM BAKERY ENCOURAGE IMPULSE BUYING.
HOME MADE NASTIES
HIGH INTENSITY LIGHTING MAKES SUPERMARKET APPEAR EXTRA HYGIENIC.
VILE BLEACH 28p
SIX DREARY SLICES REDUCED TO 45p
SUPERMARKETS ARE LAID OUT TO MAKE YOU PASS AS MANY SHELVES AS POSSIBLE. THIS IS WHY THE ENTRANCE CORRIDOR USUALLY GOES STRAIGHT TO THE BACK OF THE SHOP—BLOCKING ANY SHORT CUTS TO THE CHECK-OUT.
COLD BORE SALAD
PUSHCHAIR UNSALTED BUTTER
THE CENTRES OF FREEZER CABINETS & ENDS OF AISLES ARE CALLED 'HOT SPOTS' BECAUSE PRODUCTS DISPLAYED THERE SELL TWICE AS FAST AS IN OTHER PLACES.
IT HAS BEEN ESTIMATED THAT SHOPPERS SPEND AN AVERAGE 1/4 TH SECOND LOOKING AT EACH PRODUCT.
AMPUTATEY SPAGHETTI LIMBS 33p
PYRAMID DISPLAYS ARE OUT OF FASHION. SHOPPERS FEEL DISCOURAGED FROM TAKING A PACKET FOR FEAR OF COLLAPSING THE PYRAMID. RANDOM PILES ENCOURAGE MORE PURCHASES.
GOLDEN BLUNDER CRISPS
HI POOH TEA
THE PURCHASE OF SOME THINGS, PARTICULARLY TEA, BUTTER, PET FOOD & SOAP, IS USUALLY PRE-PLANNED. THESE PRODUCTS ARE PLACED AS FAR AS POSSIBLE FROM EACH OTHER.
£225 MILLION A YEAR IN UK IS SPENT ON CAT FOOD.
BRAIN 62p
£500 MILLION A YEAR IN UK IS SPENT ON BISCUITS.
BOUNCY BAR
WE ARE EATING 30% MORE BREAKFAST CEREAL THAN IN 1970 (FEWER PEOPLE ARE EATING A COOKED BREAKFAST).
WE ARE EATING 35% LESS SUGAR THAN IN 1970.
BIG ITEMS ARE PLACED NEAR THE ENTRANCE TO ENCOURAGE SHOPPERS TO USE A TROLLEY INSTEAD OF A BASKET (MOST PEOPLE STOP BUYING WHEN A BASKET IS FULL).
THE BAR-CODE ON THE SIDE OF MOST PACKETS WILL SOON BE USED AT SUPERMARKET CHECK-OUTS. THE CASHIER WILL RUN A LIGHT PEN OVER EACH CODE & A COMPUTER, FED WITH THE PRICE OF EACH PRODUCT, WILL ADD THEM UP. PACKETS WILL NO LONGER NEED INDIVIDUAL LABELS & THE SUPERMARKET WILL ALWAYS KNOW ITS PRECISE STOCK.
SUPERMARKETS ARE GETTING BIGGER. 60% OF THOSE OPENED LAST YEAR WERE MORE THAN TWICE AS BIG AS THIS ONE (20m × 30m).
RICE SOGGIES 48p
BEAST EXTRACT 96p
SNIFFY CAT 22p!
IN A RECENT SURVEY, SHOPPERS WERE ASKED WHAT THEY WERE INTENDING TO BUY BEFORE ENTERING A SUPERMARKET. THE SHOPPERS EMERGED WITH, ON AVERAGE, ALMOST TWICE AS MANY ITEMS. OF THE EXTRA PURCHASES 1/3 WERE THINGS THEY REMEMBERED WERE NEEDED, 1/4 ON SPECIAL OFFER, 1/3 BOUGHT AS TREATS, & THE REST THE SHOPPERS COULD NOT REMEMBER.
SUPERMARKETS EXPECT TO LOSE ABOUT 1 IN 5 OF THEIR TROLLEYS A YEAR.

slightly different form, specialising in the use of long words combined in enigmatic phrases. I once wrote down the most obvious examples from one issue of an art magazine, and found they fitted together almost seamlessly: "The over-elaboration as pragmatic method with televisually juxtaposed information tangoing through banal European tychism... That necessary metamorphosis takes place on the specially sensitised space of the painted surface."

There's really little to choose between rubbish like this and the endless "quality and good, old-fashioned excellence" language of commercial hype.

There's no escaping the world of pigeonholing and hype. I must admit I rather enjoy trying to navigate my way through it, poking fun at it rather occasionally. I don't find it too difficult to avoid the worst of it as long as I'm happy not making lots of money.

338
254

CHAPTER 12 **Corporate Fitness**

SEBASTIAN COE, OBE, is perhaps Britain's most famous athlete of the 1980s. In an illustrious career he won two Olympic golds and two silvers, and European gold, silver and bronze medals. He broke 12 world records at four distances, and along the way received numerous awards, including BBC Sports Personality of the Year in 1979. A successful businessman, in 1987 he became chairman of Diadora UK. He has written five books, and was elected MP for Falmouth and Camborne in 1992.

Could you win a gold this year? What's your training plan for next season? Is your team in peak condition, committed and motivated? Are these sporting questions or business questions? Who better than Sebastian Coe to provide the answers, we thought, so in January 1991 we invited him to discuss with us his chase for excellence – both on and off the track.

At the age of 14 I came off a rain-sodden track in South Yorkshire and my old man turned to me and said: "I've been meaning to say this to you for a few weeks - you will be going to the Olympic Games, but don't let it come as a major surprise to you, because I've seen a lot of athletes crumble when they get the selection letter." This wasn't three or four weeks beforehand, this was in 1971, and we were aiming for the 1980 Olympics.

The pursuit of excellence is much the same thing whether you're in sport or business. From my earliest days in athletics, certain rules were instilled in me that had very distinct business and management analogies.

As a coach, you have to assess your product and its best marketplace: whether your athlete is most suited to field events, to track and field, short distances or marathon. You then have to do a lot of planning, preparation and setting of targets – the basis of any form of sport that lasts.

Clearly, my targets were being set at both short- and long-term, which is related very closely to the business market. In athletics, you can't move from one market to the next without having first achieved the short-term objectives. You wouldn't go from school level to city level without something in between; you wouldn't go from city level to international level without having progressed through county, area and then national level. They are all perceivable steps. This is no different from, in business, knowing your market niche and moving on from stage to stage.

There is continual assessment, of course, of whether things are going badly or going well, because markets never stand still. A world record, when set, is not the end of the road, it simply alerts the market to the fact that you're in a wholly different environment. An area that you were operating in and a target you were going for is, suddenly, dramatically altered. There is regrouping, reassessment and continual modification.

There are issues involved in business that fall within all the areas of sports psychology: the understanding of working in a team situation; of how to get the best out of an individual without taking off some of the roughness around the edges. How do you incorporate the workings of the individual in a team without altering the fundamental direction in which that team has to go as a unit, and without removing the individual flair that makes that team so successful?

When I made the transition to business I knew one of the rules in athletics was that nothing good develops quickly. Systems take time to get in place. When I started training and competing, between 1968 and 1970, I didn't get into the national team for nearly nine years, and it took me another two or three years to make an Olympic team. So, one thing I learnt was that long-term planning (you hope!) pays off in the end.

Physical fitness will make your staff more efficient but, when it comes to fitness at work, in the UK we are very much in our infancy. If you go to America, there are very few companies who don't now have a Director of Corporate Fitness. I don't like the idea of compulsory sport in the workplace – I don't think you can, practically, enforce sport in any situation – but you can try and create an environment where people understand that there are significant benefits to physical and mental output by being that little bit fitter than they were before.

Part of your persuasive tool is, I think, introducing fitness assessments at the office. You're not trying to convert the workforce into Olympic athletes, you're trying to improve their health and wellbeing by some pretty well-understood paths. And if those paths are fun and very self-explanatory, and if you have the aid of on-site helpers, then you can turn that effort into something altogether more interesting. And, if we're talking about a corporate market, we're talking about people who, on the whole, have stressful lifestyles. So, in terms of getting fitter and healthier, you also need to work in some techniques of stress management. Because that's all part and parcel, I believe, of the overall package.

I insisted, recently, that all my staff were tested by a fitness assessor. Not only was I thinking of the wellbeing of my workforce, but also of the company overall. I don't know how any organisation that is tight in terms of manpower can ever be wholly comfortable about issues such as succession planning if it doesn't know that the people it is working with are fit and healthy enough to carry out the task that is being set for them.

Business and sport have got a lot to offer each other. I've outlined the ways in which I think business can learn from sport – assessment, planning, team-building and motivation. And sport can learn a lot from business – administration, finance, pr and lobbying. But is there ever a finishing line in either discipline?

I don't think there is a definite finishing line in sport, and there certainly isn't one in business – short of selling up and getting out. The chase for excellence is something that never finishes, because, by its very implication, excellence means doing better. And you can always do better. In sporting terms, yes, you might win a race, but next year you will have to adapt to a completely different market, a new crop of athletes coming in. You were the one that set the trend, you were the one that broke the record. You have to face the fact that there is a whole generation of athletes coming through behind you whose sole endeavour is to equal your pace and, ideally, to overtake you – which is what competition is all about. The same applies in business terms. If you have objectives and targets, then necessarily, once you have achieved something, you have to move on to the next thing.

The chase for excellence is about getting better, about continual assessment along the way. It is about that blend of short-term and long-term planning of targets and objectives; the simple determination to achieve something in the market, something which you feel you can do better than the next guy. And that is the essence of competition and the essence of achievement.

CHAPTER 13 **Poetry**

WENDY COPE wrote prose in her spare time as a child, and studied history at Oxford University. It wasn't until she was in her late twenties, and working as a primary school teacher, that she developed a passion for poetry. Eventually, she was spotted by Faber & Faber, who featured her in their *Poetry Introduction* of 1982 and then published her first book, *Making Cocoa for Kingsley Amis*, in 1986. Unusually for a book of poems, this went straight into the best-seller lists, and shortly afterwards Wendy gave up teaching to be a full-time writer.

Wendy's talk at Newell and Sorrell in March 1991 was funny and entertaining. Sitting quietly but with great presence, she gave us some background to her poems and read a selection to us. It was a wonderful, gentle evening which left everyone feeling good and reminded us just how important the English language is, especially when you have a way with words.

A talented young chimpanzee
was keen to appear on TV.
He wrote to Brooke Bond
But they didn't respond
So he had to become an MP.

That's my political poem. This is a poem about me and my sister, an affectionate poem, written in 1978, during one of the rare phases when we were speaking...

"Sisters"

My sister
was the bad one –
said what she thought
and did what she liked
and didn't care.
At ten she wore
a knife tucked in
her leather belt,
dreamed of being
a prince on a white horse.

Became a dolly bird
with dyed hair longer
than her skirts, pulling
the best of the local talent.
Mother wept and prayed.

At thirty she's divorced,
has cropped her locks
and squats in Hackney –
tells me, "God created man
then realised her mistake."

I'm not like her,
I'm good – but now
I'm working on it.
Fighting through
to my own brand of badness.

I am glad of her
at last – her conferences,
her anger, and her boots.
We talk and smoke
and laugh at everybody –
two bad sisters.

This is a love poem that appeared in the *Telegraph* as a valentine poem. That's a time of year when what I call "Dial a Poet" becomes very active. It seems odd to me to commission a love poem, because the first requirement is that the poet fall in love. But anyway, what I've learnt now is that if I have an unpublished love poem, the best time to sell it is at the end of January. It's called "Flowers".

Some men never think of it.
You did. You'd come along
And say you'd nearly bought me flowers
But something had gone wrong.

The shop was closed. Or you had doubts –
The sort that minds like ours
Dream up incessantly. You thought
I might not want your flowers.

It made me smile and hug you then.
Now, I can only smile.
But, look, the flowers you nearly bought
Have lasted all this while.

This one is called "The Orange". I'm boasting now, but a young man saw this poem in the *Telegraph*, and then lost his copy and rang up my publishers to say he wanted to read it to his bride on his wedding day, and could we possibly arrange it.

At lunchtime I bought a huge orange –
The size of it made us all laugh.
I peeled it and shared it with Robert and Dave –
They got quarters and I had a half.

And that orange, it made me so happy,
As ordinary things often do
Just lately. The shopping. A walk in the park.
This is peace and contentment. It's new.

The rest of the day was quite easy.
I did all the jobs on my list
And enjoyed them and had some time over.
I love you. I'm glad I exist.

But then, of course, love goes wrong. This one is called "Loss".

The day he moved out was terrible –
That evening she went through hell.
His absence wasn't a problem
But the corkscrew had gone as well.

This one has a similar theme. It's called "I Worry".

I worry about you –
So long since we spoke.
Love, are you downhearted,
Dispirited, broke?

I worry about you.
I can't sleep at night.
Are you sad? Are you lonely?
Or are you all right?

They say that men suffer,
As badly, as long,
I worry, I worry,
In case they are wrong.

And the last one on that theme is called "Two Cures for Love".

1 *Don't see him. Don't phone or write a letter.*
2 *The easy way: get to know him better.*

Now for something completely different. This was commissioned for a charity. A friend was editing an anthology for the benefit of the World Wide Fund for Nature, and he kept saying to me: "You are going to write a poem for my anthology, aren't you?" and I kept saying: "Well, I'll try, I'll try." In the end I wrote this poem called "Kindness to Animals", which I recited to him. Unfortunately, World Wide Nature then didn't get the benefit of it, because he felt it was unsuitable. So I had to publish it in a newspaper and be paid for it instead.

If I went vegetarian
And didn't eat lambs for dinner,
I think I'd be a better person
And also thinner.

But the lamb is not endangered
And at least I can truthfully say
I have never, ever eaten a barn owl,
So perhaps I am OK.

This is my other green poem. It's called "A Green Song to Sing at the Bottle Bank".

One green bottle,
Drop it in the bank.
Ten green bottles,
What a lot we drank.
Heaps of bottles
And yesterday's a blank
But we'll save the planet,
Tinkle, tinkle, clank!

I have a problem with fashionable causes.

When I had first given up teaching, I sometimes used to write poems for BBC programmes. And sometimes they would give me something to do and I would just think: "Well, you know, it's only on the radio, no-one's going to study it." But occasionally the commission could be quite good for me, and I would write something that I wouldn't have thought of writing otherwise. This one was for a current affairs programme that went out after Betjeman died and before they had appointed a new Poet Laureate. They asked several different poets to write poems that had something to do with the Laureateship. I think this was the very first commissioned poem I did for the BBC, and you will see it's actually rather short – I think it lasted half a minute. When I listened to the programme, everyone else had written terribly long poems, and when I got paid I realised why – because the BBC pays by the half-minute. Before 1971 they used to pay by the line – in the Sixties there were these long, thin poems; sometimes a word would be broken, like

thin-

king, but when the BBC changed its policy and started paying by the half-minute, these long, thin poems completely disappeared. This is called "An All-Purpose Poem for State Occasions", and the idea was that if there were an all-purpose poem, there would be no need for poets to write silly poems about royal occasions.

The nation rejoices or mourns
As this happy or sombre day dawns.
Our eyes will be wet
As we sit round the set,
Neglecting our flowerbeds and lawns.

As Her Majesty rides past the crowd
They'll be silent or cheer very loud
But whatever they do
It's undoubtedly true
That they'll feel patriotic and proud.

In Dundee and Penzance and Ealing
We're imbued with appropriate feeling:
We're British and loyal
And love every royal
And tonight we shall drink till we're reeling.

I will now read a parody. I sometimes get written about as if I do nothing but write parodies, but they're actually quite a small part of my output. This one is a parody of Wordsworth. It's a game that quite a lot of poets have played, where you wrap up a well-known rhyme in the style of a particular poet. It's a bit like that game on *Face the Music*, where there was a well-known tune in the style of a composer, and you had to guess the tune and the composer. Here, I have in mind the kind of Wordsworth poem where he goes for a walk across the hills and meets a rustic character and converses with them and then goes on about how wonderful they are.

The skylark and the jay sang loud and long,
The sun was calm and bright, the air was sweet,
When all at once I heard above the throng
Of jocund birds a single plaintive bleat.

And, turning, saw, as one sees in a dream,
It was a Sheep had broke the moorland peace
With his sad cry, a creature who did seem
The blackest thing that ever wore a fleece.

I walked towards him on the stony track
And, pausing for a while between two crags,
I asked him, "Have you wool upon your back?"
Thus he bespake, "Enough to fill three bags."

Most courteously, in measured tones, he told
Who would receive each bag and where they dwelt;
And oft, now years have passed and I am old,
I recollect with joy that inky pelt.

The next poem is really miserable, so I've called it "Some More Light Verse". This is a comment on the fact that, whatever I write, however miserable it is, some people still interpret it as light. I dislike the "light verse" label and believe it is often used inappropriately. I just wrote this poem because I felt like writing it. It was published in a newspaper, and I got a request from a TV company that wanted to use it. When I phoned back, I found out the name of the programme they wanted to use it in was *Midlife Crisis*.

You have to try. You see a shrink.
You learn a lot. You read. You think.
You struggle to improve your looks.
You meet some men. You write some books.
You eat good food. You give up junk.
You do not smoke. You don't get drunk.
You take up yoga, walk and swim.
And nothing works. The outlook's grim.
You don't know what to do. You cry.
You're running out of things to try.

You blow your nose. You see the shrink.
You walk. You give up food and drink.
You fall in love. You make a plan.
You struggle to improve your man.
And nothing works. The outlook's grim.
You go to yoga, cry, and swim.
You eat and drink. You give up looks.
You struggle to improve your books.
You cannot see the point. You sigh.
You do not smoke. You have to try.

I don't have fixed views on whether poetry should rhyme or not rhyme, but I sometimes think I should get away from rhyme more often. My last poem is called "An Attempt at Unrhymed Verse". It's about trying to write a poem that doesn't rhyme.

People tell you all the time,
Poems do not have to rhyme.
It's often better if they don't
And I'm determined this one won't.
Oh dear.

Never mind, I'll start again.
Busy busy with my pen...cil.
I can do it if I try –
Easy, peasy, pudding and gherkins.

Writing verse is so much fun,
Cheering as the summer weather,
Makes you feel alert and bright,
'Specially when you get it more or less the way
you want it.

CHRIS WOODHAMS

received an honours degree in zoology in London, worked on marine research in Florida and insect distribution in France, then researched the genetics of ageing in the fruit fly at Barts Medical School. After that he spent seven years as a maths teacher at a London girls' comprehensive before, in 1974, becoming an independent financial advisor. After just one year he set up his own practice, advising individuals and private companies. In 1987 he joined Greig Middleton, the independent stockbroker, as a director and as managing director of Greig Middleton Financial Services Ltd.

In his talk in May 1991, Chris explored the questions of how to develop your full potential and channel your abilities. He challenged our audience to look to the future – at what they wanted to achieve and how they were going to achieve it.

CHRIS WOODHAMS

We are all in the communications business

and our ability to communicate is going to determine how we will succeed – or otherwise – in the future.

I see two main types of communication. I would call the first type public communication – the way in which we communicate with other people and in which they communicate with us. This breaks down into two further types of communication. The first of these is verbal communication, where we use words, expressed with different tones. The tone has more impact than the words and can deliver intriguing variety. People who sound exactly the same may be as rare as people who look exactly the same. The sense of belonging to a community is enhanced by accent, which may also reflect social status. Parents might select education on the basis of how children sound in a particular school, and may also bring their own children up to speak in a certain style. You can argue there is a biological drive to pass on knowledge about how people believe social advantage can be gained by verbal communication.

The second type of this public communication is non-verbal communication. Anthropologists and we zoologists call this "body language". It is all about the things we communicate without actually using any words.

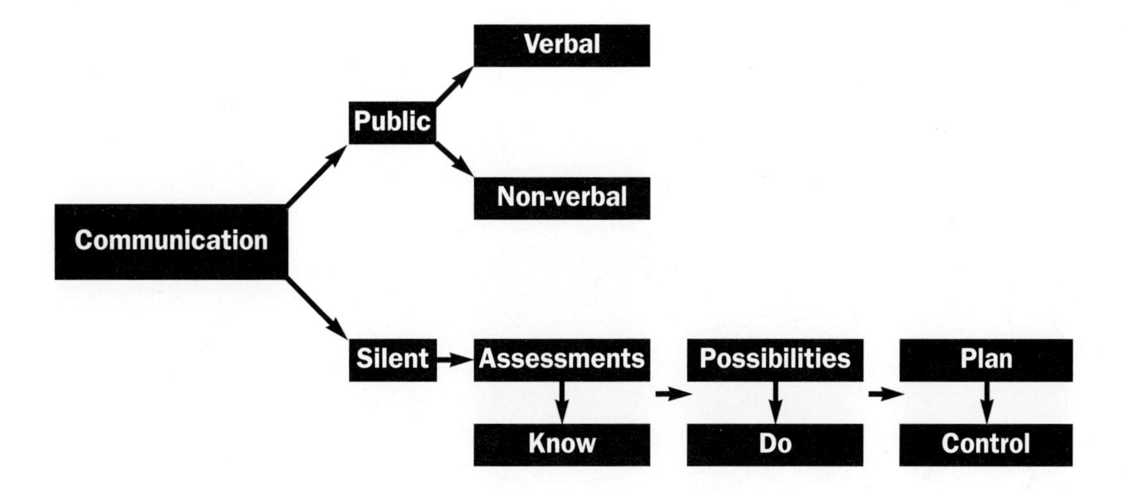

According to research, non-verbal communication accounts for about 55 per cent of the means by which we communicate with other people.

The second of the two principal types of communication is silent communication. I would define this as the communication that we have with ourselves.

Silent communication is really the foundation for all of our public communication, because what silent communication does is to build up a perception of who we are, how we see other people and how we deal with the challenge of life. According to research, about 95 per cent of the decisions we make come from our subconscious – automatic responses from years of self-programming.

Know

We use silent communication for making assessments of the world around us, such as whether we like or dislike someone. That assessment often occurs in about the first five seconds of meeting someone.

So how do we make all these assessments? We must make them from a reference point of some sort. The reference point is thought to be the

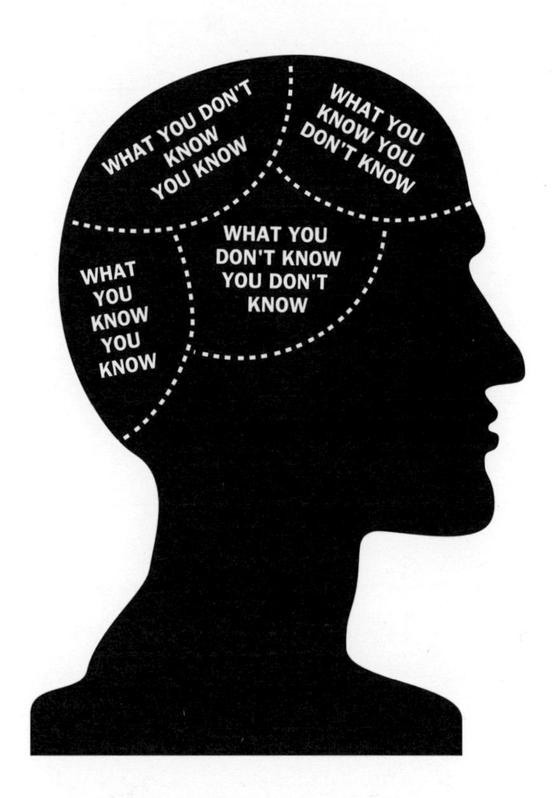

information that we have in our central nervous system, in particular the brain. All that information amounts to what we know. What we know only comes from two places. It comes from the chromosomes we inherit from our parents, and it comes from experiences. And those two things programme us. However, like a computer, we can put lots of garbage in, and we will get lots of garbage out. The GIGO principle.

We all know something different because we have all got different gene patterns on our chromosomes and all our experiences have been different. We each see things from a different point of view, and that causes the challenge of communication.

The diagram opposite represents knowledge, where the different segments represent different types of knowledge. The first part represents what you know you know. For example, I know that two plus two equals four. The second part represents what you know you don't know. For example, I know that I don't know how many people live in Moscow. The third part is what you don't know you know. In certain situations, there is a trigger mechanism, where certain words come out and you say: "I had forgotten I knew that!" The final part is what you don't know you don't know. This is the big exploration in life.

Do

In summary, we assess the world based on what we know. Each of us is different in what we know and hence we assess the world in different ways. It is not possible (maybe not even useful) to consciously recall all we know. Access is difficult. To say: "I have a bad memory" may often mean good memory, but lousy recall. The challenge is accessing what we know.

From what we know we make assessments, which lead on to identifying possibilities, like: "What shall I do tomorrow?" Out of those possibilities we select some which I shall call options: "Shall I do this or that?" The way forward into the future is about selecting some of the options from our assessment of the possibilities.

Control

Selecting options gives us a plan for our future, and that plan enables us to be in control. Here we have three key words – know, do and control. We must do a bit of knowing, we must do a bit of doing and we must do a bit of controlling. How do we balance these three? I think the really powerful people are those that have a significant bias towards control. They get leverage from other people who do things and who know things.

There has been a revolution in management. Know-how is a product that the workforce has developed, removing the need for middle management in hierarchical structures. The West has had to develop the means to export know-how as we have become less able to compete as manufacturers.

When we make a conscious plan for the future, the starting point is to ask ourselves: "What result do I want?" When we have decided on the result we want, we then decide how we are going to control our situation in order to reach that result. Then we can ask: "What do I need to do that is relevant to that result, and what do I need to know that is relevant to that result?" Most of what we do and most of the knowledge we acquire day by day is actually irrelevant to the result that we want. The challenge is constantly to increase our know-do-control effectiveness.

There will probably be three to five critical success factors to get us from where we are to where we want to be. The skill is to identify these critical success factors and then use know-how and activity relevant to that result. We can involve other people to enable us to get the result we want. People like to help, though they may not move us forward.

Getting to the result is a question of direction. Are we going to go in a straight line, or do we need to use an indirect route? Most people, if they're not into planning, probably feel that their path to the future is not in their hands. That is because they do not have a specific direction in which they want to go or do not want a specified result enough.

When deciding on direction, there are two basic things we need to know. First, where we are now, which I will call Position A. We need to know that because, if we are going to get somewhere, the first thing we need to know is where we are already.

The second thing is to work out where we are going, which I will call Position B. There are various definitions for Position B depending on where it is in terms of time. If it is a long way ahead we would call it an "aim". We aim for something which is long-term. If Position B represents what we are going to do tomorrow, it is very short-term, and known as a "tactical objective". The key objectives are "strategic objectives", where B is one to three years away.

Where do you want to be in your business, and in your life, in one to three years time? Next, can you write one strategic objective down? If you can't, how can you work in a relevant way towards achieving it?

A study at Yale University in 1953 asked students: "Do you have written goals?" Three per cent answered yes, they had something written down about what they wanted to do in the future. In 1973 the same group was asked: "How much money are you worth?" (This was an American study!) The three per cent were worth more than the other 97 per cent put together. Not because they had better exam results, richer parents, or even because they had achieved what they had written down – it was the fact that they were goal-oriented that made them more successful.

Of course, we cannot achieve either business or personal goals without having a clear view of what we need to know, do and control. One mechanism for reaching our goals is self-improvement. What skills do you need to enable you to achieve your business objectives or your personal objectives? We need enabling, self-improvement goals too.

Getting There

How to get to our one-to-three-year objective is the strategy. It should be written down, on just one sheet of paper. What is it you have to do to achieve what you want? No-one else can help you do what you want to do if you have not determined what it is that you want to do yourself. If you do not have a sense of ownership of your future you could end up resigned to your situation and feeling a victim when things go "wrong".

When we move along this journey, we need to look at internal factors, ourselves as people, our strengths and weaknesses. Or if we are planning for a business, to look for the strengths and weaknesses of the business. And externally, what are your opportunities and what are your threats? The trick of moving along the path to the future is to exploit your opportunities using your strengths. If you do not know where your strengths and weaknesses are, if you do not know what opportunities and threats are out there, you cannot link the strengths and opportunities together. Ask other people for help if necessary. Allocate enough time.

Looking at the concept of who we are, there are probably three elements that we need to be aware of.

First of all, self-ideal. We all have ideals about how we would like to feel, dress, behave or even what sort of car we would like. What, ideally, would we like to be in all segments of our lives?

Parallel to that or maybe mirroring it, or matching it, or maybe conflicting with it, is what our image of ourselves is. Self-image. Some people find it very frustrating if there is a big difference between the ideal they want to be or do and what their self-image is. For others it can be the great motivator to change. Self-image may be different to how other people see us. Investigate the difference. Is there any value or meaning in it?

The important element about the concept of ourselves is self-esteem. Self-esteem is centred on how we feel. How we feel is very much part of the fuel for driving us. If we feel good, we feel more able to do things. Some people may even be motivated by self-esteem, especially if their sub-culture rates low esteem highly. People's emotions go up and down, and it is being able to weather and enjoy that roller coaster as we travel along the path which is a key.

Self-esteem is the driving force behind attitude. Is your attitude positive or is it negative? It is very easy to be critical: it is quite hard always to make a contribution which is creative or constructive. We do not make money or progress by being negative; we get somewhere by being positive. Positive to ourselves and to others. It is the people who can break through the cloak of negativity and stick to their purpose who will succeed.

So, attitude is a driving force behind this journey to the future. Companies might employ somebody in the belief that the value of the person to the company is 80 per cent their technical ability and 20 per cent their attitude. But in fact it is attitude which is 80 per cent of our means of success in the future.

But of course, attitude is not everything. We do need a certain amount of capability. Capability relates to how much we know and how much we use it effectively. We need a certain amount of capability, but maybe not as much as we think. We can always ask someone to help us out.

The main thing we need, in our personal life and in business, is credibility. Credibility is about getting other people to believe we know something or we are capable of doing or achieving something. Your attitude may be positive, and you may be a very capable person, but if nobody believes you – if you haven't got any credibility – you cannot get across what you want to get across. Then you are unable to get other people to help you achieve the results you want. You need enough credibility to motivate other people to support your journey into the future.

So what is the challenge?

Change

Our expectations are about growth. In business terms, companies that do not grow die. And we have this belief within us that if we do not keep making progress, if we stand still, we are actually going backwards. But growth is not the challenge. We can say it is, but I think all that does is to focus our mind on the wrong thing. In practice the challenge is not growth, the challenge is change. And whatever words we use for growth, we should use for change. If we ask: "What rate of growth do you want?", the question we are really asking is: "What rate of change can you handle?" Because if we can't handle change then we can't handle growth. If we want fast growth, it implies that we want fast change. The challenge is not growth, the challenge is change. And most of us are probably not prepared to change fast enough to get what we want. That is the problem, because we cannot get something different from what we have now unless we are prepared to change. The challenge is how we direct, manage and control change, and that will deliver the growth.

How come we are not prepared to change? Well, psychologists say it is because we all live in a "comfort zone", and if we do something different it is a risk that will involve becoming "uncomfortable". I put it down to fear of failure. Fear of failure is the greatest block to our achieving what we want to achieve, because we cannot succeed in doing anything unless we are prepared to fail.

Churchill said: "You will succeed to the extent to which you are prepared to fail." A young executive once asked the founder of IBM: "What can I do to be more successful?" The answer was: "Just double your failure rate." The more we are prepared to fail, the more chance we have of succeeding.

Listen and Learn

Maybe we should re–label the comfort zone as the "boring zone" and change as the "adventure zone". And failures could be judged by the test of "Are we failing in a forward direction?"

In fact, the challenge is not about growth; and the challenge is not even about change. The real challenge is about learning. Are we willing to learn? The problem is that, when we are young, parents have the responsibility to teach us; when we are at school, teachers have the responsibility to teach us. Once we are adult, it can take a number of years to realise that we are the people responsible for our own learning. And if we wish to be successful, the key is to learn things which can help us get to where we want to go. The challenge is how we direct, manage and control learning.

There are different types of learning. The first is maintenance learning. We need to learn certain things in order to maintain our lives: how to use a knife and fork, how to dress ourselves, how to brush our teeth, how to use a word processor.

But life is not that simple and maintenance learning does not fully prepare us for a crisis. The aspect of learning that deals with a crisis is shock learning. In a state of crisis – a bereavement, a car accident – we will learn something which we would not have had to learn otherwise; we will learn about something, whether ourselves or the world around us. A crisis is the catalyst for the silent communication of shock learning.

We use these two instinctive techniques, maintenance learning and shock learning, to continue living. They maintain the momentum, but we need something more than that. The problem is the human gap. The more knowledge and awareness we have, the more informed we are, the more inadequate we can feel. The solution is innovative learning, a style of learning that can help us deal with the future. That has three aspects.

The first aspect relates to the plan we have defined, and is anticipation. We must be able to anticipate what we need to learn for the future.

Secondly, we need to be able to listen, which is different from hearing. Remember, we automatically have psychological filters like: "I know all that," which prevent us listening and picking up things which could be relevant. We must be able to listen to the people who can help us get where we want to go. That is an enabling technique, an empowering technique.

Lastly, we need to be able to get in and participate in what it is we want to do. Don't sit on the sidelines and watch the video. Participation can sometimes be threatening and sometimes making that step can be the big one. If what we want to do is radically different to what we are doing now, the way in which we participate in those events is going to be radically different. We have got to be prepared to do that and to call it learning. It may be that we have to amend the way in which we network with our personal support team of friends, contacts and colleagues.

Finally, responsibility. When we are adult, we are responsible for our learning, we are responsible for our future. There is no excuse for your problems; they are your challenges, and you have got to find the solutions. We are all individually responsible for unlocking and developing our potential. I hope for you it will be exciting and rewarding.

Have a good trip.

CHAPTER 15 **The Creature Show**

JOHN STEPHENSON

studied furniture design at the Royal College of Art then left for the States, where he came across the legendary Henson Organisation in its heyday of producing *The Muppet Show*. It was 1980, and animation technology (animatronics) was just about to take off in a big way. John worked on Henson's film *The Dark Crystal*, then went freelance to do a variety of films, commercials and pop promos. In 1986 he became Creative Supervisor of the Henson Organisation's London-based workshop – The Creature Shop.

The Creature Shop has been involved with many prestigious film and TV projects, including *The Witches*, *Teenage Mutant Ninja Turtles I* and *II*, and *The Flintstones*. Current projects include *The Indian in the Cupboard*, *Loch Ness*, *Babe* and *Pinocchio*.

When John came to us in October 1991 he had just finished making the first *Turtles* movie. He brought with him video clips and models which he used to demonstrate the art of animatronics, from pulling a piece of string to hi-tech computer wizardry. John's behind-the-scenes revelations amazed us, and our guests loved meeting the pizza-eating reptiles who were on show in our gallery.

JOHN STEPHENSON

It all started with Jim Henson.

Jim was an extraordinary man. He was a tremendous businessman, an artist and an inspiration to those around him. He gathered together a bunch of craftsmen and women, performers and generally interesting types, put them to work and left them to come up with original ideas. A television genius and a technical perfectionist, he is, in fact, probably remembered more than anything else for his own (now much copied) brand of humour. Being really silly with puppets on screen! He probably spent a good half of his 25 years in showbusiness being exceptionally silly while using technology to its greatest advantage.

The Muppet Show was immensely popular, both here and in the States, for about eight years. The favourite character-puppet of them all, and Jim's alter ego, was Kermit, and no-one but Jim was allowed even to touch him. Kermit was a very simple hand puppet, but it was quite extraordinary that Jim could make everyone believe that it was doing such complicated movements – even tap dancing.

Jim started as a man underneath a table with a "dolly" on his hand, but he was continually looking for the next step, the next thing to do, which is what The Creature Shop has been doing ever since. In the years that *The Muppet Show* was on air, production values multiplied and the whole business, in fact, snowballed incredibly quickly. By the end, there were a number of different rigs involved, some of them huge, with people operating things on strings or radio controls, and eventually a thing called a "waldo", a mechanical device used remotely, which transmits the movements of the puppeteer's hand to the puppet.

Performance and entertainment are the key to it all. A lot of special effects companies forget that, and get completely carried away with the design, the thing on the bench, the drawing or whatever it may be. When I went to the Henson Organisation I guess I was a real design purist, but this was knocked out of me terribly quickly – because those things don't necessarily work on screen. Everything we make at The Creature Shop is, first and foremost, designed to work on screen.

Jim finished *The Muppet Show* in 1979. Public demand was still enormous – he could have been doing it now. But he decided he had done everything he wanted to do with the Muppets, and he had an idea for a fantasy film (and this is where I appear, fresh-faced out of art school). I was lucky enough to be picked by Jim to work on *Dark Crystal*. It was completely different from *The Muppet Show*. The Muppets were fairly simple hand puppets, and now we were trying to do something totally different. The puppets had to be sculpted, they had to be moulded and mechanised, and this, I suppose, is where The Creature Shop had its foundations.

If the Muppets were the beginning in performance, *Dark Crystal* was the beginning technically. It was amazing, really, because we had no terms of reference whatsoever. Of course, there have always been examples of real-time animation – most of them absolutely terrible. It didn't get serious until *Star Wars* and *Alien*. *Star Wars* had just been made, and the makers had created a little character called Yoda, which was a little taster for us, but almost everything was new – materials, technology, and a whole design philosophy. Everything had to be discovered for the first time.

I got well and truly bitten by the bug. I left Henson after that year working on *Dark Crystal* and worked for seven years on my own in the film industry, designing and making, generally doing what I could. I was involved in quite a few projects, including pop promos, commercials and a few films: *Greystoke*, *Return to Oz*, *Arena*, *Max Mon Amour*.

During that period I met a brilliant man called Rick Baker, who had come to the same sort of conclusions as me, but from another direction. He was a make-up artist, and had started simply by putting make-up on people's faces, beautifully and very successfully, and then decided to augment that work with localised movement. He did *An American Werewolf in London*, which added a lot to the contemporary picture of real-time animation, and then went on to do *Greystoke*, on which I was employed for about a year trying to make a whole load of men in mechanical ape suits look realistic.

At the end of that seven-year period, in 1986, I was called back by Jim to set up The Creature Shop, which is where I am now. The idea was to turn this group of creative people I described earlier into something more commercial – not an easy task. We seem, however, to have been very lucky and quite successful!

The first project that we did was a Henson project (though we do produce our own shows as well), called *The Story Teller*.

We built four shows in about eight weeks, a phenomenal pace, and because of this enforced speed we had to change the way we worked. During the days of *Dark Crystal* we had spent hours and hours experimenting and developing, trying to get our brains around things, whereas by now we sort of had an animatronic vocabulary. We also developed our own methodology in terms of storyboards and various other aspects of production. In the good old days we would probably have built one creature that would do everything; but when it came to *The Storyteller* we built things that would do just what was necessary for the job, and nothing more. It had taken years of development and hours of work to be able to do so many shows in such a short space of time. And we managed to attain what we thought were very good results.

After that we developed a continuation to *The Storyteller – The Greek Myths*. Again, production values were very significantly improved.

Another great programme we did around this time was *Living with Dinosaurs*, about a young boy who had a huge attachment to his cuddly pet dinosaur. He was going to a grown-up school for the first time and insisted on taking the toy with him. The boy and the toy had such a close relationship that every time we saw them together the toy actually talked to him. The toy's character was interesting because it was completely obsessed with Elvis Presley.

Then we made *The Monster Maker*, about a guy who made creatures. There was a huge monster in the story who was probably about 30 feet high and, I think, had a wing span of about 70 feet. This monster represented the man's life's work, and he had it hidden away in a shed, where it occasionally came to life. There were about 22 people operating the puppet.

By now we had developed a very effective way of working. This involved sketching, then making models at one-fifth real size, using clay or Plastillene (a sort of oily Plasticine). From that we would probably work with the director quite a bit to make changes to the model before we took it any further. Then we mould a full-sized clay model and make from it a fibreglass skeleton. This would be chopped up and mechanised, using anything that would make it move – electronics, pneumatics, hydraulics, cables… even a piece of string. It could be controlled by computers or simple levers, whatever the design required. Computers have enabled us to do a fantastic amount; three or four years ago you would have needed six people to operate one puppet – now, with computers, you only need one. You can do more and more, and you cut the margin of error. And although animatronics is expensive (because it's labour-intensive), it's actually cheaper than employing a fairly well-paid American actor.

Soon after *The Monster Maker*, another project turned up. It was *The Teenage Mutant Ninja Turtles*.

There are lots and lots of stories that have been told about the turtles and how they were done. Technically, the problems were very much to do with the fact that we had four lead characters who were there for the duration of the film and who had to be able to do more acting than is usual with a puppet.

In the past, if we had wanted to make a head talk beautifully, or to do something which was to be credible, we probably would have made a close-up head, then cut away to something else, and then if we needed to see the same thing in a long-shot it would be a man in a suit running about. We would constantly be doing that sort of thing – cuts from close-ups to long shots or medium shots. But we couldn't do that on this film, so we had to get a bit clever, and very quickly.

What we had to do was create a system whereby a performer/turtle could come right up to the camera, talk, and go into a piece of action, without having to cut. We didn't have any responsibility whatsoever for the quality of the filming, but we did take responsibility for the images themselves, and I guess they are successful. The turtles were achieved using many costumes. Splinter, the rat character, was a hand puppet, but the main costumes had incredibly sophisticated heads which could do all the talking and the expressions. I think we made 59 rubber suits for that film – they're quite fragile things and they got absolutely ripped to shreds. We had three people to each turtle. One was operating the facial expressions, using a computer system which enabled the puppet's expressions to follow the actor's expressions exactly; one was inside the turtle during the main body movements; and the other one was a martial arts expert and stunt man.

After this, in many ways, we came full circle into a 30-minute television comedy series which we shot in Los Angeles. *The Dinosaurs* came from an idea of Jim Henson's before he died. They were very American characters, a family of dinosaurs, and the joke was that they were completely environmentally unaware – they were smoking and drinking and so on. The son, who was the exception, a nice, gentle sort of lad, quietly went away and ate vegetables in his room. I think that sets the scene.

We won an Academy Award, and the series was hugely successful in the States, with audiences of something like 60 million. We had to do it very fast, and we made 19 dinosaur characters in 16 weeks, then shot one half-hour show a week, using a crew of about 30 people in LA.

To give an example of how complicated it gets, with just one character, Baby Sinclair, we had to make ten rigs. Some were very simple, just bits and pieces, like a stuffed puppet that could be thrown around the set. Others were more complicated. We made various sets of hands and arms using different operating arrangements, we made a fully-mechanised head, and we made one outfit, out of foam latex, which had someone inside.

Animatronics is used more and more nowadays, and much of the time it is so sophisticated that audiences don't even realise that is what they are seeing. Not that long ago people shied away from our discipline because it was believed to be unreliable and difficult to shoot, but that is just not the case any more. Animatronics has come of age, there is a recognisable vocabulary that we can use, and if somebody comes to me with a particular type of imagery that they are interested in using we can make it work for them. We can realise people's dreams.

CHAPTER 16 **Journey to the Surface of the Earth**

MARK BOYLE was born in Glasgow. When he was 22 he met the Scottish painter Joan Hills and they began a lifelong collaboration – from beginnings in painting and assemblage, they began to develop, in 1964, their detailed and astonishingly lifelike relief paintings of the Earth's surface.

Together, they invented liquid light shows and, with their children Sebastian and Georgia now involved, put on a stream of performances, events and presentations celebrating, in a particularly vivid manner, the microscopic and macroscopic organic life that surrounds us, physical and chemical change, the fluids and functions of the human body and the social environment in which we live.

In 1967 **BOYLE FAMILY** embarked on a global project, making their pictures at random places on the surface of the Earth. They represented Britain with solo exhibitions at the Venice Biennale in 1978 and the Sao Paulo Bienal in 1987.

In November 1991 our gallery was transformed by a display of extraordinary works, loaned to us by Boyle Family to accompany Mark's talk. For most of our guests it was an immense surprise to find that what they were looking at were not slices of reality lifted from the ground, but painted fibreglass reliefs. Mark's talk was very personal, moving, funny and inspiring – but he didn't reveal the secret of their magical technique.

I grew up in an atmosphere in which the whole world seemed to be in Hammer technicolour.

An absolutely garish, Gothic luridness. All of my six brothers and sisters would agree with that. A blow could fall upon you at any time. At dinner my father would suddenly launch himself across the table and hit the person three down from me a hard blow round the ear, saying: "I told you not to take sugar with your rhubarb!" My father was a wonderful monster. Very witty, very bright, a maniac, who eventually died in an asylum. When he was up he was the greatest company in the world; when he was down he was the worst company in the world.

This was a man who believed that the things that kept people in a state of oppression were inarticulacy and not being part of the culture of your times. So he made us write in a little notebook, every day, three words that we had discovered in the course of our reading, together with the definition of the words and the actual sentence we had found them in. If your notebook was not up to date, he would batter you. He also made us go to all the concerts of the Scottish Orchestra. We sat in the seats closest to the Exit sign. This was not so we could make a quick getaway, it was so that, in the sign's dim light, we could all read while the concert was happening. In that way we unconsciously absorbed the great classics of music and literature – and sat there and looked for our three words while we were doing it.

My father also went to Workers' Educational Association classes in art appreciation and came back every week with a postcard of the picture they had discussed. He didn't actually talk about what he'd heard about that picture. Ever. He talked about the name of the artist, the date it was painted, the title of the painting and the gallery it was hanging in. We had to know these facts. He kept the postcards in a biscuit tin beside the round, brown Bakelite radio in the drawing room. Every Sunday night he would pull a picture out at random and if you didn't know the name of the painting, the artist, the gallery... Bang!

A long time went by; I joined the army, and then, in 1956, I was introduced to this wonderful girl in a Polish café in Harrogate. That evening we went for a walk round the town. We couldn't stop talking. We went back to the café. We had £1 between us. We had dinner in a Chinese restaurant. It cost five shillings each. By the end of the evening we had formally decided that this was not love at first sight. But we had also decided that we would work together for the rest of our lives. What we wanted to do was to make a kind of art that could include anything. Or at least a kind of art that would not reject anything.

When I met Joan something quite extraordinary happened to me and my life. It took me a little while to realise it, but I began to notice after a while that the world was no longer in that kind of garish technicolour. There was a wonderful vividness. Walking through the streets with Joan I saw the streets with a kind of beautiful clarity. Suddenly it was peaceful and you could see things in their proper light. It was a fantastic experience, and so began the great collaboration of our lives.

For some years, Joan and I worked side by side. We went to Paris, but never thought of making a living either from the poems or the pictures. The question never arose; we just assumed we would always have to do other jobs. We got sent back to England by the Embassy because we were destitute, and we ended up working in a restaurant. I was the head waiter at £1 a week and Joan was the chef at £3 a week, plus tips...

It was midday. Joan had cooked 90 steak and kidney puddings that morning. She said to me: "I think it's going to be today." So I took her home and eventually at about 8pm the doctor called me up and said: "Look, if you want to be present at the birth of this babe, Mark, you'd better get yourself over here fast." So I jumped onto my bike and cycled whooping and shouting through the streets till I got home, just in time to see the arrival of Sebastian. And then a short time later I was cycling through the streets whooping and shouting for the arrival of Georgia. And ever since then, in the most sentimental and joyful way possible, we have been Boyle Family.

Since then we've all worked together. Sebastian and Georgia can't remember a time when they weren't working on the pictures. From the earliest days of making these kind of Earth pictures they were there. I assume that in the first days they were just asked to find a screwdriver, but eventually they were probably allowed to paint the edges. None of us can remember when it was they started painting the surfaces with us. It's been a pretty good collaboration since then, and immediately they stopped their full-time education we established Boyle Family and everyone became an equal partner.

It's a marvellous and wonderful collaboration. That's not to say it's a

Study from the Broken Path Series with Two Paths
(work in progress, 1986)

Study for the Westminster Series with Kerb
and Pavement Light (1988)

Street Study from the Westminster Series with Yellow
and Red Lines and Pub Cellar Trap Door (1989)

Study from the White Cliff Series (1988)

cosy democracy or anything like that, far from it. We are four feuding dictators. Everybody knows exactly how it should go and says so in a loud voice. And to get your way it's not necessary to shout louder than anybody else, but to shout more persistently than anybody else. Eventually three voices die away and one is left and that's what we do.

In 1964 we had our first show at the Edinburgh Festival and we decided that we had to leave the restaurant. The boss would only believe that we were actually going to leave when we spent our last wages on two bottles of champagne and put them in the fridge on our last night. We believed we should leave at a time when we had no money at all, on the principle that if you're going to jump off a cliff, the sooner you hit the bottom the better. We had also spent a whole evening discussing with one another which of the assorted writers, dancers, actors, singers, musicians and sculptors that worked in our restaurant would actually ever manage to leave. And we had decided that none of them would, and that an objective observer from outside would have to include us in the bunch that never would. And we just had to leave, just go, and this was a good moment, because we had an exhibition – the pictures were so staggeringly beautiful we were bound to make a fortune...

On the last night we went round and thanked all the customers, explained that we were leaving, and we set off. We took the two bottles of frozen champagne back with us and when we got home we ran a very, very hot bath and got into it with these two bottles of champagne.

There is something about the juxtaposition of icy champagne, very hot water and naked human beings that creates an atmosphere that can certainly be described as friendly. Time went by. At about 2am somebody rang the front door bell. We got out of the bath giggling a lot and, as there was only one bath towel, we wrapped it round both of us and advanced on the front door in that fashion. We opened the front door and all our customers from our last night in the restaurant were there – all with bottles of wine – and they said they'd come to give us a good sendoff. They all came in and then they told us that after we'd left they'd had a meeting and they'd decided that their good sendoff was going to take the form of their buying a picture from us between them. They decided which picture they would buy and said they would each have it for a month. We were, of course, just beside ourselves. It was like a fantastic omen – we'd taken this huge risk of plunging into being professional artists at a time when we had nothing, and here we were (it wasn't even two hours later) already in receipt of our first cheque and feeling absolutely wonderful. From the time we got into that bath with the frozen champagne it was going to be 17 years before we would actually make a profit. But that night it seemed that we were absolutely on top of the moon, and there was a wonderful party that went on till dawn.

And every show that we had after that seemed to be so exciting that the idea carried on. For some reason or other it never stops, I never stop believing.

We had a horrendous time getting to that first show. We had no money and we had to get someone who had a car to drive us up to Edinburgh. We paid four guys ten shillings each, 50 pence, to help us get the pictures up the spiral staircase – some of them were 13 feet long. And then we discovered that the walls couldn't actually take their weight, so we had to build a wooden structure wedged between the floor and the ceiling in order to hang them.

At the opening, to my astonishment, the place was absolutely packed with press. I hadn't expected this; there must have been 50 journalists in the room and the cameras were flashing away. We were complete beginners and I thought well, it must be like the theatre, all the critics turn out for all the openings. It's never happened to me since – but I was a new guy then. So I said to Joan: "Let's try and keep it very cool, don't let's show that we are complete beginners." When the press conference started, this guy asked: "Is this pop art, Mr Boyle?" and I said: "No, it's not pop art." "What is pop art?" "Well, pop artists are doing what artists have always tried to do. They've tried to tell the truth about their environment. That's what the Italian Renaissance painters did, that's what the Impressionists did, that's what the Dutch interior painters did, that's what Turner did, that's what William Blake did and Rembrandt and really everybody that's any good has always done that. That's what it's about, it's about trying to tell the truth about your environment." And the questions went on, quickfire, for an hour or more. The next morning there was a picture on the front page of the Scottish *Daily Express* showing us lined up. Sebastian had fallen out of the truck on the way up and had a split head with a big bandage round it, so he looked like a battered baby. Joan was zonked-out, and she'd shut her eyes because of the flashing of the camera. I was leaning against something, smoking away, trying to look really cool and looking really stupid. And there was a big headline going right across the page saying: "I'm doing the same as Rembrandt, says Mr Boyle."

We came down to London after that and our studio was on a junk site; in fact it was a moving studio – it went from one junk site to another. We used to work there very happily, making sculptures out of the rubble we found there. One day there was one of these grey plastic frames from a TV set, the thing that holds the screen in place, lying there on the site. What lay within it seemed to us to be absolutely perfect and we stared at it with great fascination wondering why it seemed so perfect. Then we thought maybe this shape appeared to be an aesthetic object because we had all been watching too much TV. So we tried it somewhere else – didn't work, was relatively boring. And we moved it and placed it in various places, but we could never get anything that seemed as exciting as we saw in the first place. So then one of us, no-one can remember who, thought well, maybe it was because it just came like that, grew naturally, arrived naturally, in that particular way. So we took the frame and just threw it across the junk site and went to look at the place where it had fallen... and of course it was perfect.

For the next few days we spent the whole time alternately placing this thing and getting a poor result and chucking it away and getting a good result. It's most extraordinary – I'm still not absolutely sure, and people continually can't believe, that the pictures we make are random. Yet we always have a random element, it doesn't matter what kind of picture, unless it's a tiny study where we're trying to get some particular effect – the equivalent of a practice sketch. Now it seems to us so natural that it's difficult to remember how we felt then. But if you take a coloured London atlas, flick through it, pick a random page, stab your finger into it and look at the square that your finger has landed on, you'll find the design of that square is always perfect. It's an immaculate design. Extraordinary.

I'm not a philosopher, I don't understand these things, but I suspect that what it's all about is the fact that we're using this earth, in its natural state, as the basis of our concept of beauty and design, and part of its natural state is the havoc we have done to it. And everything we do is part of nature, in the same way that a cobweb made by a spider is part of nature.

The first major series we completed was on a beach at Camber Sands. We wanted to take one square of sand and make a study of it after each tide for a week, so that we would see what effect the tide had over it each time. At the same time we began to develop a new series where we sent off to people, through the post, an invitation that was a dart stuck into a card marked "Earth Probe". It was 1967.

When the people arrived at our house they were blindfolded and taken into a room where they were invited to throw the dart at an unseen target. When they'd thrown the dart their blindfolds were removed and they found themselves looking at a map of the world. That was the beginning of our world series. The process was continued at the ICA, where the darts were fired out of a gun instead of being thrown personally, because we had discovered with the original series that a lot of them dropped low and there were more of them in the southern hemisphere than in the northern hemisphere.

The first site we went to was in Holland where we had been invited to do a show at the museum at The Hague, and part of the show was a commission to make a piece there. We made the piece during the show and it was exhibited at the end. We were very, very nervous. When it was finished, the museum workers gathered round to look and were talking very interestedly to one another. I asked the director what they were saying, and he said: "They are saying this is Dutch earth." I said: "That's ridiculous, it's just ridiculous." It had been a demolition site just like we'd been on in the early days, except that there was hardly anything on it. There was a bit of a broken pipe, otherwise it was just this grey sandy earth. I said: "It could be anywhere in the world." And he said: "No, no, you're wrong. Take a look." We went over to it and he said: "You see where you painted all these little shells? At one time the whole of The Hague was under the sea – this is Dutch earth." It gave me a real shock to realise that they had discovered something in it which I didn't know was there.

We had the same experience some time later in Norway when we were showing in the Oslo Museum. We had made some snow pieces and taken them back to London to finish them in our studio. But when they were finished and lit, suddenly they didn't look like the snow as I had seen it on the site any more. I saw there were patterns in the snow, but when I had seen it on the site it had looked like cotton wool, like snow does. I was really embarrassed. At the opening of the show I wouldn't unwrap them until everyone had gathered. I pretended that I didn't want them to get dirty – but in fact the truth was I was just frightened of what these guys would say; snow is their religion. It was a big moment when I unwrapped them – a whole series from pure snow through to pure earth, during the melt of the snow. There was total silence and then somebody said something in Norwegian. Again I grabbed the director's arm: "What did he say?" And he said: "He wants to know how you keep them cold."

Herbert Read, a famous critic, once said of art that it should be wonderful, original in concept, innovative in technique, significant, powerful. What we look for when we're looking at art is something which should be unique. It should be delicious and I'm not talking about chocolate-box lids – I'm talking about the way Francis Bacon puts paint onto the canvas, which is, to my mind, delicious. It should be amazing, it should be blazing off the wall. It should feel necessary or inevitable.

I can't ever forget the night after Martin Luther King's death when we were travelling with Jimmy Hendrix and Soft Machine. Hendrix's concert was packed to capacity, but he abandoned his regular set completely, came to the microphone and said: "This number is for a friend of mine." Then he played the most heartbreaking music I've ever heard. Within a few minutes, the entire audience was sobbing – even the old redneck stage hands came and stood around the back, listening with tears running down their faces. At the end of it he put his guitar down and walked off the stage, and we got into the limo and drove away through the deserted streets. That seemed to me to be an artist speaking to his people in the most necessary way.

The final thing that we're looking for in a work of art is that it should be true, or be about truth, or be about the possibility of telling the truth – it should address that question. There are many kinds of art and I love all of it, I don't make any kind of barriers.

Finally, I'm not going to put forward any theories or intellectual arguments in favour of our work. Our work is what it is. You can see it for yourself. You don't need to understand it – it's just there.

CHAPTER 17 The Heart of the World

ALAN EREIRA is a historian who spent 18 years in educational broadcasting before deciding to move to a medium with broader appeal. His many projects range from a commemoration of the French Revolution to a series on the Armada, which won the 1988 Royal Television Society Award for best documentary series.

In 1989 the South American Kogi, an ancient tribe who live on a virtually inaccessible mountain in Colombia, were seeking to relay an important warning to the outside world. The Kogi were convinced that the balance of life on Earth was threatened – and they chose Alan to transmit their message.

In January 1992 Alan came to Newell and Sorrell to give an intriguing account of the time he spent living with the Kogi, their way of life and their beliefs. And, using a selection of slides together with the Kogi's own, powerful words, he explained why, after four centuries of isolation, they had decided to break their silence.

"We are the Elders. We are the Elders of all. With greater knowledge, Spiritual and material."

There is a mountain called the Sierra Nevada de Santa Marta on the north coast of Colombia, facing onto the Caribbean Sea. It's a separate tectonic plate from the rest of South America, and it's very small, as tectonic plates go, only 90 miles long. One side is sea, the other two sides are rift valleys, and in the middle is a wedge, quite a neat equilateral triangle, which rises 18,000 feet straight out of the sea. There is no other mountain like it; it is the highest coastal mountain in the world. It has equatorial forest at the bottom and glaciers and snow at the top. In between it has every climate on the surface of the planet. Anything that will grow anywhere will grow somewhere on that mountain. It is a complete ecological model of the whole planet. The Sierra has still not been fully mapped, especially the north side, which is the most difficult side to get into. At the bottom is an area of pretty dense jungle, along with cocaine farming in private army territory. Most of the beaches are inaccessible to ordinary mortals because they're used for drug shipment. There's also a lot of banditry, and guerrillas operating in the area.

High up on this mountain live the Kogi, the only surviving high civilisation from pre-Columbian America. There once were a large number of similar cultures – highly developed, highly sophisticated – but most of them were decimated by the great empires that developed in the years before the Spanish arrival. However, in this particular area that didn't happen. Neither Inca nor Aztec actually reached in, so their civilisation was more robust than the others when the Spanish arrived. For various reasons it was not brought into a state of instant collapse by contact with the Spanish, but co-existed with them for 75 years. Then, when things became too hot, they had a heartland to which they withdrew... and there they still are.

I got involved with the Kogi because I was in Colombia making a film about the Spanish Armada, and while I was there the BBC asked me to check out an archeological site that had been discovered on the lower slopes of the Sierra Nevada. It was called by the Colombians the "Lost City". It was very big, around 2,000 acres, buried in the jungle, but apparently in immaculate condition. As I started to read up on the area, I began to hear more and more about the Kogis being present on this mountain, and that they were the descendants of the people who had built the Lost City. I heard that they had similar cities, though on a smaller scale, which they were still living in. So I thought the thing to do, if we were going to make a film about this Lost City, was to get in touch with the Kogi and ask them to cooperate in the filming.

Everybody said I was wasting my time, because the Kogi didn't speak to outsiders. But I succeeded in getting a message to them through intermediaries. The message was: "If you want to speak to the outside world, I can help you." And a message came back some months later: "We're waiting to work with you."

After months of preparation and research, I arrived in a Kogi village, a set of woody glades high enough not to be too hot, and not so high as to be cool – the climate was paradise. Coming into this small town of circular huts were men wearing long white robes, with dark hair flowing down over their shoulders, some of them riding magnificent black horses with red woven harnesses – the whole thing was like a mythological dream. I was swept away, with a government official, to wait in a building set aside.

That evening I was summoned. I tried to explain who I was, what a film was, and what I wanted to do; and also all the reasons why I thought they might not want to do it, and then why I thought it might be a good idea for them to do it. And I said that of course they would also have their own reasons, which I wouldn't understand. All the men were carrying a gourd with a stick in it, and at that point there was a rattle of all the gourds. I was told: "We have listened to your words, we will analyse them and consider them and tomorrow we will divine on the top of the mountain and then we will tell you."

When they came back we were summoned in. The men began to speak one at a time: "All of those who are present here from the community of Mamas made divination up there on the hillside with their knowledge. They concentrated and analysed up there. Now we will speak to our Younger Brother, we who are the elders, we who are the elders of all, with greater knowledge, spiritual and material." And they began to spell out their whole idea of creation and the history of the world, what their civilisation had been, and how Columbus had come and all but destroyed it.

In the beginning *Aluna* (memory, possibility, past, future) was a cloth, laying flat, then a corner of it was lifted up, and as it unfolded a space appeared, and in this space was everything. Creation was the process of opening up the space between past and future, making the present. *Aluna* is also the mind and the life force itself. The two things are one and the same as far as the Kogi are concerned. Everything is alive; they don't have a concept of inanimate. Everything is part of the universal mind which is life energy. The process of creation is a process of differentiation out of this life energy, particularly differentiation between masculine and feminine. The idea of differentiation means that the Kogi perception of nature is of a delicately maintained balance between a set of careful separations. The function of humanity is to be the bridge between the material world and *Aluna*, the world of mind and spirit, and the essence of potency. The function of the *Mamas* (the Kogi elders) is to work with *Aluna*, to meditate, to concentrate and actively to manipulate the spirit structure of the world, to be its guardian, to prevent the world from getting out of balance. The Kogi see themselves in a kind of Adam-and-Eve story in

which they still live in the Garden of Eden. We are the Younger Brother, lacking the ability to understand or get inside the essence of nature. In their mythology we were excluded, sent away to another part of the world, where we work without any perception that we have to balance the consequences of our actions.

Having built a whole new world in isolation, the Kogi had anticipated that they would be able to continue living in it, without any contact with us, from then on. This is what they had done for four centuries. But they had now come to the conclusion that this was no longer an option, that the Younger Brother, whose nature was destructive, was now so destructive that he was affecting the very future of the world itself.

The Kogi know a surprising amount about the outside world. Any information that crosses their frontier is gathered in. If an individual felt that he or she were out of harmony – say, if they were having bad dreams – he or she would go to a *Mama*, who would ask them to describe, in great detail, their whole life since they last had this kind of conversation. In this way the *Mamas* learn everything that their people have seen and done, which, of course, will include a certain amount of contact with the outside world. They also gather information through trading, through dealing with government officials in Santa Marta, at the bottom of the mountain (which is, incidentally, the oldest city in South America, and the place in which the Spanish first discovered the continent, 15 miles from the Kogi), and through contact with other related tribes on the mountain who are much more acculturated. They add all this information together with the information they already have about the Spanish period of contact between 1525 and 1600. Their knowledge can be startling. I knew an archaeologist who was working in the Sierra on a grave area. One day the Kogi approached him and said: "We hear you have developed a bomb which will kill people but not destroy buildings. What do you intend to do with it?" He replied: "No we haven't, I don't know what you're talking about." It was only when he got back to Santa Marta and told the story that he heard about the neutron bomb, news of which had only reached Santa Marta while he was up on the dig. Somehow the Kogi had got hold of this story.

In their speech to me they went on to explain how, in their view, there must be massive deforestation taking place, and that there must also be large-scale mining of minerals and fossil fuels. They believed that the deforestation was causing the Earth to heat up and the water to dry up, and that the excavation of minerals was causing the Earth to lose its strength. They were certain that if this continued all life on Earth would perish. Therefore, they had to find some way of speaking to us, the Younger Brother, to try to get us to change the way we were behaving. That's what I was there for, and they now proposed to work with me to do this.

What was very clear right from the start was that these were very serious, very intelligent people, who had a profound idea of what they were talking about and whose minds were very fast indeed. There is nothing primitive about them; in fact it was a shock to be confronted by a group of people who – I have no doubt whatever – have better minds than I do. They not only thought faster, they also thought much more clearly. This has to do with a number of things. One is that they deliberately don't use writing, regarding information acquired through writing as being defective. Secondly there is the extraordinary education of the *Mamas*. Extraordinary because it is an education in darkness. Children are taken, ideally from birth, and kept for at least nine years in complete darkness. The child is left to discover what he is interested in and is helped to pursue that by a teacher. He is only allowed out at night and, traditionally, even then he has to wear a large woven square over his head to prevent moonlight and starlight falling onto his face. The world, for him, is an exercise of the imagination, and he is taught to meditate and to contemplate and to make offerings. It is only at nine years old, at the earliest, that he will actually see a chicken, a tree. This is a completely baffling process; all my understanding of child development is that this should produce a highly damaged personality. I can only tell you it doesn't. The evidence that I have seen of the *Mamas* is that they are in no way damaged – they are remarkable people, whom the whole community trusts.

Incidentally, the Kogi society works rather effectively in a material sense. They reckon their average life expectancy to be about 90. The agriculture that we saw looked extremely capable. They concentrate a great deal on what plants go with each other and in what location.

Everything has to work with everything else. They are acutely aware of the effect of a single plant on the ecology of the whole mountain. Things grow well, and the animals are healthy. The Kogi explanation is that this is because they maintain the harmony. When things go out of balance (and everything we do in the material world tends to throw it out of balance), it produces some kind of disease. As far as the Kogi are concerned, that disease could be parasites in animals, illness in individuals or illness in animals or plants, or even social breakdown – they are all the same thing, the product of the world being out of kilter. You have to find ways of correcting what you've done wrong. They are balancing all the time, both materially and spiritually. The Tairona civilisation sustained 300,000 people on that mountain. Today modern agricultural methods operating on two of the three slopes of the mountain have completely eradicated its agricultural potential. It is now only capable of supporting 20 per cent of the population that it supported before America was discovered.

The message the Kogi wanted to send out to the world was an ecological message: "Look at how you're treating the world." On a deeper level they saw us having to learn a notion of respect; respect for the rest of the world. They see us as people who have no respect. Up to now, their experience was that they had not been treated with much respect. What they would be looking for now was some gesture from us that would indicate that we were capable of having respect.

The Kogi worked very hard at putting themselves onto film. They have no concept of film, and of course they've never seen television. They viewed what we were doing as a curious marriage between technology and spirit, in which we were attempting actually to place a human presence inside the camera. They spent months preparing themselves mentally and spiritually, making offerings, meditating, building up their strength to put a human presence in this box. It seems a strange idea, but we also have this word "presence", and we know what it means. I don't know where we get it from, but I do think that on the film the Kogi have it.

When I went back to Colombia with the finished film I invited the Kogi to come to Santa Marta to see it. To my amazement, 70 Kogi came down. The following day I went back to the compound where the Kogi were staying to discuss the film with them. By then they had worked out a grammar for understanding film. They had analysed it according to their own rules of rhetoric, which meant that they had gone through the whole film counting the number of times that the same theme was returned to, in order to work out how much weight was being given to different parts of the story. They were able to discuss the film on an intellectual level and raise some questions about the way in which I had made it. Quite honestly, there were more interesting and helpful things said by the Kogi than by anybody at the BBC. A conversation would begin: "The photography was absolutely beautiful but I would like to ask you…" It was as though this man was a lecturer in a film school! And he was someone who didn't speak Spanish and who had never seen a film before!

But the man who I regard as the wisest of the *Mamas*, Mama Valencia, didn't come down the mountain to see the film. Instead, he sent a message: "I'm not coming down until I can see that something good is happening, and I haven't seen it yet."

And that's where we're at now with the Kogi. The Kogi want nothing from us, but they do have needs. I have established the Tairona Heritage Trust, which acts on the advice and at the request of the Kogi *Mamas*. The primary thing that we are trying to do is to help the Kogi buy back land from the settlers who have been moving in, to give them access to the sea and to the lower areas of the Sierra again so that they can grow the crops they need. We also support medical projects, and aim to help stabilise the frontier between the indigenous people of the Sierra and the outside world. I hope this frontier can become a point of exchange, where the Kogi can sell their produce and buy the things they need from us. It should also be a place of cultural exchange, for they have much to teach us – if we are prepared to listen.

CHAPTER 18 **Off the Record**

BERNARD INGHAM

was born and brought up in Hebden Bridge, Yorkshire. He failed his 11-plus, but his parents paid for him to go to grammar school, where he worked hard and excelled. He played cricket and soccer, and became secretary of the local Labour League of Youth. On leaving school Bernard trained as a junior reporter at the *Hebden Bridge Times*, before moving on to the *Yorkshire Post*, followed by the *Guardian* and then the Government Information Service. He became Chief Press Secretary to Margaret Thatcher in 1979 and, during 11 years at Number 10, established himself as a controversial and powerful figure. He was knighted in December 1990 and wrote a 140,000-word autobiography, *Kill the Messenger*, in three months.

Sir Bernard's talk at Newell and Sorrell in May 1992 concentrated for the most part on an insider's post-mortem of that year's General Election. A no-nonsense man with strong opinions, Sir Bernard expressed powerful and outspoken views and stimulated strong debate among our audience. We have reproduced some extracts of his talk here – with the addition of his comments on the current political scene.

Sir Bernard on **Mrs Thatcher**

The plain and simple truth is that she came at the right time and was very much needed by Britain. The history of post-war Britain is of a sort of pale pink political consensus – "Butskellism" – and it didn't work. We declined steadily as a nation and it became terminal in 1978-9 with the Winter of Discontent. Thatcher came into power and stopped the rot – albeit at some price, with the rise in unemployment.

She was astonishingly successful until Nigel Lawson experimented with running the economy. It went wrong and she came a cropper due to rising inflation and the imposition of the poll tax – which I think would have been accepted grudgingly if interest rates had not gone through the roof. But Mrs Thatcher will go down in history as one of the two great post-war British prime ministers. Attlee changed the nature of Britain and so did Mrs Thatcher.

As a person she was the world's top executive woman. And, because she was a woman who knew what she wanted to do, was very decisive and didn't brook any interference, she was labelled with the imagery of a woman who went round handbagging men. Undoubtedly, she was a very tough cookie, but that doesn't mean she wasn't very concerned about people, which she would show if you knew her.

Sir Bernard on **John Major**

He is an extremely acute politician but incredibly self-effacing, and is unlikely to be able to present himself as a tremendously powerful man. But in a sense his reputation belies him, because he can be very firm and stubborn.

I think his great success so far is to have won an election at what is now known to have been the absolute rock bottom of a very deep recession, and to have held his party together through a very difficult period. He was handed a poisoned chalice economically, and it's only recently that he has begun to enjoy the prospect of economic success. To go for three years without economic success is a problem for any prime minister, but it looks as though the economy is coming right now.

Sir Bernard on **Tony Blair**

As one who publicly urged the Labour Party to elect Tony Blair as their leader rather than the late John Smith, I ought to be pretty smug about how things have turned out. He has done well as a leader – he's certainly been tough on his own party – as a personality, as an orator and as a public relations strategist. Like John Smith, he has removed much of the electorate's fear of Labour. In short, he has made Labour electable. And there are not many who are disinclined to bet on his making Number 10.

And yet I have my reservations. British politics was crying out for a Labour leader who could reinterpret the old socialism for the 21st century; who could make Labour relevant to the age in which we live. Instead, Mr Blair has simply pinched Mrs Thatcher's clothing. His transvestism is deeply worrying to old-fashioned Labour folk who stand for something else. This raises serious questions about the future.

Is Mr Blair simply proposing to manage Britain better than the Conservatives? If so, he will have to work hard to persuade the voters he can run a Conservative Britain better than the Tories. Or is he simply proposing to give Conservatism a human face? Or is he just a means to an end for the real Labour Party who, understandably, feel they have no political future if they come clean about their aim to level rather than lift Britain?

These questions flow inevitably from Mr Blair's utter refusal to put a cost on any concept or policy. Until he does, I cannot be sure I was right in backing Mr Blair before Mr Smith. I reserve my judgement.

Sir Bernard on **the Conservative Party**

The modern Tory Party is nothing like the old Tory Party. When Mr Heath took over he broke decisively with the landed gentry and the privileged classes, and Mrs Thatcher continued in that direction. Indeed, there is not a great deal, socially, to choose between the two main parties any more, although the Tories have had far more business experience than Labour, who have traditionally been in the public services and the unions. Modern Tory MPs are much more complicated than they used to be. They are not easily typecast – they may be right-wing on economics and wet on social matters. As a consequence, they are very much more difficult to cope with and the party is more complicated and difficult to manage: in one sense more attractive and, in another, more fractious.

Sir Bernard on **the Labour Party**

The Tory Party desperately needs a better opposition – governments perform best with a small majority and up against a real, hard opposition. The problem for Labour is to find a new, not Socialist way, appealing as a crusade to the mass of people. They are therefore looking for a new niche, and if they find it they could give the Government a hard run for its money. But for me the Labour Party represents the outstanding political failure of the Western democratic world. It's been in opposition for 15 years and it still hasn't got a clue what it stands for.

It went through moments of acute madness when it elected first Michael Foot and then Neil Kinnock – although Mr Kinnock turned out to be far better than anyone had expected. He forced the party to look at itself, and tightened up the machinery. Superficially, it now has a leader in Tony Blair who is very attractive, capable of saying the right things, a master of the sound bite. But I don't think he has very much in common with the rest of his party, and I foresee a great deal of trouble.

Sir Bernard on **the Unions**

I take a complicated approach to trades unions. I think they were once necessary, coming about because of a desperate need to deal with an abuse of employer power and to strive for some form of social justice. But, as so often happens in society, the institutions became more important than the members and their leaders abused their power.

Mrs Thatcher tamed the unions just as surely as she tamed inflation for a time during the 1980s, and I don't see much future for them in their present form.

Sir Bernard on **the Media**

The press, to my certain knowledge of 25 years, is less prejudiced against Labour than many people imagine, although it is weighted towards the Tories. The *Mirror* Group, the *Guardian*, the *Observer*, the *Financial*

Times, are all lined up on Labour's side. To varying degrees the *Daily Star*, *Today* and the *Independent* try to steer a middle course. But there is no evidence that I know of that conclusively proves that the press decisively influenced the last or any previous election. For example, some recent research suggests that half the *Sun*'s readership voted Labour against its editorial line, which raises the question of whether they read the editorial. The support for the Tories among *Mirror* readers was slightly greater than the national average, which again begs the question whether readers of the *Mirror* read their editorial.

A colleague in Newcastle University, Martin Harrop, thinks that the Tory slant of the press, over a parliament, is worth, at most, ten seats to the Tories during an election. I am not aware that he has done any discounting for the BBC, but then he perhaps has no need, because in my experience the BBC is as chronically determined to test Labour governments to destruction as it is Tory governments. In all my 23 years in government service I have yet to work for a government, and shan't do now, which believes that the BBC is the soul of impartiality. Labour governments I have known (I ought to write a book about that!), and individual Labour ministers, have been convinced that the BBC was a hotbed of capitalist vice. Tory ministers I have known have, just as passionately, (well, not quite because they tend to keep their passions to themselves), believed that the BBC is a Trotskyist cell, determined to undermine the very fabric of our society. I don't believe a word of it. I don't believe that the BBC collectively is Labour or Tory. Quite simply, as Brian Redhead made clear every morning on the *Today* programme, the BBC is determined to submit the centre of power, the Government, to the closest possible scrutiny and provocation. Which begs the question: Who polices the BBC? But we won't go into that.

My second point is that I neither know nor care whether this talk is on or off the record, unattributable or distorted. Most of the press these days don't know the difference and didn't for all those years that I was Press Secretary. Correction – some did but found the distinction inconvenient. Personally, I am very worried about intrusions of privacy. It's perfectly reasonable for the media to say that they must be allowed to expose abuses in public life, but that can't excuse many of the things they do. We are looking at an abuse of media power, and it's an unresolved question whether the media – and we are talking principally about newspapers, because radio and TV tend to follow – are capable of disciplining themselves and regulating themselves. But no government, Tories rather less than Labour, wants to regulate the media, because they know there's only pain and suffering along that route.

Sir Bernard on **How to Run the Country**

The answer lies, in my view, with the passion to run an efficient government, which enables the Government to deliver what the populace want. Good public services at reasonable cost. Good health care and good education. A good environment. A good safe, sensitive, society. A nation which stands tall in the world. It is not enough to talk about compassion. I've had enough compassion from politicians to last me two lifetimes. You have to do something, and doing something demands you take the difficult decisions and make unenviable choices – and generate the wealth to fund your compassion.

Sir Bernard on **the Next Election**

"I will tell you who will win the next election after Christmas 1995," I have repeatedly told people who have asked me for my tip.

Why Christmas 1995? Well, I don't think the Labour Party, even under Mr Blair, is capable of winning the next election. But the Tory Party is eminently capable of losing it, especially if it carries on as it has done, self-indulgently and self-destructively, for the past three years.

In my view, Mr Blair and the Labour Party have peaked. We are not going to learn much more from them before the next election, because I do not believe they have much more to tell us and because, if they did, they wouldn't dare to do so. Having established Mr Blair as an impressive leader, they are relying on the Tories to self-destruct.

But that is one thing I would not count on. Tories like power. Mr Major lanced the party's boil in July with his back-me-or-sack-me challenge to his silly Parliamentary Party. He is now in command. If Michael Heseltine can, unusually, demonstrate his loyalty and support for his Prime Minister and bring his formidable presentational qualities to bear on Government policy – and the opposition – we shall soon see a change in the political weather.

But that change of climate will only be sustained if the Tory Party as a whole can convey to the nation that, far from being worn out by nearly 17 years in office, it is determined to put the last three years behind it and make a real effort to win a fifth term.

It will, in any case, be a far closer contest than the opinion polls have been predicting for years. And I would not put it past Houdini Major to confound everyone. Whatever else may be said about him, he is a dab hand at winning elections.

What They Have Said *about Sir Bernard*

I have been called many things in my time: "Mrs Thatcher's personal Rottweiler", by Tim Condon in *Scotland on Sunday*, who clearly thought that I ought to be put down for my antisocial behaviour. "A cross between Heathcliff and a pit bull terrier", by the late lamented Jean Rook. I worked with Jean 30 years ago on the *Yorkshire Post* where I called her "A fugitive from the Serengeti", on account of the extremely colourful nature of her coat. When, 30 years later, just before her sad death, we were next door to each other in the *Daily Express* office, I reminded her of this and, if I may say so, this is one of the more interesting commentaries upon women: she remembered the coat but not my remark. I was also called "That rough-spoken Yorkshire Rasputin", by John Biffen in a moment of generosity. He also called me "The sewer, but not the sewage". I think he was getting his own back on me for my calling him that "Well-known semi-detached member of the Cabinet". I should finally say that I have also been called "A menace to the constitution" – by Sir Edward Heath. Well, he should know.

CHAPTER 19 **Earth Summit**

JONATHON PORRITT

wrote his first book, *Seeing Green*, in 1984. It remains one of the most important expositions of green politics to have appeared in the UK, and since then numerous appearances on TV and radio, countless public lectures and many articles in newspapers and magazines have made Jonathon one of the best-known "greens" in Britain today. He was co-chair of the Ecology Party (now the Green Party) from 1980 to 1983, and director of Friends of the Earth from 1984 to 1990, during which time he increased membership from 15,000 to 200,000 and turned the group into an influential lobbying organisation. Jonathon is now a special advisor to Friends of the Earth, and holds many positions on other environmental organisations while remaining committed to getting his message across to as wide an audience as possible, from church groups to civil servants, schoolchildren to scientists.

In June 1992, 130 heads of government as well as thousands of officials, scientists, environmentalists and a host of assorted guests flew to Rio de Janeiro for the Earth Summit. Jonathon was there, too. Just a few weeks later he came to Newell and Sorrell to give us a hard-hitting, behind-the-scenes look at what went on in Brazil, and to discuss how best to turn talk into action.

JONATHON PORRITT

The Earth Summit

was an amazing aggregation of initiatives and energy flows coming together in Rio for a two-week period. Forty thousand people descended on the city to stir the ecological and development pot in one way or another. Following all this excitement, the questions now are these: what were the benefits of the Summit? And, in terms of implementing and building on what was actually done there, how much can we hope to achieve?

I think the intangible benefits of the Earth Summit counted for as much as the tangible benefits.

A lot of non governmental organisations criticised the Earth Summit as being nothing more than a media circus. This was pretty ironic coming from organisations that are almost entirely dependent on those self same bits of the media circus to amplify and magnify the voices that they raise – but it was, all the same, a media circus. Some things that went on were deeply offensive. For instance, the way photographers pursued representatives of different tribal and indigenous groups, trying to catch them in what they considered to be anomalous poses, as if to say: "The picture editors will like that." And the way in which the media slavishly followed the world leaders as if they thought they were going to get anything interesting or original out of them was slightly peculiar. But nonetheless the media did an amazing job, and stimulated increased awareness of environmental concerns around the world.

That was one intangible benefit. Another was the extent to which world leaders gave an imprint of official international solidarity to this whole environment business. For example, the first paragraph of the Convention on Climate Change says that the climate is changing as a direct consequence of man-made impacts on the physical environment. Remember that 152 countries, including the United States, signed up to this. For the first time those countries acknowledged that global warming was an identifiable phenomenon, or series of connected phenomena, and that we were responsible for it. And that the speed of change was something that we now had to address, otherwise we would end up in all sorts of trouble.

So while we were right to be angry about the fact that all the specific targets about stabilising and reducing carbon dioxide were taken out at the behest of President Bush, the point is that the foundation stone was laid, and within two to three years (at most) those targets will follow on as complementary protocols to that convention. There is now a very detailed and intensive process to keep the momentum on climate change and global warming moving forward.

However, there were some pretty grim and grisly things going on at the Earth Summit, too.

The first thing was the extent to which OPEC, the oil-producing countries, and in particular the Gulf countries, decided that it was time to do away with all the usual subtlety and quiet diplomacy that they had been engaged in behind the scenes, and come out into the open and say that any policy initiative, including a carbon tax or energy tax, that offered up a threat to the sale of hydrocarbons – particularly oil – around the world, would be opposed by them tooth and nail. I think this ought to remind us that there are many fierce and furious fights in which we will be engaged over the next few years.

Equally, the business community was playing a most peculiar role at Rio. Everyone likes to think that the business community is now with us rather than against us, and it is right to acknowledge that, as far as the market leaders are concerned, there is a process of internal change that is absolutely valid, way beyond the PR-led initiatives of the sort that we had in the late Eighties, and which will lead to substantial changes in corporate behaviour. But that is not necessarily the case for the entire business community.

The American delegation, for instance, was unapologetic in its defence of American business interests. They lobbied furiously to ensure that the United States did not sign up to the Convention on Biological Diversity. President Bush said time after time the Convention was a threat to American biotech and genetic engineering industries. At three separate press conferences he was quizzed to give an indication of precisely how one American scientist, or one representative of an American biotech company, would lose his or her job as a result of the Convention. There was, of course, no answer, because there is no way to demonstrate how that legislation would cause a loss of jobs in America.

In general, the business community kept on trying to say that regulation had no particular contribution to make in advancing the environmental agenda. This was transparently stupid – regulation is critical to advancing the agenda. The people who are causing much of the damage tend to be smaller companies, not in the public eye, not vulnerable to bad publicity or consumer pressure in the same way that big companies are, and who are getting away with absolute hell.

Behind the scenes, the more regressive and reactionary business elements were assiduously involved in hunting down references to regulation, taking out from the core documents any suggestion that the problems had been, in part, caused by the unregulated operations of trans-national corporations. And they really did work hard. It was a coordinated effort, and a very successful one: not a single one of the formal outputs of the Earth Summit contained any criticism whatsoever of multinational companies today. Now that's pretty peculiar. Because although the business community, or bits of it, is moving in the right direction, to pretend that it hasn't been implicated in the pattern of damage done to date is frankly unbelievable.

The role that Japan played was equally worrying. Everyone thought they would go there as the new saviours of the international environment, put billions of dollars on the table, and dramatically snub America by saying: "OK, you're not up to the challenge of leadership in the area of sustainable development. Well, we are." Well, they didn't. They produced a small amount of additional funding for some of the sustainable development items in Agenda 21 – which is a sort of extensive wish-list of what we should all be doing to save the Earth – but, by and large, they almost floated through the Earth Summit as if they were hardly there. There is a great deal of worry about the role that Japan intends to play in the international economy.

The funding issue was itself deeply grim. Most countries couldn't even sign up unequivocally to the old United Nations commitment to spend 0.7 per cent of GNP on overseas aid. As was said right at the start: "The rich countries have never felt so poor," and that was exactly how they behaved all the way through the Earth Summit, much to the consternation of the developing countries who still believe the rich North cannot go on denying their problems while at the same time asking them to do something about global warming, ozone depletion and whatever else it might be.

So, you can only say that it was a pretty mixed picture that emerged from Rio. I personally think that the positive things marginally outweigh the negative things, but it is marginal.

So where does the environment movement go from here? I would like to indicate one or two changes that I think are absolutely critical if we're going to make progress over the next few years.

First, cooperation. Let us hope that the parochialism, the persistent territoriality which currently determines the operations of some organisations, will be a thing of the past. Because unless we learn to work more effectively together, the amount of pressure we will be able to bring to bear on governments will be strictly limited.

The second thing is developing the expertise that we need. We are no longer living in an era when simply talking about one's worry about conservation, or about marine issues or about ozone depletion, will carry any weight at all. It is only those organisations that are able to bring economic expertise to bear on how we find solutions to those problems that are going to be in positions of influence in the near future. And yet, if you look at the staffing of environment and development organisations today, and you ask how many professional

For the Earth Summit Jonathon Porritt initiated a "Tree of Life" project. Designed by Peter Avery, the tree's leaves were made from letters containing pleas for the end of environmental destruction sent by children all over the world.

economists or economic experts they actually have on staff, you would be hard-pressed to find more than a handful among all of them.

And thirdly, there is the whole question of how we reach out to wider audiences. How is the Green Movement going to move out of the ghetto that it is currently inhabiting? Its inability to find ways of talking to a wider public is becoming more and more difficult for the green groups to deal with. But I see no strategy at the moment in their efforts to come to terms with that.

Those are some of the challenges for the environment groups. The challenges, however, don't end there. Whatever else may have happened at the Earth Summit, it has set in train a series of processes which will eventually percolate through into the life of every single business and the life of every single individual. It's no good blaming the Government for a failure to respond to the historic moment, because that failure was a reflection of the level of awareness that could be seen in the UK. If we didn't get what we wanted out of the Earth Summit, it was because not enough people said they wanted it. Not enough people were out on the streets, out there at the ballot box, out there as green consumers, making their choices in a way that the Government couldn't ignore.

The survival instinct is a more powerful instinct than any other. If we can eventually trigger the survival instinct, we may see a process of change unravelling which will defy our worst expectations about the future. But how near to the edge do we have to get before the survival instinct is triggered? Just how close do we have to be? How many people must drop over the edge before we find ourselves driven to change our ways by a fear of extinction and a fear for our children?

I don't believe there is any prospect of making sense of the dilemma we have got ourselves into after 250 years of industrial progress, unless we engage the free, unfettered participation of the human spirit in that process. Change will only come when people are engaged spiritually as well as politically.

If we rely on fear, rage and compassion, I think the planet will disappear down the plughole before we've had a chance to find other creative psychological elements. If we can sow seeds of hope about alternatives, about different ways of living, about celebrating our role on Earth today, then we may have a chance.

CHAPTER 20 **Going for Gold**

FRANK DICK is president of the European Athletics Coaches' Association and a highly regarded performance consultant. A former international athlete, he was Director of Coaching for the British Athletics Federation between 1979 and 1994. He was chief coach to the British team at four Olympic Games, and has coached athletes to European, world and Olympic honours in a wide range of events. He specialises in sprints and, during his 15 years in charge of our international relay teams, Britain enjoyed an unprecedented period of international success. Frank, who was awarded the OBE in 1989, has written several books on training and performance management, and has been performance advisor to Gerhard Berger, Katarina Witt, Rob Andrew and the West Hartlepool Rugby Football club.

Frank's highly motivational talk took place in September 1992, just after the Barcelona Olympics, and his words were accompanied by video clips of British successes which stirred our audience to some patriotic cheering. Frank explained how his coaching experience can be applied with equal success in the business arena – to unlock the potential of individuals and companies with a training package that can help people *win*.

It's the athlete's job to go into the arena, any arena, and make a total statement about who they are. It's not just about their arms or legs, the quality of their heart, the quality of their muscles, or even of their skills. It's who they are. They actually choose their arena deliberately. You've chosen yours. Daley Thompson chose his. Linford Christie chose his. You take your arena to make a total statement about yourself.

I believe there are two kinds of people in this world: valley people and mountain people. Valley people are the people who go for safety. The people who believe that not losing is important and therefore the draw, as far as they're concerned, is all that matters. The people that bump into you at parties and start off their sentences with: "I would have...", "I should have..." or "I could have...". They are life's "might have been" people, and they are non-achievers. The tragedy is that they don't even know they are losers.

Mountain people decide that way of life is not for them. They decide to go up the mountain. They know before they start they're going to fall a couple of times, there are going to be a few bumps and bruises, but they take the risk of winning.

You often hear the expression "take the risk of losing". There's no such thing as a risk of losing. You can lose any time you like; you don't have to practise for it or train for it, you don't have to put years behind you for it. It can happen completely naturally. So I don't see that there's any kind of risk in that at all. The risk only comes when you go for the win. People who do that – mountain people – are winners.

Where do winners come from? To spot a winning athlete, I am convinced you must look first and foremost for athletes with the passion to achieve, the desire to be the best in their chosen arena. If an athlete is a genius in the high jump but is actually in love with basketball, the probability is that basketball will be his best arena. Talent always comes a poor second to this kind of passion.

I first really understood about where talent stood in the scale of things when I discovered what I thought at the time was a unique problem. The National Schools' Athletics Championship in England produces outstanding champions every year. However, in the late 1970s it was commonplace for us to lose up to three-quarters of those champions within a couple of years. No-one can afford to lose high-quality people at such a rate, and the mystery preyed on my mind. In the end I mentioned it to a friend, Miroslav Vanek, who at that time was president of the International Federation of Sport Psychologists. "It's like this," he said. "Your young champions are so because they are talented. They're not yet long enough into the discipline of training to be reaping its benefits, so it's clear they are more talented than those who are seconds, thirds and fourths. On the other hand, those athletes have a different kind of motivation. In particular, although they win more often than they lose, they lose more often than the champions. This makes for a valuable learning experience. Coaches can use it to help the athletes develop a resilience to defeat and this is something more than talent alone can do."

Suddenly, it is no longer a case of just talent spotting, but also motivation spotting. Talent alone simply isn't enough to get to the top. It comes down to establishing and developing the right profile of talent and motivation. We might not all be able to alter the natural talents we're given, but athletes and coaches can create and manage a motivational climate in which we can achieve anything.

In this respect, what really separates the achievers from the "almost" people – the mountain people from the valley people – is mostly what goes on behind the eyes. The winning edge lies here. It is a state of mind, a philosophy if you like, but a simple one. In general, achievers need only three qualities – what I call "winners' life skills" – to create their motivational climate: you must want to win enough; you must believe you can win; and you must persist until you do win.

Just as it is the athlete's objective to make a total statement about himself or herself in the arena, it is the coach's objective to guide the athlete towards making that statement. Since I believe that real achievers, the people who win in their arena, are made, not born, and that their "making" comes down to quality coaching, achieving the objective of being a great coach is, for me, a statement in itself. Don't underestimate it. It's a uniquely difficult statement to make.

You must prepare the athlete by developing him or her towards a freedom and competence to make their statement. When an athlete or new member of your team meets you for the first time, motivation is high. After all, the athlete knows who you are and that you are going to help him or her fulfil their ambitions.

On the performance front the athlete may well be better than his peers – this may be what has made him want to develop in this sport or business and come to you in the first place – but chances are he won't be too developed yet.

Against this background, you set the ground rules for how you and the athlete are to work together. You are very much in charge at this point, applying experience and expertise to make an early assessment of where the athlete is heading and to plan how he or she will get there. Early personal preparation plans leave very little room for interpretation, with the athlete following them almost as a set of instructions or orders.

Next, motivation goes down, even though the athlete is gradually improving. There are two reasons for this, in my experience. The first is that most of the novelty of what was a new situation has disappeared. The next is that I've never met anyone who improved as fast as they thought they should.

You need to change tack to combat this and introduce what I call a "sleeves-rolled-up" approach, applying specific technical knowledge and people knowledge to help the athlete work on strengths and accelerate development where this is needed. Importantly, you begin to involve the athlete more in designing his personal preparation plans. These now proceed with some feedback, more like demonstrations and examples than orders. They are not given life only by you, the coach. Part of the heartbeat is the athlete's.

You then cross a line. You've been in charge, you've had the motivation, you've seen the potential. Out of nowhere the athlete begins to go up in steps – not in a straight line; if that happens they're history because it will flatten off and come back down again – and you build them up; you take time to develop them, to accelerate and stabilise, accelerate and stabilise. Day to day, week to week, month to month. You don't keep pushing and pushing and pushing, because that will destroy them. Motivation varies, with far more ups and downs than before. But the biggest difference now is that control of things rests far more with the athlete. He or she has accepted greater responsibility for performance development and motivation.

Now the athlete understands where he or she is heading and wants to

Overleaf: Linford Christie wins the men's 100m final at the 1993 World Athletics Championships

NIGERIA
TDK
932
TDK
444

TDK
USA
TDK
1319

be involved in how to get there. Coaching style is adjusted again in this new climate. The athlete is fitted into the role of decision-maker and the coach works to equip him for this role and to guide the athlete through the more difficult decisions. Coach and athlete design, evaluate and review their preparation plans together. This certainly is not the easiest stage. The athlete has to take a few bumps and bruises in exercising responsibility for his or her decisions, and the coach's supportive style must strike a balance between catching the athlete before a fall, picking the athlete up after a fall, and letting the athlete pick himself up. This involves sensitive judgements in using the opportunity of problem situations to develop resilience while avoiding serious motivational injury.

Eventually motivation is up, confidence is up, the athlete is in charge, and at this point you simply counsel. You stand back. A family friend, Beatriz Bolton, said she wished me the strength to give my children the two gifts that were mine as a parent to give: roots to grow, and wings to fly. And that's not just about bringing up kids. That is about developing anyone. A coach developing an athlete. A manager developing a member of staff. The point is, having the courage to stand back and let them fly.

We all need to take the lead, to be coaches, at some time in our lives, as friends, parents and colleagues to one another. All these areas are important, but I believe there is one area where a coaching approach is often neglected but, if applied, could transform not only our personal lives but the economic life of our country. This is the area of management.

Every company in this country is presently experiencing culture change on a huge scale. Part of that change, I believe, must be a shift in management skills – leadership skills – towards those of coaching. These skills are necessary because every one of them is to do with people and preparing them to achieve more in their lives in general and, in particular, for the organisation to which they belong. This is nowhere truer than in the case of the one organisation we all belong to, Great Britain Plc. A country's greatest resource is its people and using them to their full should be any country's highest priority.

Many companies now recognise the need to maximise our human potential and I fully support this greater application of coaching skills.

What I have trouble with is how the process of change is delivered in some companies and by some managers.

It's not enough to coach an athlete by announcing that you're going to do so with a fanfare and a roll of drums, explaining what you are going to do and then leaving them to get on with it. You have to go through the process of personal preparation already described, updating that plan from time to time, and delivering on personal coaching for months, even years, till the athlete wings his or her way into the arena.

There are no hard-and-fast rules to coaching. A good part of your effectiveness as a coach must come down to knowing the people you work with and knowing yourself. Even if you have absorbed everything the manuals say, you must still add something personal to your coaching. After all, coaching as a business is all about people and personalities, and this goes for coaches in sport and in business. If you have mastered this, you are ready to apply your skills as a coach to the organisation you serve and to the badge you follow.

As I said at the outset, you've got to take the risk of winning. But don't get that confused with being careless. Of course you'll make mistakes – but that comes with the territory of the Risk Business, so don't back off because you might make a mistake. I never met any top achiever who didn't make quite a few. The trick is to learn from each and not to make the same one too often. Jimmy Greaves reminded me some years ago that he still held the record for the highest number of goals scored in First Division football. "I've got another record, too," he said. "The highest number of misses in the same season!"

It's up to you. Take the risk, because if you never try, you'll never know.

CHAPTER 21 **The Dynamite Kid**

BRIAN BLESSED is one of Britain's most respected actors. Since his TV debut as PC Fancy Smith in *Z Cars*, he has played countless leading roles in theatre, television and film, including Augustus Caesar in *I Claudius*, Richard IV in *Blackadder*, Old Deuteronomy in *Cats* and Voltan in *Flash Gordon*.

But, while acting has been Brian's career, climbing is his passion. From the age of seven, when he read in his *Hotspur* comic about George Mallory's 1924 ascent of Everest, Brian dreamed of recreating the historic climb. At the age of 53 his dream came true when, in 1990, he led an expedition up the North Face of Mount Everest.

Brian gave a powerful performance for us in October 1992, roaming from stories of his wartime childhood in rural England to hilarious backstage anecdotes, from his dramatic experiences on Everest to his encounter with the "Dynamite Kid". He roused and inspired our audience, who responded with a standing ovation.

In 1993 Brian climbed the South Face of Everest, reaching 28,000 feet without oxygen – a world record for a man his age. In October 1995 he returned for an encore at Newell and Sorrell, with a thrilling talk that described his second confrontation with Everest, and revealed how he was preparing for his ultimate challenge – a daring ascent of the North Face's remaining 1,000 feet to the summit...

I have always been in love with adventure, the universe and space.

I was born in a marvellous place called Goldthorpe, halfway between Doncaster and Barnsley. On one side of my house in Probert Avenue was the London and North-Eastern Railway, where trains like the Flying Scotsman, the Mallard and the Golden Arrow ran. On the other side was this huge railway embankment with lots of swings, where we could enact Johnny Weissmuller as Tarzan. We had nothing, and we had everything.

They were marvellous days. When I was six years old, Bruce Woodcock, the best heavyweight boxer ever – the "Dynamite Kid" – was due to appear seven miles away, in Doncaster. I'd seen him at the cinema, on *Pathway to the Stars*. He looked like a giant Jimmy Cagney, and he was unbeatable, brilliant. I was six years old, and I took my tiny little Mickey Mouse tricycle and cycled out of Goldthorpe to Doncaster to try and find him. This was my first Everest.

The police were looking for me everywhere. My mother was absolutely furious. I cycled for miles, for hours and hours, with a face like a beetroot. I got lost under the gas lamps, and when I got to Doncaster I was crying my eyes out, saying: "I don't know where he is." People said: "What's the matter with you, lad? Six years old, what's tha doing lad?" "I'm looking for Bruce Woodcock, he's going to be the world heavyweight champion, he's the European Champion, I've seen him in the cinema, and he trains at the Plough Inn. But I don't know how to get there, I'm lost." "We know where he is, lad, we'll find him." And they carried me and my tricycle and took me to the Plough Inn. And I heard: "Last ten seconds Bruce!" and I went up this ladder with this man called Reg and I went in, and there he was sparring in a corner; there was this Hector, with these immense shoulders, with this tremendous accuracy, this tremendous right hand, and he was hitting a swing ball. Elastic to the ceiling and to the floor with a ball in the middle – made boxers look idiots. He turned round and there was Woodcock. I said: "Th'art better than Joe Lewis, th'art better… I've seen you on the films… you're wonderful… you're going to be the world heavyweight champion." And the emotions were just running down my spine. A trainer came forward and said: "Would you like to get in the ring with Bruce?" So they gave me these gloves (which were bigger than me) and said: "Hit him in the knee, lad, hit him in the knee." And I hit him on the knee and knocked him down, and he picked me up and he said: "By gum, Brian, tha can't half punch."

I've always been adventurous. As a kid I met Picasso at the second World Peace Congress which was held in Yorkshire in 1950. Wonderful. And I didn't believe he was Picasso: "Tha's not Picasso, tha sounds like Carmen Miranda, let's see you draw if you're Picasso." And he drew this little dove of peace and it was a load of shite – "You're not Picasso, that's not a dove," and he offered it to me and I turned it down! And I drew him a dove of peace and he accepted it.

My life was full of people like that. Great people who influenced me, people of imagination. From an early age I read all about adventure in the *Hotspur* comic. All my life is Everest, and I think that all of our lives are Everest in varying ways.

It was in the *Hotspur* that I first heard about Mount Everest, and about Mallory and Irvine. Mallory and Irvine were last seen in 1924, 28,250 feet

above sea level, 700 feet below the summit of Mount Everest. That was 30 years before it was climbed by Sir Edmund Hillary – and Mallory and Irvine climbed in Norfolk jackets, homburgs and puttees. The mists came down when they were approaching the summit, and they were never seen again. Whether they ever reached the peak is a great mystery.

In 1852 a member of the Trigonometrical Survey of the Plains of India shouted: "I've found the highest mountain in the world!" He told the Surveyor-General, Sir Andrew Waugh, who decided to name the new discovery after his predecessor, Sir George Everest; and so it's called Everest, a lovely name. But at the time they didn't know that it's called Chomolungma in Tibet and Sagarmatha in Nepal, and that the Dalai Lama calls it the Turquoise Mountain.

In 1913 a wonderful man called Captain John Noel, one of the best of the British explorers, dyed his hair, dyed his skin, got leave from North India and went right into forbidden Tibet – really dangerous country. He got within 40 miles of Everest when the Tibetan troops turned him back with their machine guns. Captain Noel went to the Royal Geographical Society after the war in 1919, and he said: "We've conquered the North and the South Poles, now we must look to the third Pole, Everest." They got in touch with the Dalai Lama, and they got permission to go. All our best climbers had been lost in the war, but one day this man appeared, a man who, in looks, was a cross between Kevin Costner, James Mason and Rudolph Valentino. He was noble, self-effacing, unassuming, and he believed in all that was good and noble in life. And they christened him Sir Galahad. His real name was George Leigh Mallory. Not only was he beautiful to look at, but he was also a great mountaineer. And he was selected to spearhead the expedition to Everest.

They left Britain in 1921 for the reconnaissance. They filmed in Darjeeling and Sicimb, they went through the Tister Valley, and then they stepped off the map. Isn't that what you've always wanted to do? Step off a map! And they went hundreds of miles towards where they thought Everest was. There were mists everywhere. Mallory took his binoculars up and then gradually, very gradually, over two or three hours, visions of great glaciers and ridges and mountain sides started to reveal themselves. They started to see a whole range of mountains until, as Mallory said:

◀ Bruce Woodcock: The "Dynamite Kid"

"Unimaginably higher than imagination dare to dream, the top of Everest revealed itself." And that was it, he was Mallory of Everest.

Now when I was seven, I read that in *Hotspur.* It was a good comic. Incidentally, I used to read *Flash Gordon* in those days, and I always played Voltan in our gang's games. I never believed that, 30 years later, I would actually play Voltan professionally. It was a very difficult part to play. Voltan had these wings which took half an hour to screw on, so they made me a perch because I couldn't sit on a chair, and all the cameramen would go: "Pretty Polly, pretty Polly." Then they gave me this bloody great bazooka: "Action Brian." "Freeze you turkey! Bang, Bang!" "Brian, we do the special effects." Flash Gordon was worse, he'd come on going "Ptang, ptang, ptang!"

I've always treated great actors with terrible disrespect. I remember in the canteen one day Gielgud said to me: "Oh Brian, Brian, I had a terrible night last night." He was doing a play called *Coming Home* with Ralph Richardson. Gielgud said: "You modern actors, we never know what you're going to do. Terry Rigby, last night he did a line in an entirely different way and Ralphy went straight into the third act. We couldn't get him out. And so I said, 'Ralphy, Ralphy, Ralphy, you're in the third act.' And he said: 'Johnny, it's such a terrible play, I don't think it makes any difference.' "

I'd just like to say that I think acting is a great art. It requires immense bravery. Ninety-eight per cent of our profession are out of work and, as an actor or an actress, your eyes, your ears, your nose, your heart, your soul, your mind, your imagination are judged frequently, are shot down frequently, and then you have to stand up and face the world. I have never in all my life seen anything to equal the bravery of Peter O'Toole when he played Macbeth and I was Banquo. After about four weeks I found Peter in my room, looking as if his veins were hanging out of his head – I have never seen a human being in such an awful state. He was screaming like a banshee and saying: "Look what they're saying about me!" He was one of the greatest Shylocks ever, a great triumph, noble, tall, beautiful and still, and suddenly the Macbeth didn't measure up (for all kinds of reasons) and they butchered him from here to the Stock Market in America. No actor could have taken that, and he was on the floor. I had to laugh, it was so horrible. I said: "You're dying, you're bloody dying. I'm going to tell the audience to go home, Pete, you're dying." But he stopped me, and he went on that night – and he completed the run. I'd never seen bravery like that.

Everest and other great mountains are very special. If you go into their rarefied atmospheres you find you are totally changed. It is life on a grand and refined and total scale; it points elsewhere to dreams and revelations. There's nothing I've experienced in acting quite to meet the reality of it.

Anyway, I read about the Everest expedition when I was young. Then when I was older, 24 or 25, and I was in the TV police series, *Z Cars,* I used to talk to explorers and to actors and explain the whole story. I used to wax a bit lyrical, and sweat blood, and they said: "Brian, you must go and follow the expedition, follow in their footsteps, you must make a film of it, you must do it. Because we know about Scott, we know about Laurence of Arabia, but we don't know about Mallory and Irvine."

I became 27 and then 37, then when I was 40 or 45 I started looking for sponsorship so I could actually do this wonderful project. I found a fantastic BBC director called John-Paul Davidson, and we managed to get half the budget from the BBC, but we still needed the other half. I went all over the place looking for backers, but I kept getting turned down. Eventually I was selling the film of *Henry V* in Brighton, and talking a lot of nonsense with a lot of passion, and Stephen Evans, the producer, said: "I've enjoyed doing this film so much, Brian, would you mind if I financed the rest of the Everest exhibition?"

And that was it! I was off! And all of a sudden I was scared. I was in my 54th year.

I trained hard. I did a marathon every five weeks, and I trained with the army, running with sand on my back. But in the end we had nothing, nothing among all our science to protect us from Everest. Even with all our most modern gear, if Everest was in her worst mood we would not be able to fight her. The temperature can reach 70 degrees below zero with the wind factor, and there can be winds of 100 to 180 miles an hour. So you just have to train like hell, pray, obey the laws, get into condition, hope she will give you a window, and hope she will spare you, let you up – then release you as well.

We went into Bhutan, the whole reconnaissance group, with me dressed in Twenties gear in order to recreate Mallory's expedition properly, and we

The 1924 Everest Expedition.
Left to right (standing): Irvine, Mallory, Norton, Odell, Macdonald; *(seated):* Shebeare, Bruce, Somervell, Beetham

trained like hell. Charlie Clark, the Everest doctor, said: "You're not the right physique at all, mountaineers are usually long and thin." "Not small and thin?" "That's right Brian." "Can't a big fellow like me go to Everest?" "Yes, yes – Don Williams was big... and he died."

Eventually we began filming. We filmed in Darjeeling and then we went back to Delhi and on to Kathmandu. We had a high altitude team of David Breashears, a great big massive man called Jeff Long, and a sherpa called Wongchu. They were waiting for us in Kathmandu, and just as we set off to meet them we discovered that we couldn't enter because there was a revolution going on! After five frustrating days there was one plane from Dumdum airport, but then its bloody dashboard fused! I was thinking of parachuting in, but they said I couldn't because the air was too thin.

Anyway, eventually they mended the dashboard, and we got into Kathmandu. It was dark and there were soldiers everywhere. There were guns all over the place. We were frogmarched into the airport and suddenly I could see David Breashears and the giant. I thought: "Everest is only 180 miles away, we must get close to the mountain." The British Ambassador appeared with a great big lorry: "In you get then, fellows. Hold a torch on the front there, Blessed, on the Union Jack, otherwise they'll shoot us."

The next day, suddenly, there was democracy in Nepal, and that was it, the revolution was over. We set off across the fields, through Nepal, and we started to get up onto the roof of the world.

All mountaineers want to go high; there's a change at 5,000 feet, there's a change at 10,000, a change at 15,000, and a change at 20,000. At 22,500 feet life stops. If you've never taken a breath at this height, then you've never taken a breath. Normally, you have 14,500 tons weighing your body down, but at 22,500 feet this disappears, and for the first time in your life you learn to breathe, you learn to live. You've got 14 days to live at 22,500 feet. At about 25,000 you've got five days; at 27,000 two days; at 28,000 feet one day.

I was the first to see Everest and I was astonished at how big it was. It's five-and-a-half miles high! And it's red! I was crying like a child.

We lost our cook on the first day. He had a cerebral haemorrhage, and it took seven days to save his life. One of the Soviet climbers had pulmonary oedema; his lungs were full of liquid. One of the Americans also had a cerebral haemorrhage – and I was 20 years older than any of them.

But there we were on this colossal mountain, and after about three weeks of filming we started to move up, onto the Rongbuk Glacier. It is the most stupendous place, five million years old; it has corries and blowholes, and black and purple flowers. We moved across it: 17,000, 18,000, 19,000 feet. We moved towards the fairy kingdom, with its giant shark fins of ice, where Mallory said Alice's white rabbit would get lost. (Mallory said some marvellous things. He said: "Because it's there," and he said: "The greatest danger in life is not taking the adventure.") I couldn't believe what was happening to me. I could feel my brain and my heart opening; it was as if I suddenly used the right-hand side of my brain. Reinhold Messner, the world's greatest climber, said: "You will find your instinct will develop totally, and you will be changed." And I am.

We reached 21,500 feet, the highest in my life, and then we had to go all the way back down to base camp, because if we hadn't, we wouldn't have been able to get higher. Then we discovered one of our biggest blows: we'd lost our oxygen. We'd paid £48,000 to the Chinese for it and they'd sold it to another expedition. They were bastards. We saw other climbers being brought down – one with a collapsed spine, two with cerebral haemorrhages, but I felt that we would be more lucky because we were there for the right reasons, we were there offering prayers, attempting to find the spirit of the Twenties and pay tribute to those tremendous climbers and to pay tribute to the mountain. So we started back up again.

Halfway up the North Col my heart stopped three times. My blood was the consistency of glue. I was dying – I had to hit my chest to get my heart going again. Gradually, I got to the top of the Col, and there, in front of me, was the whole North Face, miles across – the most dramatic sight on earth. There was the North East ridge where Boardman and Tasker had died, and there was this huge face, with great couloirs, and Everest all golden in the sunset with her dress of sandstone. I went into my tent and stuck my head out. As it became dark I could see the Milky Way almost sitting on us, and every seven seconds there was a meteorite storm, a constant firework display. The next morning Jeff touched me, and he looked at me and said: "I'm not coming on with you, Brian, I've got to go down, I'm blind." I said: "It's snow blindness, it's nothing." "No, no Brian, I've haemorrhaged behind the eyes."

I said: "It's me, my bloody vanity, it's me that got you all up here, me following this silly expedition." "No, Brian – we're here because we love it, we would do anything to be on Mallory's route. I'll be OK, you concentrate on the climb, go as high as you can, you'll be all right." And he went down.

David Breashears set the tripod to film an amazing moment: a middle-aged actor on the North Ridge. We went up to 25,000 feet; my heart was fine, my breathing was fine; I took small steps as Messner said. And I got higher and higher.

I was up there in Twenties gear, weighing about nine stone (I was 16 stone before we started), and I could feel the mountain breathing with me. I felt as if I were a lung; I felt that death died – approaching 26,000 feet without oxygen, life and death were fluid. And it was at that moment that I saw the whole of the 1924 exhibition in front of me, all of them. I said: "You're not real," and they said: "We are, we are, Blessed, you're doing very well." And I said: "Where are you going, what are you doing?" And they said: "The adventure is absolutely unlimited, Blessed. Limitless possibilities. You're doing very well, but now you must go down, you can come back next time. You have completed the film, you must go down soon." I said: "Where are you all going?" "We're going off for lunch." And they disappeared. David joined me after about an hour, and we found a young French climber dead in the snow. We turned his body round and cleaned his eyes so that he could face the summit. I'd broken the world record for a man of my age. David said: "We must go down now, or we'll die." And then, as if to make up our minds for us, there was a great storm, short and sudden from the mountain, which drove us down.

I got down to the North Col after about four hours – I'd been climbing for about ten and I was dehydrated. The expedition carried me down the rest of the way bodily. I couldn't move; I was like cardboard. They put me in my tent, unzipped me, put me in my sleeping bag, fluffed up my duvet and gave me a great big mug of tea with Nestlé's milk. I said: "Thank you. Thank you for saving my life." At that point I realised a very simple thing – that other people exist.

In 1921 Mallory got to 23,000 feet up the North Col. In 1922 he got to 26,800 feet, and then in 1923 he was ready for the big push. The pressure was on him, and other climbers were astonished that he was going up for the third time with 22-year-old Irvine. They had primitive oxygen apparatus, yet they ascended the Col in fast time, just two-and-a-half hours. They got to 25,000 feet in record time, to 27,000 in record time. Then they set off for the summit. Captain John Noel was a backup climber. He looked up and saw two ants ascending the second step, and he knew it was Mallory and Irvine only 700 feet from the summit. Then the mists came down and they were never seen again.

When I was up there I was very close to where Mallory and Irvine were, very close, and I instinctively felt they'd made it. It was good weather, and Mallory would have got up at 2 o'clock in the morning to get on the second step. The big proof for me, though, was a chance meeting I had at the Alpine Club with a Chinese man named Mr Chu. The Chinese always said that they'd climbed it in 1960 on Mallory's route, and the West now accepts they did do it. Mr Chu was on that expedition, and he said: "Yes, I am not good, Mallory climbed it, I am not good climber." His group had photographs taken at 28,000 feet, but no higher, because they claim they climbed it at midnight. Anyway, Mr Chu said: "I took my shoes off on the second step because I couldn't climb it." He took his shoes off and got up it. And of course by the time he'd put his shoes on and he'd got back down, he was going to lose his feet. That's why he's called Mr Chu (shoe). But a great climber could climb it: there are hand jambs, and it's only 15 feet. Mr Chu said that at 28,500 feet he found hemp rope. Mallory's hemp rope. Well, as Messner said to me, if that's the case then he climbed it, because there's nothing left on that side; that's the hard bits done. It was just an easy snow slope to the top, he'd have done it on all fours. I'm quite convinced they got up; they just didn't get down.

But I just hope the mystery always remains, because mystery is a rare commodity these days. The sight of those two climbers is a clarion call to our materialistic age. The greatest danger in life is not to take the adventure. So I say to you, ladies and gentlemen, God's speed, follow your dream, we'll all get there in the end, we're going to make it.

Let us probe the silent places, let us seek what luck betide us,
Let us journey to a lonely land I know,
There's a whisper in the night wind, there's a star, a gleam to guide us,
And the wind is calling... calling... let us go!

Sir Walter Scott
From the *Reconnaissance Book of Everest*, 1921

CHAPTER 22 **Voices for a Better World**

LIVE WIRES is an opera group for children aged eight to 12 from all over London. As part of English National Opera's Baylis Programme, which aims to make opera accessible to everyone, Live Wires devise, perform and sing their own musical works.

This was an extraordinary and exciting musical evening in December 1992. First, opera singer **JANIS KELLY** sang *Lorelei* and *The Mermaid's Song* from Dvorák's *Rusalka*. Then **LIVE WIRES** gave us their first semi-staged performance of a new piece, under the direction of Sean Gregory, called *Voices for a Better World*. A comedy with a message, the mini-opera's theme was a journey to four planets in search of a better way of life, loosely based on the Janácek opera *The Adventures of Mr Broucek*. Finally **DAVID JOYNER**, a freelance voice coach and pianist, led an energetic and hugely enjoyable audience sing-along of Christmas carols. Proceeds from our evening went to the Great Ormond Street Hospital for Sick Children.

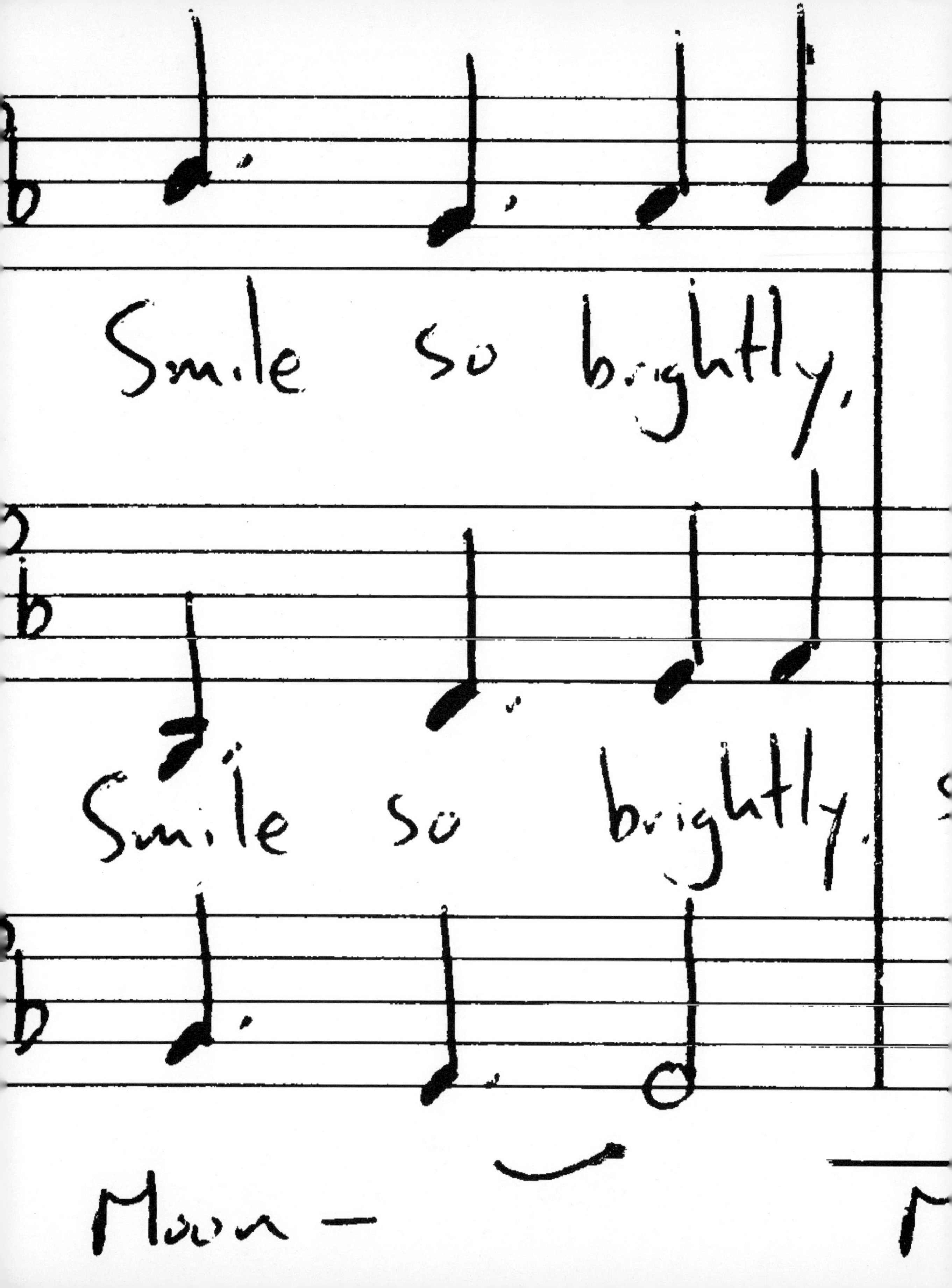

Smile so brightly,

Smile so brightly.

Moon —

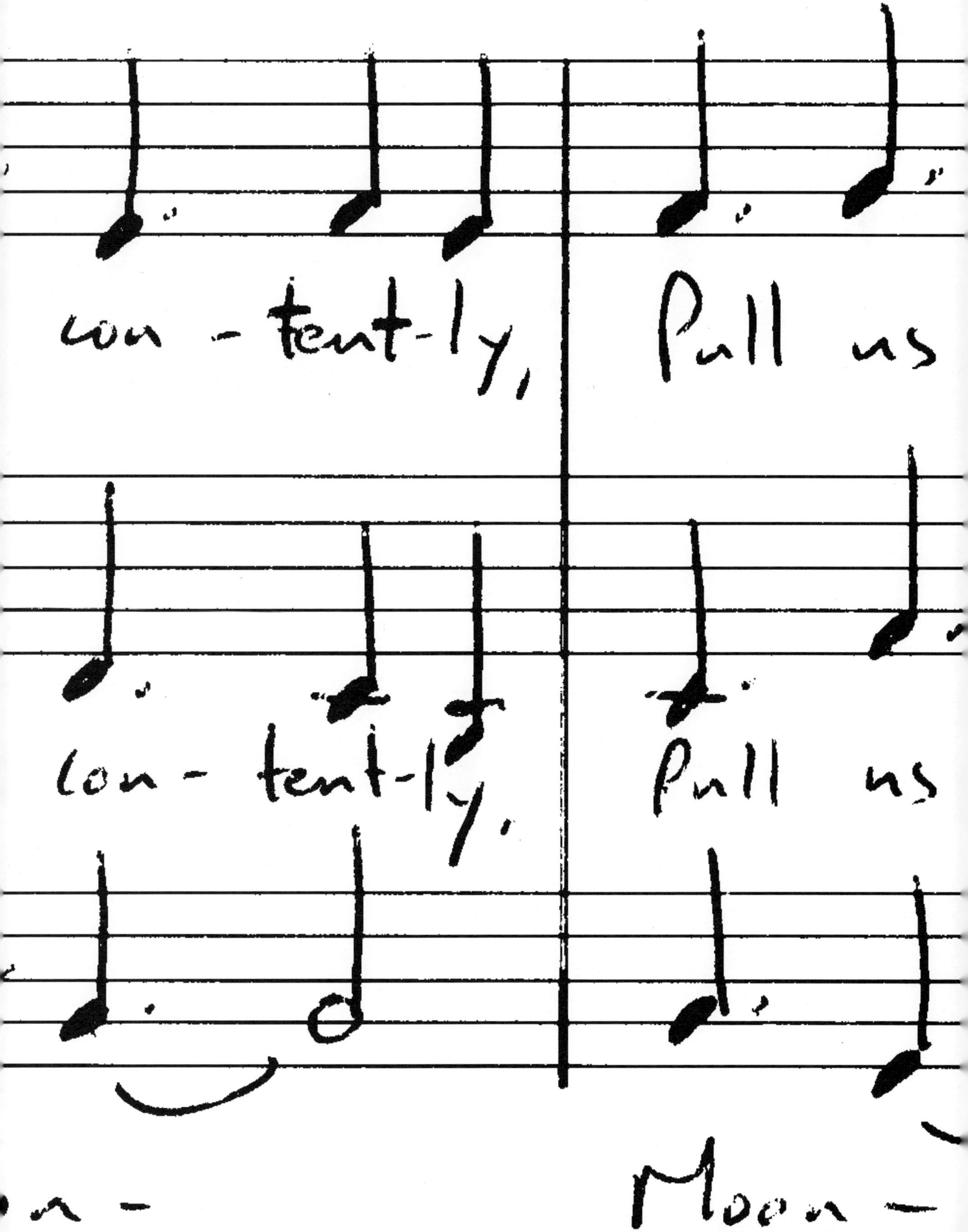

con - tent-ly, Pull us

con - tent-ly, Pull us

-on - Moon -

VOICES FOR A BETTER WORLD

SCENE ONE: **ON EARTH**

Boy *(spoken)*: Life on Earth's been pretty predictable.

Girl: School, school, school is bad,
Anyone who likes it must be mad.

Chorus: School, school, school is bad,
Anyone who likes it must be mad. *(Repeated.)*

Chorus: Smash! Crash! Smash! Crash!... *(Repeated.)*

Boy *(spoken)*: It was him! It was him!

Chorus *(spoken)*: It was them! It was them! It was them!...

Voice *(from offstage)*: STOP!

Chorus: Smash! Crash! Smash! Crash!... *(Repeated.)*

Boy *(spoken)*: But I'm always breaking things.

Chorus 1: Maastricht politics, everywhere –
On the TV and on air.

Chorus 2: In the House of Lords and in your home.
(Repeated.)

Chorus 1: Pain, famine and disease...
Put our minds at ease. *(Repeated.)*

Chorus: Brothers and sisters always get their ways –
I'll be washing up for the rest of my days!
(Repeated three times.)

Boys: Brothers and sisters... *(Repeated.)*

Boy *(spoken)*: I'm so bored – let's go to the moon!

Chorus: Will you take us into Dreamland,
Pale and wistful friend up there?
Smile so brightly, so contently,
Pull us up tonight? *(Repeated twice.)*

SCENE TWO: THE WOBBLY WORLD

Boy *(spoken)*: We're here!

Chorus *(spoken)*: Where are we? Is this the moon?

Wobbly Boys 1: We are the people from a wobbly world
And the language is...

Wobbly Boys 2: Wobb-e-l-o!
We are the people from a wobbly world
And the language is...

Wobbly Boys 1: Wobb-e-l-o!

Wobbly Children: We are the people from a wobbly world
And the language is...
Wobb-e-l-o! *(Repeated.)*
You don't know how excited we are –
We've never had visitors,
We've never had guests!
Come and see our trifle tower,
Our leaning tower of French bread!
Our wonderful opera's our national anthem –
Our Wombley Stadium, too!
A jelly a day keeps the doctor away!

Earth Children: How much is this? How much is that?
Can we buy that wobbly cat?
Shall we go up? Shall we stay down?
How many flavours do you have now?
How much is that jelly in the window
(wobble, wobble) –
The one with the cherry on top (wobble, wobble)?

Wobbly Children: Ssssssh... Ssssssh... Ssssssh... Ssssssh...
Wobb-e-l-o... Ssssssh... Wobb-e-l-o...
Ssssssh... Wobb-e-l-o... Ssssssh... Wobb-e-l-o...
WOBB-E-L-O!
We are the people from a wobbly world
And the language is...
Wobb-e-l-o! *(Repeated three times.)*
You don't know how excited we are –
We've never had visitors,
We've never had guests! *(Repeated; gets faster, eventually collapsing into a wobbly jumble.)*

SCENE THREE: **THE PLANET OF SNIFF**

Guide *(spoken)*: Hello, and welcome to the planet of Sniff. Our first stop on this tour will be the national galleries. Here we will be joined by Leonardo the Sneezer, and Vincent van Snot. And here is the famous painting of the Mona Sneezer. Can we have a few words on this please?

Grunter: *(Grunting noises.)*

Guide *(spoken)*: Aah! It's a famous painting of the Queen. We now move on to the Sniff Laboratories, where you pick up all your nasal necessities and nose bits. What are we making here?

Grunter: *(Grunting noises.)*

Guide *(spoken)*: Aah! We are making a machine to remove unwanted nasal hairs. Will you give us a demonstration please?

Grunter: *(Grunting noises and demonstration.)*

Guide *(spoken)*: And we move over now to the favourite pastime of the people of Sniff – spider racing. And this is a great event. And I think they're off! And... and... that spider's won! Oh! And now we are going to hear the beautiful national anthem of Sniff.

Chorus:
God bless our nose, God bless our nose,
God bless our nose.
Our favourite sport is spider racing;
We like to sniff and snort.
But most of all we like to blow our nose!

We ride around on termites;
We worship satellites;
But most of all we like to blow our nose!
Our houses are all made of junk –
We're very proud of that –
But most of all we like to blow our nose!

Boy: Aaachooo! Aa... aaa... aaachoo!

Girl *(spoken)*: I told you to take your injections against colds, and to bring your tissues.

Chorus: *(Sniffing noises)*: Na... sal... na... na... na... na... sal! Aaachoo! Na... sal... na... na... na... na... sal! Aaachoo! AACHOO!

Boy *(spoken)*: It's all cleared now!

Girl *(spoken)*: That's because you've given it to them.

Chorus: AACHOO!

SCENE FOUR: **THE SWEET PLANET**

Chorus: Chocolate trees, marshmallow houses,
Treacle rivers, stuff, munch, chomp! *(Repeated.)*

Eat the cafés, eat the houses –
Our insurance is quite cheap!
But if you eat our dear palace
You'll find you're in trouble deep.

Boy: Right ho, golly gosh!

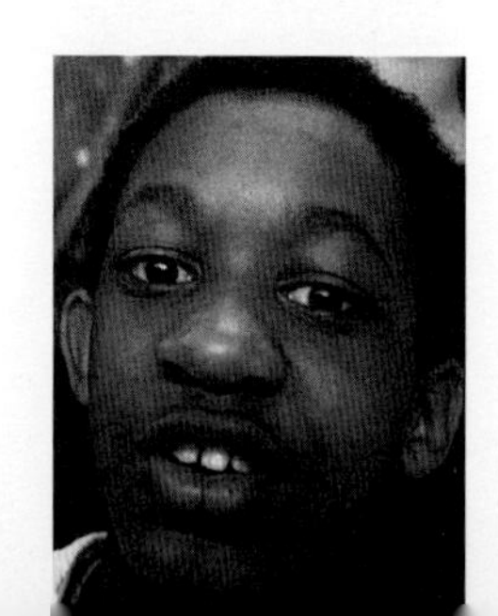

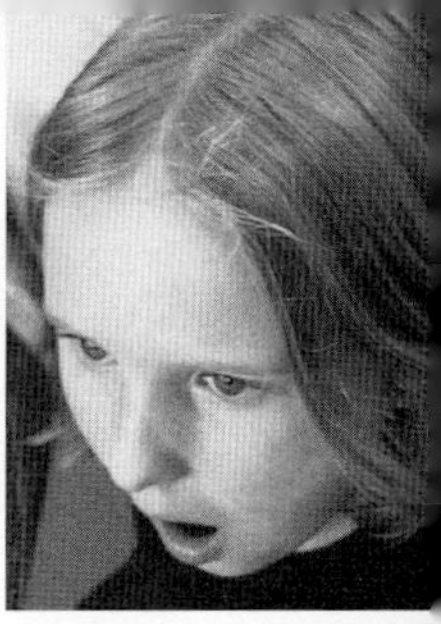

Chorus: Right ho, golly gosh!

Boy: Lots of food for little dosh!

Chorus: Lots of food for little dosh!

Boy: Rather splendid, quite supreme!

Chorus: Rather splendid, quite supreme!

Boy: Look at that building made of ice cream!

Chorus: Look at that building made of ice cream!
(They eat, greedily.)

Boy: Golly gosh, I'm still hungry!

Another Boy: Crikey – look at that mansion!

Chorus: Stop! Don't eat that! That's our palace, not a snack!
(They eat it anyway.)

Oh, no – look what you've done!
Now the melting has begun!
We don't want you on our planet –
Go away you greedy gannets!

SCENE FIVE: **THE PLANET CHAIR**

Boy *(spoken)*: Look at that planet – it looks like a chair!
We go visiting Planet Chair.
We're sitting on a chocolate bar,
Whizzing through the air!

We are going
We know not where,
To find the aliens that live out there.
Oh yeah!

We learn everything from watching TV,
It's better than paying the human school fees!
Our money is cheese,
It grows on trees.
No pain or disease,
No bugs or fleas.
Oh yeah!

It's better up here than it was down there,
So let's stay on the Planet Chair.
Marshmallow houses,
Choco treats,
It's all very tasty
But we don't eat
Vegetables, sweets, not even meat –
So it doesn't really matter if it doesn't keep!
There's no food here, there's no food there,
So let's get off the Planet Chair!
Oh yeah!
Oh yeah!
Oh yeah – tickety boom! *(Repeated.)*

Voice *(from offstage)*: TICKETY BOOM! *(Chaos.)*

SCENE SIX: **FINALE**

Girl *(spoken)*: When are we ever going to find a place good enough to live on?

Boy 1 *(spoken)*: Maybe it wasn't so bad back there after all.

Boy 2 *(spoken)*: I wish I was back on Earth.

Chorus:

Pain, famine and disease…
Put our minds at ease. *(Repeated.)*

Brothers and sisters always get their ways –
I'll be washing up for the rest of my days!
(Repeated twice.)
Brothers and sisters… brothers and sisters.

Will you take us into Dreamland,
Pale and wistful friend up there?
Smile so brightly, so contently,
Pull us up tonight? *(Repeated twice.)*

THE END

CHAPTER 23 **Bagpuss, Nogs and Clangers**

OLIVER POSTGATE AND PETER FIRMIN

created *Bagpuss, The Clangers, Ivor the Engine* and, of course, *The Saga of Noggin the Nog* – for many people, programmes that represent all that was best about children's television. Yet these classics were all produced in a converted pigsty in Kent, on a budget of practically nothing. Oliver, who had trained in acting, wrote the stories, made the films and provided the narration, while Peter, who studied illustration at the Central School of Art, did the drawings and made the puppets. Oliver and Peter have been awarded honorary degrees by the University of Kent, and new editions of their books and repeats of their TV shows are currently enjoying renewed success.

Oliver and Peter talked at Newell and Sorrell in January 1993 about how they created their stories and characters, and revealed how they developed their innovative techniques of animation and puppetry. They were accompanied in their hilarious double-act by some non-speaking old friends – the Clangers, the Iron Chicken and the inimitable Bagpuss.

Once upon a time...

OLIVER In 1958 I was working as a stage manager at ITV, as a sort of director's runner, really for the purpose of seeing where there was a hole. And I saw there was a hole in the children's department, so I wrote a set of stories called *Alexander the Mouse* to go with this marvellous new animation system called "visimotion".

PETER Oliver wanted someone to do the drawings, and they could only afford to pay £30, so he went to the Central School to look for a hard-up student. I was teaching evening classes and struggling to earn a living doing illustration, and I got the job. And we started doing things together from then on. *Alexander the Mouse* was a live, animated story which was produced by fixing magnets to bits of cardboard. The animators would sit at a table with a magnet underneath and move the mice across the picture.

OLIVER It was a very thin table, and you approached it with a magnet, got hold of a mouse and moved it about. If you had the polarity reversed when you approached it, the mouse turned it on its back. If you managed to approach it vertically in the wrong polarity the mouse would leap into the air, turn over and show its Sellotape on the other side. All you could do was to reach in with a hand and turn it over. This was live television and none of it was ever seen again – thank God the video recorder hadn't been invented. So then, partly out of desperation, I asked if we could do the next series on 16mm film. The budget was only £120 a programme, but rather than go on with the magnets I took a contract to make six silent films for the hard of hearing at that price. It was accepted, paid for, and we were in business. I set up our company, Smallfilms, and we paid for the camera, built the animation table and set about what was to be the main work of our lives – creating worlds.

I hadn't the slightest idea how to make animated films when I took the contract, not the faintest idea, but I found out. And in those days there was no money anyway, so they couldn't expect too much. And they didn't get it! What we did was to find the cheapest possible way, and the method we used was to make the soundtrack first and shoot to match it, which meant that we shot one-to-one, so that we only used as much film as we were actually going to sell. I've often worked with people who've said: "Oh we'll do a post-synching for that," and I've said: "A post-synching? That'll cost you 60 quid for the studio time, that's the profit gone!" All the time, I was working out how to make the film while I was actually doing it.

The important thing was to avoid buying equipment. I rang up the BBC and said: "Do you want the tracks with the sound on the edge or the centre of the film?" And they said: "Well, which do you want it to be?" and I told them: "I don't mind, I haven't sawn up the tape recorder yet." My editing equipment would usually cost £20,000 if you bought it in a shop, and I don't think it cost me anything. Every time it broke down, which was about once a week, I comforted myself with how much money I wasn't paying in instalments on the hire-purchase. The pièce de resistance was the animation table. It would probably have cost about £30,000 to buy, and it was made partly from pieces of bicycle. The height measurement, a tape measure, was glued to the wall and the camera drive had this amazingly ancient piece of Meccano with a motor.

PETER For one character you needed many bits and pieces, different legs, arms, faces with different expressions and that sort of thing. And Oliver put them on the table on top of the background, their arms and legs Blu-Tacked to their bodies so they could be moved, with his camera pointing down at them. These days when they make films they make storyboards... of course, we didn't know that, so on the first film Oliver scribbled beside the script and I made the bits, and he made them perform on the table. I worked in the cowshed. And Oliver worked in the pigsty which, as he put it, "had been made bigger for taller pigs".

> *Once upon a time, in the top left-hand corner of Wales, there was a railway. It wasn't a very long railway or a very important railway, but it was called The Merioneth and Llantisilly Rail Traction Company Limited. And in a shed, in a siding, at the far end of the railway, lived the locomotive of the Merioneth and Llantisilly Rail Traction Company Limited. Which was a very long name for a little engine, so his friends just called him "Ivor"...*
>
> So began the series *Ivor the Engine*, which was to become one of the best-loved of all Oliver and Peter's works.

OLIVER We knew that the English loved railway engines far more than cuddly bunnies, and I had always wanted to do a series about a railway engine. I knew it had to be set in Wales because Welsh railways run along the tops of hills through beautiful countryside, but we had absolutely no idea for the story – what could the series be about? What on earth do Welsh railway engines want? What do they care about? Then suddenly it came to me... in the bath, actually. I jumped out of the bath, ran to the telephone, rang Peter and said: "Ivor wants to sing in the choir!" Peter said: "Of course."

PETER I had only been to Wales once, so I got together loads of pictures – all the landscape is imaginary, really. We made 32 *Ivor* films at the same time as *Noggin the Nog*, in black-and-white for ITV, and then between 1975 and 1977 we made another 40 films of *Ivor* in colour for the BBC.

M&L
RTC°L°

In the Lands of the North, where the black rocks stand guard against the cold sea, in the dark night that is very long, the Men of the Northland sit by their great log fires and they tell a tale. They tell of Noggin, the young king who reigned over a land of ice and snow in the far Northlands, they tell of Graculus, the green bird who was his guide and counsellor, and they tell of Noggin's wicked uncle Nogbad the Bad, who tried to steal the crown of the Northlands and was banished forever from the Land of Nog...

This was the beginning of what is perhaps their most famous series, *The Saga of Noggin the Nog*. As the films started, Oliver's sonorous voice was accompanied by Vernon Elliott's original music, a series of icy chords on oboe, bassoon and clarinet, which evoked the place and time with a startling intensity.

PETER I had been doing lots of drawings of little chessmen in the British Museum. It was around the time of our last programmes before Rediffusion dispensed with the visimotion technique, and they had asked for a programme they could do very cheaply, so I thought of several ideas. I was on my way to work one day when my train stopped at Neasden, and I thought: "Noggin, now that's a good name." I don't know why, but it just came to me. And I started looking at the meanings of "Noggin": a little brick, a small drink, a little tub, all sorts of things like that. It seemed to suit my chessman. So, obviously, they were called the Nogs, and this fitted nicely because the villain was called Nogbad the Bad. When my daughter Hannah was little we watched a film on television called *Nanook of the North*, about Eskimos. And that night Hannah went to bed with no pyjamas on and said: "I want to be a little Nook," and so I thought: "Nook, that's good – the Nooks and the Nogs."

OLIVER *The Saga of Noggin the Nog* was, slightly to our surprise, in spite of its clumsiness, a great success, and became something of a cult in the Sixties. In all, over a period of years, we made 30 ten-minute films.

> *Supposing we look away from the Earth and travel in our imagination across the vast endless stretches of outer space. There we can imagine other stars, stranger stars by far then ever shone in our night sky, and other, stranger people too. People, perhaps, whose civilisation, skill and efficiency may be far in advance of ours...*
>
> Thus, to the accompaniment of Vernon Elliott's eerie, space-type music, began *The Clangers*, the series that has recently achieved cult status and which, at its first showing in the Seventies, was described by a NASA scientist as "a serious attempt to bring a note of realism to the fantasy of the Space Race".

PETER The Clanger moon was made from a football bought at Woolworth's, which was covered with plaster and little buttons. The Iron Chicken was made mostly of Meccano.

OLIVER We made the Iron Chicken's nest out of bits of old iron, and it took just five minutes to collect up the pieces to make it out of.

PETER We tidied our studio and workshop, and the things we found we just tied together and sprayed silver, and that was the Iron Chicken's nest. Joan, my wife, knitted the Clangers, and I made the skeletons. All the puppets that we use in single-frame had to have a skeleton, so that they could be put in a certain position and stay there. They had quite complicated structures, with a long nose, and they had socket joints so Oliver could put them in position when he was doing the animation.

OLIVER They had holes in their toes, so I could spike them down. The "world" was made of expanded polystyrene mixed with plaster and you could actually spike down into it – I had very sore thumbs after a while – so they could stand in any position; otherwise they'd fall over when they were walking. My twins invented the Soup Dragon, years and years and years ago. They said there was a giant called Edward who lived in the moon, and I asked: "What do they live on?" and they said: "Tomato soup, out of volcanoes". So that was it.

PETER Major Clanger was the father. The male Clangers (this is very sexist) wore armour, because they spent a lot of time on the surface of their planet, and this was to protect them from all those little bits of meteorites flying around in outer space. Whereas the lady Clangers had rather pretty costumes made of felt, decorated felt, mainly because Joan had just got a new zigzag sewing machine. When they went to bed, they lived in these little bed-holes with lids, and they'd go inside and curl up really tight, tuck their noses down, and put their ears over their eyes because they had no eyelids. My favourite, I think, is the Iron Chicken. She laid an egg – a very bumpy egg – it was riveted; it must have been very uncomfortable for her.

OLIVER To make the Soup Dragon noise we had a lot of echo and things to put over the top. When we first thought of *The Clangers* I wasn't going to have my voice over the top, but the BBC said: "No darling, you've got to have a voice over the top, the children will just turn away and ask what they're saying." And I said that you could tell what they were saying by listening to it, but the BBC wouldn't agree. The script was written out in full, in English, and Stephen Sylvester and I would sit down and play the words through swannee whistles. It was quite easy to understand. When we went to Germany a few years ago, I took with me a *Clangers* film,

without any of my chat over the top – and I asked them afterwards if they could understand what they were saying. They said: "Yes of course, they were speaking perfect German!"

Bagpuss was just a saggy old cloth cat, baggy and a bit loose at the seams... but Emily loved him.

So ended each episode of *Bagpuss*, a series of 13 which was shown 27 times during the Seventies and Eighties. It concerned the life and times of Bagpuss, a saggy old cloth cat, Madeleine the rag doll, Gabriel the toad and Professor Yaffle, who was a wooden book end in the shape of a woodpecker. They shared the window of Emily's magic shop with a family of busy mice who lived in a "marvellous mechanical mouse organ".

PETER Bagpuss has visible thoughts. Emily brings something in at the beginning of the film and puts it down in front of him. Then the puppets tell stories and sing songs about the thing she's found. One story was about a ship in a bottle – a few bits of wood and cloth and a dusty bottle and, by telling stories about it, they make it as good as new and put it in the window in case somebody should come along who had lost a ship in a bottle. When I made the marvellous mechanical mouse organ I didn't know what to do about the music rolls; I didn't know whether I should try to make it by some mechanical means. And then while I was thinking about it I went out for a walk with my dog in the woods opposite my house, and the University of Kent had been having a paper chase and had hung all these bits of paper in the trees, these computer strips or something, and they were just right for the music rolls.

The end of an era...

OLIVER Smallfilms has now more or less ground to a halt. I've got too old, and the actual sitting down in front of this animation machine with 25,000 frames to attend to has become a prospect I am no longer able to entertain.

PETER But there's been a sort of revival because of the videos of some of the series, and the fact that Channel 4 and The Children's Channel have used our things. They've come around again, so we've done a *Noggin* book and a set of *Clangers* books.

OLIVER We have been a cottage industry all our lives. Our American agent came to us about 25 years ago and said: "I'm going to make you big, you're going to give up these crappy little films, I'm going to make you rich." I said: "You're going to give me ulcers." And I wouldn't do it. He was going to put money into us and give us responsibilities. I mean, the point about our work is if we want to stop making films then we shut the door of the studio and walk away. As a matter of fact, the agent came back about seven or eight years later and said: "You were right about the ulcers."

I have never felt that the worlds which Peter and I have put together are new in any absolute sense. We may alter the scenery a bit. We may change the arithmetic of life here and there, looking at it from a different angle perhaps, but the worlds are all variations of this world with troubles and joys that we can all recognise – they wouldn't be interesting if they weren't. Only very rarely have we come anywhere near to what I would call pure creation. There was one day when Peter and I stood up in his big barn and wondered how we were going to build the small blue planet in outer space that was to be the home of the Clangers. I must confess that that moment felt a bit like genesis... In the beginning was the void, and the void was dark and without form, being large eight-by-five-foot sheets of hardboard painted midnight blue. And on the first day we took big brushes and pots of white emulsion paint and threw stars thereon even unto the uttermost corners. And we looked upon it and saw that it was terrible. And so, on the second day, we painted them out and started all over again.

CHAPTER 24 **Bellamy Unleashed**

DAVID BELLAMY was almost lost to the world of ecology at the age of 13, favouring instead a career in the classical ballet. However, having grown too tall, he ended up taking a degree in botany at the Chelsea College of Science and Technology, and first hit the headlines in 1969 when he was consulted as a pollution expert after the Torrey Canyon disaster. Since then, his regular TV appearances and numerous best-selling books have conveyed to millions of people his boundless enthusiasm and concern for our natural environment. Thanks to him, every eight-year-old knows about the plight of tropical rain forests.

The long-term problems of conservation in Russia may seem a long way from an evening in Primrose Hill, but David's talk in May 1993 showed in an informing and inspiring way just how vital it is for individuals and businesses around the world to play a part in caring for the global environment.

I'm going to take you on a journey around the world,

and the story I'm going to tell you starts, I suppose, a few years ago when I was sitting at Heathrow Airport and a little girl came up to me and spoke to me in Russian. I said: "I'm sorry, I don't speak Russian," and she said: "But sir, you do on our television sets." I didn't actually know I appeared on Russian television and nor did my agent! Not very long after this, a guy from Kamchatkan Television turned up in the offices of The Conservation Foundation, which exists to provide funding and publicity for a range of conservation projects. He hadn't got a return ticket, he hadn't got any money, and he was looking for me, having seen me on TV back home. This guy said: "I've come to ask you what to do with Kamchatka."

Now Kamchatka is that great piece of land which pokes down from Siberia towards Sakhelin and Japan, and it's where many intercontinental ballistic missiles are sited, pointing towards their targets in the old world and the new. But for a botanist it's a most amazing place; many of the plants down there are called something or other Kamchatkensis, which indicates that they don't grow anywhere else. It's also got some of the best peat bogs in the world; some of the few peat bogs that I've never actually seen. So I said to the guy: "That's easy, we'll turn it into an international nature reserve. It's got 27 volcanoes, 11 of them active, three of them among the nastiest in the world, and lots and lots of hot springs." He said: "Yes, but how do we make it pay?" Well, in the south part of Kamchatka there is the most amazing volcano that is taller than Mont Blanc, and for six months of the year you can ski down it like a helter skelter. It has, potentially, some of the best downhill skiing in the world, it's where downhill skiers from Russia train, and it's not that far by air from Tokyo. So that's how you can finance a regional nature reserve there. A "pie in the sky" idea, perhaps – but better than having no plans at all.

That was one brief encounter with conservation in Russia. Not long afterwards a guy called John Massey Stewart turned up in the Foundation and said: "I want you to help me get to Russia and run a non-governmental organisation summit on the environment." He'd been to everybody else and they'd told him to go away, but of course we said: "What a wonderful idea."

When we got to Moscow, we went along to the Kremlin and met Professor Yablokov, Boris Yeltsin's adviser on health and environment. "Professor Bellamy," he said. "You come from a group of small offshore islands which have totally ruined their economy in the last ten years. You have no untouched environment left. How can you give me any advice?" We rather had our backs up against the wall, but we talked, and 35 minutes later he said: "You're the first people to come over here actually understanding the problem and not trying to make lots and lots of money. You can have access to the Kremlin's data banks on the environment – come back at the end of the week."

The first thing I wanted to ask was what had happened to all the country's peat bogs, because I knew that Russia had 62 per cent of the world's peat lands. We found out that all the ones they had which were easily exploitable had already gone. I actually wanted to go home and cry, because peat bogs are very important things, helping to control not only local water supply, but also regional and global climates.

The next question was the life expectancy of the average Russian. And up it came that, in three areas of Russia, the life expectancy was below 42 years. That's worse than any third world country. And then we asked for correlations. The best correlation that came up was that where life expectancy was lowest there were no endangered species left. Now think about that: those areas of Russia where everything had been so destroyed, where there was nothing natural left, where there was not one rare species to be cared for, people were dying. Of course there were other correlations; radioactivity, air pollution, water pollution, it's all there on a grand scale. But the main thing was that, where the natural ecosystem had been totally destroyed, people were dying, and dying very early.

The data banks warned us that 12 per cent of Russia was an environmental catastrophe. If you want problems, Russia has them. The world appears to be turning away and saying it can't solve the problems because they would cost too much money. The real problem is that if the world doesn't help pull Russia back onto its feet, the cost to the northern hemisphere and to the world would be too horrendous even to think about.

Let's take a look at the Urals. The Urals are one of the richest sources of metals in the whole world. In fact, inside the Ural mountains there is every element in the periodic table, including all the very rare ones. During Peter the Great's time the Russians started exploiting their potential, but they never bothered about what they did with the waste, so there's something like 1,600 square kilometres of land covered with waste, containing very high concentrations of everything you could ever think of. One area we were asked to look at contained about 20 per cent chromium. Now chromium is a very nasty thing, even stuck on the front of a motor car, but when it's in solution in the environment it kills plants, animals and people. What can you do about it? An international consultancy was asked what they could do with it. They said: "Well, we could dig a big hole and line it with very thick polythene, put all the stuff back and cover it up with concrete. It'll cost you x trillion roubles." So they went away. The real answer is not to look at this "waste" as a problem; what you have to do is look upon it as a resource: the richest chromium deposit in the world. We currently mine chromium at 0.2 per cent, so get in there and get it out: exploit the chromium. Problem solved, with a profit too. Both environmental and fiscal into the bargain.

I fly to New Zealand quite a lot, and one route takes you up the Baltic, where you hang a right, and you go down across Russia. Russia owns about 64 per cent of the world's soils, including some of the best agricultural soil in the world. On three occasions there wasn't a cloud in the sky all the way down through Russia, and from the plane I could see all the various types of soil down below, stretching for miles on end. Absolutely amazing, but another catastrophe, for most soils have lost their organic matter and are eroding, blowing away. Let's take a sideways look at this: Russia could actually help feed the world if only those soils could be put back into working order. One way we could do that is with sewage sludge. At this moment we in Britain are chucking our sewage sludge into the sea. It's very high-grade organic material. Okay, some of it does contain heavy metals, but using prokaryotic organs, bacteria and blue/green algae you can get those heavy metals out and export a very good soil conditioner. I dream of great tanker loads of our sewage, not being dumped in the sea and killing off the inshore marine life, but reviving those soils. Russia, of course, has her own sewage and, with the new technologies now available, not the old technologies being offered (or rather sold) to Russia by vested interests in the West, they could do the job themselves. Many of the people who first went out to Russia to give environmental advice were those with vested interests from the past, the people who had already done it the wrong way. Companies with the new, innovative technologies just don't have the money to get there, and what we're trying to do at The Conservation Foundation is to link them up. We can, I believe, act as a catalyst.

Our dream is to see the creation of, say, Russia Plc, so that anything which comes out with a Russia Plc label makes a profit out of solving problems. A company may say they'll clear up a great big heap of pollution, but will share in the profit from the metal they extract. Using

"The new corporate identity has a softer look..."

new bio techniques it can be done moderately simply. There is an initial outlay, but there's real profit to be made, with the added benefit of leaving Russia with a modern metallurgical industry so that she can move on to sustainability, a world share in all its resources.

My apologies. I said I would take you on a journey round the world, and I have dallied too long in Russia. So now I will jump to the end of my journey, and to my favourite mountain. It's called Mount Hikoragi, and is right over on the other side of the North Island of New Zealand. It's a sacred mountain for the Maori people, because it's where the first rays of every new day fall and, because we put the international dateline not very far away, it's the first place that every new day starts. As the Earth rolls through space, the first beam of sunlight of every new day lights up the Hikoragi's summit. On three occasions of my life I've sat there, watching the eyelid of the world lift up and say: "Good morning, world." As I sat there I thought: "Goodness gracious, it took me 21 hours to fly here, there was a three hour wait at Gatwick, so it's taken me a day – what's happened in that day?" In that day at least 100 species of animals and plants have gone to extinction. By the end of this century we will have sent one-and-a-half million species into extinction. One-and-a-half-million. And we didn't even know that most of them existed. But a lot of the bigger species are following – why, if it wasn't for captive breeding programmes in our zoos, then 6,000 species of vertebrate, including most of the big game of Africa, could be extinct by the year 2025.

So how are we going to solve all these problems? We need to take a sideways look. Conservation is about stopping bad things happening; it's about doing things in the right way. It is about reaching into and working with the diversity that is the Earth. That's why I'm a conservationist; that's why we've got to look after the Earth. It's not all doom and gloom, there are immense bright lights at the ends of tunnels. The tunnels were getting longer, but I think that they are now beginning to shorten. They're beginning to shorten because industry is on our side. It's not greenwash, industry is beginning to try to put its house in order. Why? Because it is beginning to realise that it's the only way it's going to survive. Economy, ecology and environment are one and the same thing.

CHAPTER 25 **From Gravestones to Graffiti**

NIGEL REES has written and presented many programmes in the fields of news, the arts and light entertainment. He is probably best known for devising and presenting Radio Four's *Quote... Unquote*, which has been broadcast worldwide for 20 years, and he has also written more than 30 books, including three novels and the immensely successful *Graffiti* series. His special interest is the popular use of the English language.

Nigel's talk in June 1993 discussed two types of inscription which depend for part of their impact on the physical appearance of the writing – gravestones and graffiti. He illustrated his remarks with photographs and gave a tour of fascinating, humorous and touching epitaphs, from "In loving memory of Frank Stanier of Staffordshire who left us in peace in 1910" to a plain and simple "Gone but not forgotten." Then he moved on to the world of graffiti...

NIGEL REES

Graffiti – the Italian word for "Scratchings" – is people being unable to resist the lure of a surface upon which to put something. The basic graffiti urge is to say that you exist: "Sam woz 'ere;" "Susan and Jennifer woz 'ere and will always stay." If you belong to a group, say The Shed, part of Chelsea Football Ground, you demonstrate that you belong to this group of people by writing the name of the group on the wall. The Cerne Abbas Giant carved on the hillside shows that graffiti goes back to cavemen writing or drawing on walls, following this primeval urge. When they

excavated Pompeii, they discovered things that had been written by the Greeks (who were there originally) and the Romans, all of which were the sort of things that we now think of as being graffiti material – political slogans, comments about people's performance in bed, those sorts of things. Slightly ironically, there is now a notice up in Pompeii: "Please do not write or scratch anything upon the walls; cause no damage to walls."

What other things do people write on walls? Well, they write their names, and things like: "To the girl in pink, with brown boots, at Gemma's party, I love you, C." In 1977 I found: "Sod the Jubilee, yeah." And then underneath: "Don't spray it, say it." That, in fact, is an old catchphrase, addressed to people who spit when they speak!

Much graffiti is either political or social in its sloganeering, such as: "Hands off Vietnam" or "Down with Thatcher." George Davis was a small-time crook from south of the river and he was charged and sent to prison for something he apparently didn't do. An enormous campaign was launched in the mid-Seventies. People dug up the cricket pitch at Lords and went round London putting up slogans like: "George Davies is innocent." (The spelling varies a bit, he's gone and got an "e" in there.) All this pressure led the then Home Secretary, Roy Jenkins, to release him, but not to pardon him. And then, lo and behold, he was done for robbing a bank, so it was all rather sad. That was graffiti for a cause, as is this example: "Reject the crime abortion – Joseph." (Signed graffiti is a rarity; it seems a rather foolish thing to do.) Joseph went around with his little pot of paint in the middle of the night putting that slogan up, and also this one: "Slay the pagan monster porn... ", and again signed: "... Joseph."

There was an organisation in Australia called "Buga-up", which stands for "Billboard utilising graffitiists against unhealthy promotions". They went round defacing cigarette and alcohol advertisements, usually not with a great deal of humour. In fact, humour can be surprisingly lacking in graffiti: "Raging in this queue the carbonic plague." This is another very unfunny one: "It's not what they say but what we do," which is topped by a slightly wittier one from New Zealand: "The riotings on the wall."

Sometimes graffiti appears to be religious: "Jesus lives in heaven, love God and each other, and The Valves." The Valves were actually a group in the late Seventies, and they've somehow been added on to this Biblical expression.

Sometimes graffiti is very odd. What are these people trying to say? "E£i$abeth II rains OK." Have they just misspelt it? Why have they put dollar and pound signs in it? I think we should be told. "Nicholas Parsons is the neo-opiate of the people." This was written in the late Seventies out near Harrow, where there's a very big roundabout. It stayed there for years and years and became quite famous. It certainly pleased Nicholas Parsons.

Around the Portobello Road is the sparse: "The Wall". I suppose that's the Pink Floyd song; and: "Max Bygraves killed my mother." But "Stump" is a real puzzle. At first I thought it was a Magritte sort of thing: "This is not a stump," or "This is a stump." Perhaps if you were playing cricket and couldn't afford a real stump, you wrote "Stump" on the wall. And then I found out that Stump was the name of a Punk group. But they didn't start recording until 1988 – and this was 1979, so the mystery continues.

"Mr Chad" arose during the war. There are various explanations as to how he became famous, but he was to appear usually with a little slogan, like: "Wot, no jam?" or "Wot, no beer?" There are various stories told as to how the "Kilroy" expression arose. The obvious one is that he was a foreman in a shipyard in Massachusetts, and when he had inspected each part of the ship he would write on it: "Kilroy was here" to show that he had inspected it. But with these bits of folklore one's never really going to get to the truth.

I'm afraid to say there is some graffiti which is just an eyesore, which doesn't say anything, which cannot be forgiven or pardoned in any respect. People just make a mess by spraying their names or their football club initials on walls. In Central Park and in the subway in New York it really is like a disease. It is not decorative, it doesn't say anything; it is just making a mess for the sake of it. It seemed as if it was going to spread over here at one time, but it hasn't really done so to such an extent. In New York there are trains literally covered with not only words, but also "designs". I think they have managed to diminish it a bit by putting electric fences round the subway trains at night so graffiti artists can't get in to do this sort of thing, but I find it hard to forgive.

But I find it easy to forgive graffiti writers if they actually are funny with it. A straightforward political slogan gave rise to lots of jokes: Astrid Proll was suspected of being a terrorist and arrested in this country. "Free Astrid Proll" of course led to: "Free Astrid Proll with every three gallons."

Or what about: "Avenue Road, what's the matter with the old one?" Or a basic one: "Bill Stickers is innocent." A feminist slogan which has been tampered with: "End violence to women now." Somebody else has added: "Why?" And somebody else has put: "End violence to women now... Yes, dear." You just can't do anything with these graffiti writers; they're not very politically correct.

In New Zealand there was a Prime Minister called Robert Muldoon, who was known as Piggy Muldoon because he looked a bit that way. On a bacon factory in Auckland I saw this: "Pigs disown Muldoon." And this one is a bit of history: "Princess Anne is already married to Valerie Singleton." It obviously dates from 1973 at the time of Princess Anne's first marriage. She was quite famous at that time for having gone on some *Blue Peter* jaunt with Val.

"Ooh look, there goes Concorde again," is what we used to say in Chiswick. Here's a funny one: an advertisement for tights. The slogan is: "Where would fashion be without pins?" and somebody's written: "Free of little pricks." Graffiti like that isn't earth-shattering, but at least it tries.

A very famous graffito was written on a wall by the railway line coming out of Paddington, and was there for very many years. Someone went out and wrote, in beautiful lettering: "Far away is close at hand in images of elsewhere." People went past every day and said: "Uh?" Peter Simple, the *Telegraph* columnist, created a whole persona for the man who'd done it. He called him "The Master of Paddington" and discussed his work very learnedly. It is, in fact, the first line of a poem by Robert Graves, called *A Song of Contrariety.* "Far away is close at hand in images of elsewhere."

Another famous one is below an enormous mural under the Westway: "A woman without a man is like a fish without a bicycle." The saying originally came to us from Germany.

Finally, we get to the commercialisation of graffiti. There's a hotel called the Devonshire Arms in Derbyshire. The manager bought a selection of graffiti from me and had them turned into tiles. Then they put them where graffiti would have been written if people had been allowed to write there – in the gents.

You could say that the epitaph on a gravestone gives you a bit of immortality. And I suppose that graffiti writers might claim that they also acquire a touch of immortality by scribbling something on a wall. People always ask me whether I do it myself. No, I don't, but I have appeared in graffiti by other people. When I was embarrassingly well known for the graffiti books, somebody told me that there was one in Cambridge at the bottom of a graffiti-strewn wall. A great big arrow pointed at it and someone had written: "Here's a good one Nige."

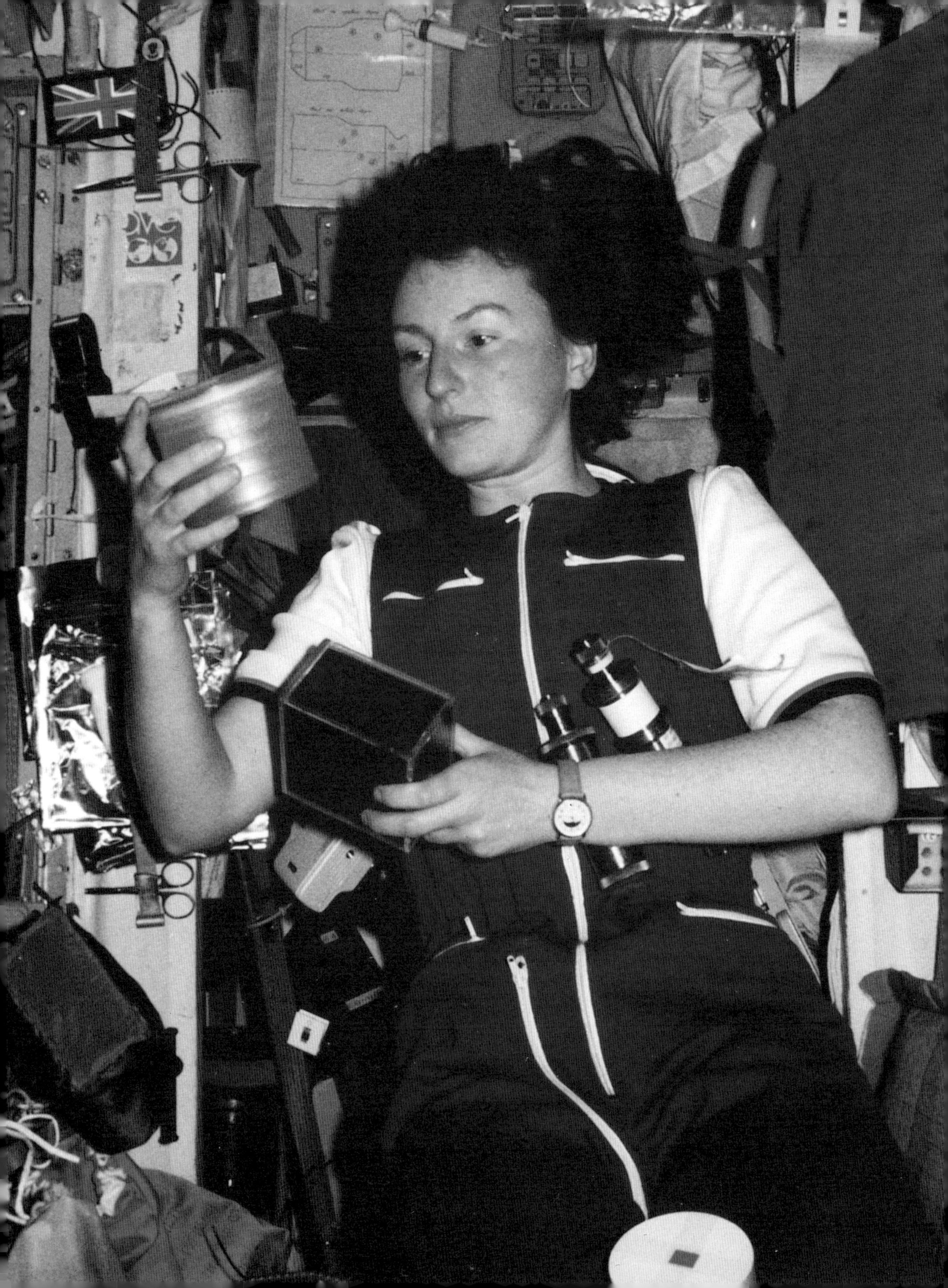

CHAPTER 26 **From Mars to the Stars**

HELEN SHARMAN

became Britain's first astronaut on 18 May 1991. Helen was working as a research technologist for Mars confectionery when she was chosen from more than 13,000 applicants to represent Britain in a joint space flight with the then Soviet Union. After 18 months intensive training in Russia, Helen found herself conducting experiments on board the Mir Space Station, travelling at a speed of eight kilometres a second over the Earth.

In September 1993, two-and-a-half years after Helen took her place in the history books, she made the slightly less arduous journey to Primrose Hill, where she told us her unique story of achievement, motivation, determination and teamwork. Her courage, intelligence, sense of humour and down-to-earth outlook impressed us all, and her talk was much more than an invigorating tale of space exploration, but also a real-life lesson in achieving your dreams.

I never expected to be an astronaut.

I enjoyed science and that's what I had decided to do with my life. However, one day I was driving home from work, flicking through the stations on the car radio, when I heard an advertisement: "Astronaut wanted. No experience necessary." I got home and I applied, as if it were any other job, to be an astronaut.

Well, after lots of tests they eventually chose two of us to go to Russia to begin our training. I was given four days' notice to leave, in which time I had to sell my car, get rid of my house plants, buy thermal clothing, meet Margaret Thatcher, have photo calls with sponsors... I arrived exhausted and couldn't understand a word anybody said. We started with three months of learning Russian, followed by lessons in the planetarium, learning about the stars – in an emergency I would have to steer the spacecraft using the stars as a map. Then we had lessons in classrooms: astronavigation, ballistics, the theory of flight, leading on to more practical subjects: the space station itself and the technologies involved in operating a spacecraft. There was emergency training to prepare for what would happen if we landed in the sea, and physical training to teach us how to manoeuvre our bodies when we became weightless.

This involved what the astronauts call their "hamster wheel". You stand inside this wheel, your feet are tied to the base, your arms stretched out, and you make the wheel spin by moving your body sideways, eventually flipping the wheel all the way over. Then you just keep it spinning and spinning as fast as you can. It makes you so dizzy that you don't know up from down.

In February 1991, about 15 months after my initial training had started, I was selected to be the prime candidate from Britain to go into space – much to my surprise. Even when it was the day of the launch, I still didn't believe it could be me. After a last-minute press conference we made our way to the launch pad. By now the rocket was erect, full of liquid fuel. We said our final farewells and climbed inside our capsule. We strapped ourselves in, closed our hatch and, with a thud, they closed the hatch on the outside. And then there was this wonderful, ultimate sense of relief that at last, after 18 months of training, we were now getting on with it.

After sitting on top of that rocket for two-and-a-half hours we felt a very faint rumble from a long way below us. There was this slight vibration and slowly, painfully slowly at first, we started to move away from the launch

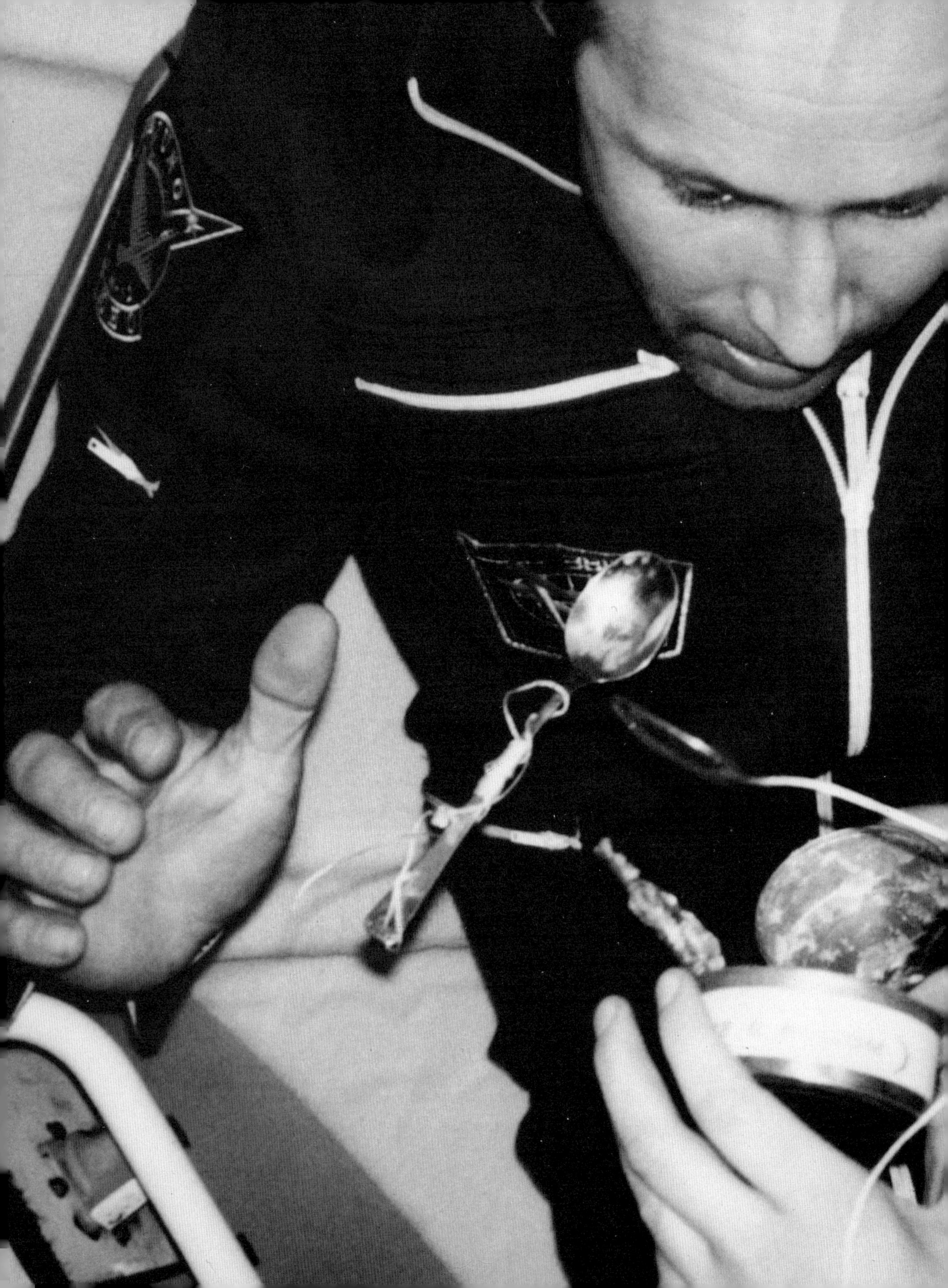

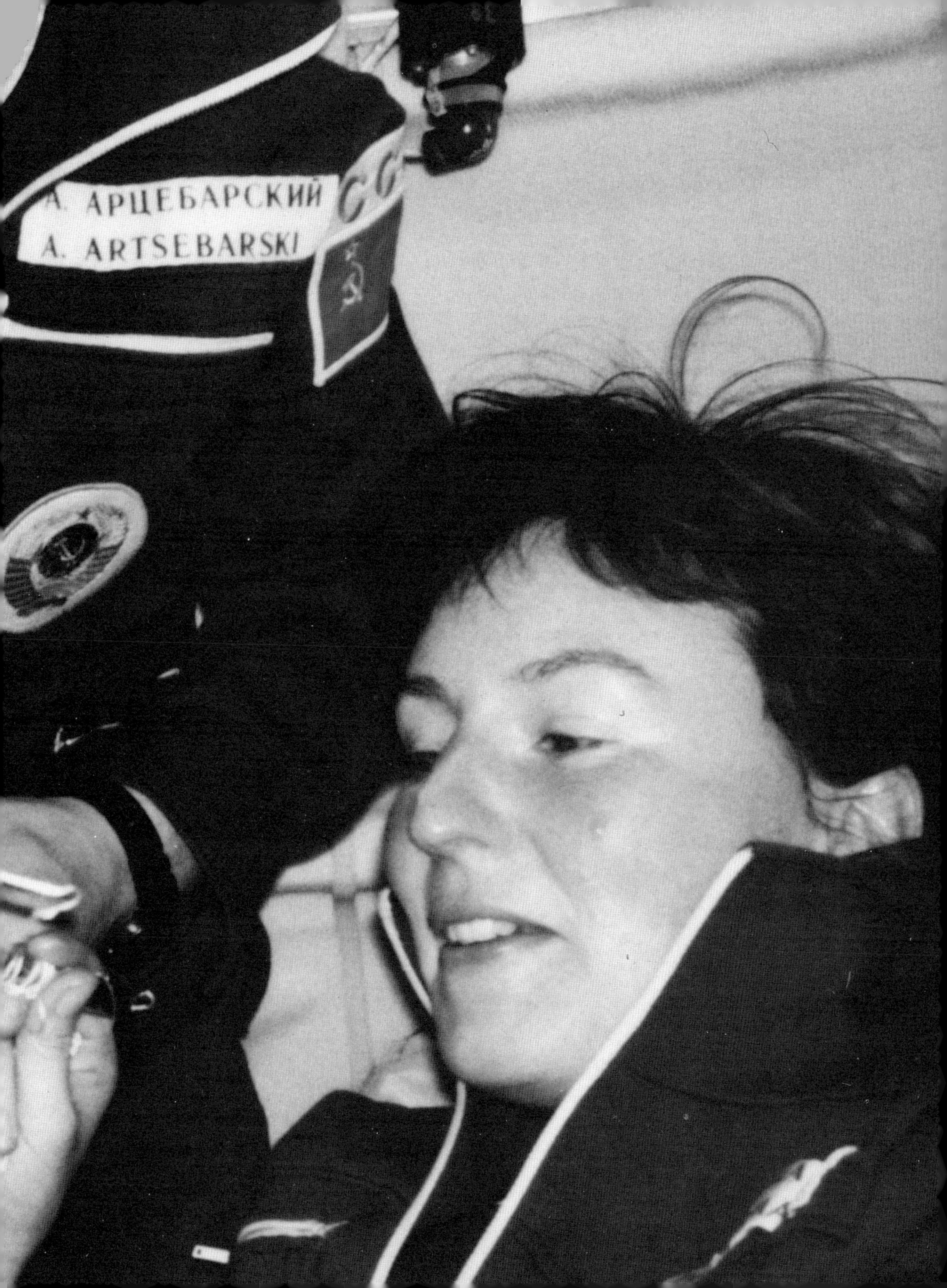
А. АРЦЕБАРСКИЙ
A. ARTSEBARSKI

pad. It took 530 seconds before all the fuel had been used up, but at that second, as we jettisoned the final rocket stage, instead of being pushed down into our seats under three-and-a-half G-force, with a bang we were floating, feeling weightless, above our seats. I didn't sit down again for eight days.

We spent two days inside the Soyuz space capsule, gradually increasing our orbit of the Earth so that we would catch up with the space station. But as we approached the station, Sergei, the engineer, looked out of the window and said: "Something doesn't feel right." We kept checking all the monitors and screens. Still something wasn't right. The amount of fuel that we'd used compared to the time taken and the speed we thought we had just didn't add up. So when we came into contact with mission control over Soviet space, we requested that we should use manual control to dock onto the space station.

I operated a periscopic television camera so that Tolya, the commander, could see where he was going. Sergei looked at what information we knew was correct, and then Tolya literally manoeuvred the spacecraft up a bit, down a bit, left a bit, right a bit. We knew this wasn't just a test that we were going through, but that if any of us made a mistake we would all be dead. If you miss by a mile it doesn't really matter because you and the space station can orbit the Earth again and have another go. But if you miss by just ten centimetres you will blast a hole in yourselves and also in the space station. When we eventually made contact with the station, we floated in and we knew that we had done it together.

The station was huge, 25 by 40 metres. There was plenty of room for us all to get on with our work. My job was to do experiments, one of the reasons I'd applied to go into space. (Another reason was that I wanted to feel the exhilaration of the launch!) You can grow protein crystals large enough so that you can analyse them back on Earth and then base future medicines on them. You can grow seeds in different magnetic fields, and you can mix lead and aluminium, a brilliant bearing material which would simply separate upon cooling if you tried to mix those metals on Earth.

Everyone always asks how we went to the toilet in space. Well, a space toilet is not very dissimilar to a toilet on Earth, except instead of flushing it with water, we flushed it with air. If you're in space, however – and especially if you're Russian – you don't waste anything. Through a series of filters and other processes we cleaned the contents of the toilet into water, so that we could (if we wanted to) drink it. Luckily for me, we'd taken 60 litres of drinking water on board our Soyuz, so we didn't need to drink our toilet water, but even if you don't drink it you still don't waste it. So much ingenuity has gone into the Soviet spacecrafts. Water – H_2O – consists of hydrogen and oxygen. Oxygen is pretty useful to people in space, so you go to the toilet, collect everything, clean it into water and then electrolyse the water to separate the hydrogen from the oxygen. We didn't need the hydrogen so we vented that into space, but we used the oxygen to breathe. That's neat!

In my bedroom was a sleeping bag, tied to the wall. You don't really need a sleeping bag; you don't need a bed, you can just float if you want – the most wonderful, relaxing feeling. However, air was being circulated around the station and, had we just fallen asleep in mid air, we would also have circulated around the station and maybe bumped into something and damaged it. We tied our sleeping bags to the most comfortable surface we could find.

The views I had from my bedroom window were spectacular! We were orbiting the Earth 16 times a day, so for us 16 times a day it was dark, 16 times a day it was light. Something I'd been looking forward to seeing, 16 times a day, was sunrise, which lasted just eight seconds. The Earth wasn't a globe in the distance, as in pictures from the moon. I was only 220 miles above the Earth's surface, and the moon is about a quarter of a million miles away, so the Earth was quite close. I could just about make out its curvature.

I didn't want to come back; I wanted to carry on up there. One of my favourite memories is of looking out of one of the larger windows on the floor of the station. If you look away from the Earth you can see the stars. When you look into space, at first all you can see is inky blackness, because your eyes are used to the very bright lights inside the station, but gradually the stars start to appear, and the more you look the more stars you can see. There are millions and millions of stars out there. I really did feel as though I could look straight through them, through those stars, right to infinity. And I know that I was able to experience all that because one day, as I was driving my car home from work, I heard an opportunity. I realised that some opportunities come our way only once. Sometimes you have to take a few chances. You get out there and you go for it.

CHAPTER 27 **Eve was Framed**

HELENA KENNEDY

has been introduced as representing "women and other criminals". One of Britain's most dynamic barristers, she was called to the Bar in 1972 and became a Queen's Counsel in 1990 – an unexpected coup for an outspoken, radical lawyer, and a woman to boot. Helena initiated an Equal Opportunities Committee to counter the handicaps facing women at the Bar, and received the UK Woman of Europe Award in 1995. She is Chancellor of Oxford Brookes University and Chair of Charter 88. Helena is equally well known outside the courtroom as a journalist and broadcaster on law and women's rights.

Helena doesn't pull her punches and, as we expected, her talk in October 1993 was a no-holds-barred insider's view of the law, its strengths and its weaknesses. In an impassioned exposé, she reached far beyond "women's issues" to the injustices and needs of society as a whole.

The whole subject of the law is very much at the forefront of many people's minds at the moment, and the way in which I have sought to address it is by asking the question:

"Is the law male ?"

And, of course, many people have replied: "Is the Pope Catholic?" More and more women are remarking on the failure of the law for them, including the way in which judges say all kinds of mad things. The judge who took the prize recently said that £500 compensation would put right the trauma of a particularly awful rape, and that a little holiday in the sun might help the victim to get over it. Needless to say, quite a lot of people were upset by that. This was followed shortly by a child sexual abuse case, where the judge commented that the eight-year-old victim was herself "no angel", and therefore this allowed for him to give the defendant a rather minor penalty.

The response from the legal establishment is that these chaps are mavericks, they practise in the provinces, they don't know about the real world, and they're very few in number. But the problem about the law is that it is very powerful symbolically. It sends out messages which resonate throughout society. Certain messages come through those kind of judgements and people take them on board – and are either outraged or take them as some kind of support for their own value-system.

So, we have begun to see a much more openly declared criticism of law. And I see that as being no more than the kind of change that's taking place generally across society: we have a much better informed public; we have people who are better educated and who are not as deferential as they used to be. People expect more of their professionals, whether they be doctors or lawyers, and are actually now criticising judges. And it's no bad thing, because one of the things about democracy is that we should expect accountability. But I also see this critique as something that's alarming, an indicator of a degree of crisis. Because law has to keep in tune. One of the things about law is that it's a social contract – we go to the law with our grievances rather than sorting them out for ourselves. We don't have pistols at dawn any longer; we pass over to the state the right to, if you like, take our wrongs on board for us, and to deal with them through a proper hearing; and, ultimately, we give to our judges the right to remove the liberty of the subject.

Now, passing that responsibility to the state means that we have to be very cautious. It gives great power to the state, and the contract is kept alive and healthy by the state's allowing for proper procedures (having protections for defendants, not removing liberty too readily), and by its being in tune with public concern about levels of crime and the seriousness of different kinds of offending.

In that social contract there's another very important element, which is how victims are treated. The victims' lobby, which is now a generalised force within our society, actually grew out of women's criticism of law. Women in the Sixties and Seventies were better educated, a female population who were combining careers with families, who were moving into every arena, and who started expecting those arenas to reflect the reality of their lives. And so women started criticising the law and the way that it failed them, particularly as the victims of crime. They put the microscope on the conduct in cases in court, cases like rape trials, domestic violence cases, cases where women, invariably, were the victim, and what they showed us was an abuse of power in which women were, for the greater part, the people who were powerless.

In the last few years a debate has raged over provocation. Does the law of provocation work for women – particularly for battered women? Is it availing itself properly to people who deserve to be able to claim it, particularly where there has been long-term and cumulative provocation? In fact, the definition of provocation doesn't take account of cumulative provocation, and doesn't take account of the way in which women tend not to be able to snap and respond with their bare hands in the face of some kind of insult but, almost invariably, are likely to postpone tackling the person who is affronting them. In many of the cases where the woman might have been able to avail herself of provocation as a defence, she has not been able to, because the definition itself involves a sudden and temporary loss of control.

What I was trying to do in writing *Eve was Framed* was not just to talk about the experience of women within the system; I really wanted to address something that I thought was even more fundamental than that, which is that, if the law is failing large sections of the community (and the same analysis could be made from the perspective of black people or of homosexuals, or anybody who doesn't have a voice within the dominant culture), then *we* are failing, because the law has to embrace all of our society.

I think there's something very difficult that the law has to do to maintain public confidence. It has to be more than just a mirror of society – it has to actually lead society. In dealing with, for example, something like discrimination, the law has to do better than the rest of society; it has to set a standard. It has such an important role that it actually can't allow itself to say: "Well, of course you'll find discrimination in the courts, because we are but human like the rest of society." It should do better.

When judges are presented with the debate about how law is failing women, they present a number of arguments which are very easily destroyed. One of them is that women do far better than men out of the legal system; that women in the criminal courts get off lightly. Indeed, they will give you the impression that if you have a good pair of legs and a snub nose you don't need a defence lawyer at all. And they point to the small number of women in Holloway Prison as an example of the fact that very few women get sent to prison because judges are so nice to them.

But the reality is that, of course, women don't go to prison in anything like the numbers that men do, because women don't commit serious crime. We don't have women committing armed robberies or being involved in the serious end of crime in anything like the way that men are. In fact, some studies have just been done by the Howard League which have found that women end up going to prison much earlier on in their criminal activities than men, due to the fact that the system isn't designed for women. Because they don't have money to pay fines when they come before the courts, they're often given a conditional discharge. But if they commit further offences, then they suddenly run out of alternatives and, because women don't have the resources to pay financial penalties, the courts use imprisonment earlier on than they do with male defendants. Also, community service was created with men in mind. It isn't geared to women, and certainly not to women who have families. So there are often fewer recommendations made for women to work in the community because they're just not the kind of jobs that women can do. The Howard League study found that 78 per cent of women who came before the courts were there for minor offences of dishonesty, and that 78 per cent of women in prison were there for non-violent offences, and were not in the high-risk category. Home Office statistics showed recently that 33 per cent of women – as against 11 per cent of men – were in prison for a first offence.

So it isn't true, this chauvinistic hypothesis that judges are nicer to women. I thought it would be interesting to turn everything on its head and ask the question: "Who are the women that are sent to prison?" And I have come to the conclusion that the women who are sent to prison are women who do not conform to the stereotypes of "good" women – the stereotypes of "the good wife and mother". A good analogy is not from a criminal case at all, but from the infamous case of Jeffrey Archer, who sued the *Daily Star* for libel when he made a donation of £2,000 to a prostitute. Monica, the prostitute, was called to testify on behalf of the newspaper, and Mary Archer was called into this morality play by the defence, in my view to counterpoint a different kind of womanhood.

You'll remember what Mr Justice Caulfield said to the jury in that case – clearly bowled over by Mrs Archer and the pussycat bow at the neck of her blouse: "Members of the jury, you have heard from Mrs Archer; was she not fragrant?" It was quite an extraordinary business that we should be considering the scent of the lady in question, but what I suspect is that many of the women whom I represent are not "fragrant" women. And by that I don't mean that they don't use deodorant, but that they do not conform to ideas of "good" womanhood.

When I was researching for the book I came across the work of Pat Carlen, a very fine sociologist, who had done some work asking judges what criteria affected their decision as to whether to send a woman to prison. And these were the sorts of answers that she got back:

> **"Women who live more ordered lives don't commit crime, because with a husband and children to look after they don't have time."**

"It may not be necessary to send her to prison if she has a husband; he may tell her to stop it."

"If she's a good mother we don't want to take her away, and if she's not a good mother it doesn't really matter. If you discover a woman has no children, it clears the way to send her to prison. If she has children but they're in care then I take the view she's footloose and fancy-free and I treat her as a single woman."

"If she's left her husband and her children are already in care, it may seem a very good idea to send her to prison, for three months."

What one is seeing is a definition of "appropriateness". Women who are "inappropriate" are more likely to be sent to prison. We have to recognise that those sorts of attitudes run very deep. There is still a notion that somehow we expect more of women, that women are the moral cornerstones of our society and that somehow women are the guardians of what is good. And if a women doesn't live up to those expectations she's committing more than a crime.

Women are not my sole preoccupation: there's also many a free man out there who will testify to my efforts on his behalf. The case that I will always remember was some years back, where I was representing a husband who'd killed his wife. We went in to see the judge because I was going to try to persuade him to consider a manslaughter plea. I explained to him that I thought he might consider this plea because there had been a sudden loss of control. And he said to me: "Yes, but he drowned his wife in the bath, didn't he?" I said yes, and he said: "It was a brutal, vicious killing", and I said yes, it was. "He held that lovely young woman down in the water!" And I said I know, it was really awful, and he said: "He applied all his male force to her neck, her young neck." And I said it was appalling, it really was terrible. And he said: "He was a bully." And I said yes, he was a bully, but it was obviously a "crime passionnel"; it was clearly not premeditated, they were in the bath together and he was at the tap end, and she was at the other… "The tap end, he was at the tap end! How long had this thing been going on?" Needless to say, my client was not convicted of murder.

ALAN DAVIES belongs to the new breed of stand-up comedians. His baggy rambles about his day-to-day, metropolitan life, and his energetic use of his body in joke-telling have earned him prime-time television appearances and masses of bookings on the London circuit.

ANDY SHEPPARD taught himself to play the saxophone in three weeks and is recognised as both a virtuoso performer and a brilliant composer. He has had an enormous impact on the international jazz scene, writing for theatre, dance, radio and TV, as well as for his own groups. Keyboard player **STEVE LODDER**, classically trained at Cambridge, is the other half of the duo Small Co-Motion.

This was a special evening with Newell and Sorrell in December 1993. Part Christmas party, part seminar and, especially, a fund-raising event for the Macmillan Nurse Appeal, we turned the office into a café, with seats for 200 people and a stage for Small Co-Motion and Alan Davies. The music was extraordinary, featuring extracts from the group's album *Rhythm Method*, a mix of funk and rock, lyrical ballads and free jazz. And Alan made us cry with laughter, running the raffle in a way that made people giggle as they handed over their money.

I am Alan Davies. I do stand-up comedy. I went to Newell and Sorrell and did what we in the comedy world call *"an office Christmas party"*. We roll our eyes a bit, but we go. Café Cabaret was not your average Xmas do, however. **There was no snogging** and it's going in a book. Doesn't happen every day, does it?

I've been on the telly a bit and on the radio, but live shows are best, even if you do sometimes get roped into doing a raffle draw. Go to see some live comedy. Something good, an established club on a Saturday night. Give it a try. Come and see me – *I'm pretty funny.*

You have to be there, you see. Have you seen Dave Allen live? Or Billy Connolly? I have. Have you been to the Comedy Store late at night when it's packed out? People are shouting and laughing and laughing and laughing. I have. I've been on there. I've been called back to do more. People cheering. And I've gone off to the sound of my own footsteps. Two hundred and fifty people and I can hear my feet. And my heart.

Café Cabaret was a rowdy old night at times. Andy Sheppard said so at half-time in no uncertain terms. But he went back on and was stunning and they laughed at my jokes. So it was good, and the food was jolly nice, too.

You had to be there, really...

"Let's just get on with the raffle, shall we? Pay attention, this is for the fruit hamper. It is red 77. Well, I say red – pink, I suppose... There it is over there – pink 77, he's won it! What a fruity looking gentleman he is. Congratulations. You don't have to eat the cellophane..."

"Sometimes in the theatre if you're not enjoying the show, you can start an interval. This is very easily done. Often during the play there will be a blackout between scenes, and the actors will go off and other actors will be all keen to come in, just throwing their hair out, getting a bit nervous, shaking it out a bit, and then just before they come on, if you're at the back of the auditorium, if you start applauding, people around you will start applauding, thinking it probably is an interval. It will catch on across the whole auditorium, the guys operating the house lights will whip them up, people will come out with ice-cream trays, like robots, and you will have an interval on your hands. Just try it next time you're at the theatre, if you're at a boring play. The actors will come out and say, "I'm sorry, we've got another scene." **Just ignore them...**"

"I've never seen so much dead meat in my life. I hope you're enjoying that chicken leg, because he's just sitting on the floor outside – he can't walk about any more, you know. He's nearer the ground, but he wants to get about..."

"We had a budget recently, which I didn't understand either. I don't understand much, as you probably noticed: it's sort of a theme in my life. I don't know if I like Kenneth Clarke; I'm a bit scared of him. He's a mixture isn't he? He's got a big bum, I noticed that, nearly as big as David Owen's, which is quite huge. Have you got David Owen doing a talk? He could talk about large pants. I don't understand it. I mean with Kenneth Clarke I'm not sure about it. **With Norman Lamont you knew you didn't like him because he had funny eyebrows,** and that was easy, wasn't it? Norman Lamont kept saying we were better off since he left REM. Correct me if I'm wrong, but he wasn't in REM was he? "That's me in the corner, that's me in..." It's bloody not, Norman, you weren't in it, you liar! It's ridiculous...”

“When I was at school, you had the fastest runner in the school and that was it. You ran from here to the end of the playground, not from here to Reading. Can anyone explain the marathon to me? *What is the point of the marathon?* Get a cab, what are you doing...?”

“**Well, you've seen a genius at work this evening.** And I thought Andy Sheppard was quite good as well, I don't know about you. Thanks a lot and goodnight!”

CHAPTER 29 **African Laughter**

DORIS LESSING was born in Persia and spent her childhood on a large farm in Southern Rhodesia (now Zimbabwe). She first came to England in 1949, when her first novel, *The Grass is Singing*, was published. Since then Doris has become a highly acclaimed and prizewinning writer, and her works include novels, short stories, science fiction, non-fiction and an operatic libretto.

In 1950 Doris was made a Prohibited Immigrant, forbidden to return to Rhodesia because her political views differed from those of its white rulers. Although she was allowed back once, in 1956, she did not return again until 1982, two years after the War of Independence.

In January 1994 Doris came to Newell and Sorrell to read extracts from her latest book, *African Laughter*, an account of her return visits to the land of her upbringing. Our audience was held spellbound by the quiet voice of this renowned author and her storytelling, as ever, was evocative and compelling.

WHEN I RETURNED TO ZIMBABWE after that long absence, I expected all kinds of changes, but there was one change I had not thought to expect. The game had mostly gone. The bush was nearly silent. Once, the dawn chorus hurt the ears. Lying in our blankets under the trees on the sandveld of Marandellas, or in the house on the farm in Banket, the shrilling, clamouring, exulting of the birds as the sun appeared was so loud the ears seemed to curl up and complain before – there was nothing else for it – we leapt up into the early morning, to become part of all that tumult and activity. But by the 1980s the dawn chorus had become a feeble thing. Once, everywhere, moving through the bush, you saw duiker, bush buck, wild pig, wild cats, porcupines, anteaters; koodoo stood on the antheaps turning their proud horns to examine you before bounding off; eland went around in groups, like cattle. Being in the bush was to be with animals, one of them…

Just to remind you, Zimbabwe is right down at the bottom of what is actually rather a large continent. Below it is South Africa, to the left is Botswana, to the right is Mozambique, and above it is Zambia. And that southern African block, in my personal, optimistic view, will be a very remarkable place in a few years.

I went back in 1982 after the country had suffered a ghastly war. None of us knew how awful it had been, I think because our picture of it was a bit simple: whites on one side, blacks on the other; goodies and baddies. It wasn't like that at all. There were lots of blacks on the white side, fighting in the white armies, and on the black side there were different armies which sometimes fought each other. There were many different strands of belief, and people were not nice to each other, let's put it like that.

The war left an aftermath of great bitterness, hate and despair, which was very evident in 1982. There was quite an extraordinary mix of

Nyanga, Eastern Highlands of Zimbabwe

optimism, ebullience and a bleak, post-war feeling. It's very hard to convey these mixed emotions, so I'm going to read a short piece which I hope conveys the optimistic side, the feeling that anything could happen and probably would, and the feeling that Zimbabwe was taking off. It's called "The Restaurant".

This is the Jameson Hotel, which was inter-racial years before Liberation, and has always been a good-natured place. In the restaurant, a husband is urging his wife to order food she's never tried. "You can't eat only sadza," says he, like a schoolmaster. She is a fat woman, laughing helplessly as she points to an item on the menu, then covers her mouth with both palms and sits shaking. The waiter stands smiling, other waiters interrupt their work to watch, the restaurant manager comes over. Everyone, black and white, is involved in this moment of social evolution.

She tastes a cheese dish, wrinkles up her face, shakes her head then shudders with her shoulders, so that a collar of tangled necklaces flash and tinkle. But we can see she's committed in principle to liking only sadza, and we do not have to take the rejection seriously. A waiter removes the cheese dish with a great philosophical shrug. Another dish is set before her. She pokes her finger into it, rolling her eyes. "No, no, you must use a fork," said her husband, with appropriate severity. She compromises with a spoon, takes up a little edge of whatever it is, lifts it to her lips, makes a big astonished face, purses her mouth, shakes her head, sits back wheezing out laughter and pressing her napkin to her whole face.

By now everybody is laughing.

The waiter sets down a plate of pudding, with a flourish and a last-ditch gesture that involves us all. Her eyes stretched wide, she stands bravely at the precipice edge, she plunges in a spoon, she takes it in slow jerks to her mouth, groaning with apprehension, she encloses the spoon with her lips, she tilts back her head and allows a look of ecstasy to overcome her, she removes the spoon from her mouth, and uses it to eat up her pudding very fast, with little cries of

> *appreciation, while the waiters reel about laughing. "My dear", says her husband smiling, "you are a very foolish woman."*
> *"Yes, yes, I am a foolish woman, my dear, but I will have some more of whatever it is. I like it."*

That scene showed something of the excitement of that year, that time.

I didn't go back for six years. And, you know, when you go back to a place you always expect to find what you saw before. Far from it. There was a new generation which was already yawning when the grown-ups were talking about the war. Everyone was extremely jolly and optimistic and happy, and it was as if the war had never been. Yet, again, there were these extraordinary contrasts of enormous optimism and ebullience with bad things that had happened.

One bad thing was that, in that very short time since independence, a new boss-class had been created, called by the locals "the Chefs". I don't know why everyone is shocked about the corruption in Africa, because every government that comes in after a civil war, or "troubles", grabs everything it can get for itself. I don't know why the Africans are expected to be any different – it's what the Tudors did, for example.

However, everyone was happy because the Unity Accord had been signed. I got involved with something called the "book team", people rushing around Zimbabwe making books for use in the rural areas. These people, having won a war, running their own country (or so they liked to think), knew perfectly well that they were ill-educated and untrained. They desperately wanted to know more, and the book team decided to make books, which would provide the most basic kind of instruction, like how to open a bank account, how to talk to a bank manager, how to use a post office.

In Europe, from the age of about six, we all take absolutely for granted that we know how to use buses, the underground, post offices, telephones – anything. But these are people who, even now, are mostly brought up in houses without electricity or any technical equipment of the kind we take for granted. So these books were designed to instruct people in how to cope with ordinary life. And I came in on the women's book. Now this is absolute dynamite. Because Zimbabwe is supposed to be a communist country it has a pretty good legal structure for women – which has never been put into practice, mainly because the women don't know about it. (Zimbabwe shares the fate of Iraq, for example, which, I'm told, has got a good legal structure which has nothing to do with what happens to women in practice.) I went out with the book team and I was in on a lot of meetings with women. They were extremely lively, energetic meetings, with men and women in full argument, in a way that was good-natured. And the things they said to each other were absolutely unbelievable.

Some points were made all the time: "Why is it that we bear the children, we bring them up, and then our husbands can die and their families can come and take away the children we have brought up and we have nothing?" "Why is it that we work the land, we look after the land, but we have no legal ownership? Why can we not own the land that we work?" These are the two big points that go right to the heart of Zimbabwean legal structure.

I'm going to describe a little meeting, which must stand in for a lot of others, to try and give a feeling of the kind of arguments that were going on.

Sixty or so people, mostly women, are on or around the big veranda where for so many years a thousand tea trays, drink trays, were brought by black servants for the farmer, his family, his guests. Presumably that square shed at the back was a kitchen. In front the bush is sparkling and fresh, and a dozen goats are making the most of it...

There are five men present, one the village chairman. They sit quietly while Cathie and Talent (the two chief women, one black, one white, of the book team) say this book for women will be written by the women themselves, and ask them to suggest subjects. Which turns out to be the same as we have heard at the other meetings.

The tone changes when a woman demands to know why they are not allowed to do other kinds of work: why can't they drive buses for instance?

The chairman says that women are not built physically for driving buses: they can't climb up to the top of buses to lift down luggage.

A woman: "Suddenly we hear about our weakness. No-one mentions our weakness when we are planting the crops and growing the crops and hoeing the crops and harvesting the crops and cooking the food and bringing up the children and building the houses and putting roofs on the houses..." she would go on but the chairman stops her: he is not the chairman of this meeting, and some women shout at him, saying so.

He says, "It is your duty to do these things for your husband."

"And whenever we criticise the men for being lazy, then suddenly the talk is of Duty."

"But," the man insists, full of calm conviction, "it is your duty."

At this, in comes that old woman who has to speak for tradition: she says there was good in the old days and the baby must not be thrown out with the bath-water, freedom for women was for outside the home, but inside the old ways are best. "Well spoken, mother," says the chairman.

Groans and laughter...

And so it all goes on, in meeting after meeting, these marvellous, lively discussions. It's like seeing life being rebuilt as you watch it.

So we've got to 1988. In 1989 I was with the book team again. Things had happened by then which were not so good. A lot of the ebullience had gone. This was partly due to the role of aid in Africa: the World Bank and the International Monetary Fund always seem to tell Africa what to do. I'm one of the few people who think that Africa could have done very much better without them, because when advice is given to the farmers by businessmen, they're always taught to think about how they can repay interest – instead of getting on with feeding themselves.

Here is an extract from a book called *Lloyd Timberlake, Africa in Crisis*. Please note "Africa in Crisis", as if it were the size of the Isle of Wight.

Advising Africa has become a major industry, with European and North American consulting firms charging as much as $180,000 for a year of an expert's time. At any given moment, sub-Saharan Africa has 80,000

> *expatriates working for public agencies under official aid programmes. More than half of the seven to eight billion spent yearly by donors goes to finance these people. Yet in the two-and-a-half decades since African independence, Africa has plunged from food self-sufficiency to widespread hunger. Is Africa getting the right advice? is the query.*

What then happened was what they called ESAP: Economic Structure Adjustment Policy. Which became a source of many jokes – a new verb: "They have esapped us, I'm going to esap you, I shall esap her," and so on. The citizenry does not like this new economic policy which has devalued the currency and caused unbelievable poverty in already poor villages, leading to, among other things, women going in for part-time prostitution in order to feed their kids. ESAP has also caused school fees to be reintroduced; a great many other things that used to be free now have to be paid for.

In fact, in some ways, some Africans say they were better off under the whites. I think it is a passing phase, and an expression of a desire to irritate. I don't think they mean it.

What happened next in Zimbabwe was a total disaster. The drought. The once-in-a-hundred-years drought. And I heard the Africans say they felt as if God himself was punishing them. In fact, a lot of Africans believe they're being punished for the unburied freedom fighters – it is their custom to bury people properly with rites, and the people murdered by Mugabe's armies in the war against dissidents remained unburied. During the droughts people went hungry for the first time in the whole history of that area. There wasn't food saved in case of drought, although long before whites came they knew perfectly well they had to save food for drought.

I was up in Stirling University last year, where I talked to a number of African experts. The chief question was, why is it that the population of the area grows exponentially the whole time? There were a quarter of a million blacks in that area when the whites came, before the end of the last century – which is a very small number. They now think there are 12 million, and their horrific forecast is that the population will treble by 2010. If that happens it will be an utter disaster, because the country has a very fragile ecostructure.

There are other big questions which nobody can answer. Is the climate changing? Was that drought just part of the cyclical droughts that they always have in that area, or was it something out of the ordinary? Because if you look back over a couple of hundred years, this was a particularly bad drought. I have white farming friends in the area that I grew up in, and one of them said to me when I was there last that when he goes out into the bush there are plants there that do not belong to the high sveld, they belong to semi-desert areas. Do the plants know more than we do? Is the country drying up? Some of the experts think it is and others say it's merely cyclical.

The other big question is, of course, Aids, which I don't have to go into. Nobody knows how many people have Aids. They don't know how many people will have Aids, or how many people will die of Aids. The only thing that is certain is that Aids is attacking other parts of Africa, and is now beginning to attack Zimbabwe and other countries around it. And it's attacking the most highly trained and valuable part of the population – the people between about 20 and 40 who have had education and training. This is a tragedy, because we're talking about very poor countries who can't afford this kind of thing.

Finally, here is something that cheers me up every time I think of it. When I was in Zimbabwe last it was as a journalist, and I interviewed David Hasluck, the representative for the Commercial Farmers' Union. It was the middle of the drought, and I said to him: "Apart from the drought, what do you think is the most important thing happening?" And he was so angry with me. "How can you say 'Apart from the drought'? I can't talk to you if you think like that." And he started talking about the dying hippopotamuses, the dead trees and the dead river beds and so on. Then he forgave me and he said: "This is the most important thing. The drought has exposed that layer of layabouts and incompetents for what they are, and no-one can ever have any illusions again about them." (He was talking about the government.) And he added: "But underneath there, there's a whole layer of young, clever, competent and non-corrupt black people who are, in fact, running this country. These are the people who will save Zimbabwe."

Patrick Barclay
Gary Mabbutt
Andrew Shields
Alex Fynn
Tom Watt

CHAPTER 30 **So What's Wrong with Football?**

ALEX FYNN, GARY MABBUTT, TOM WATT, PATRICK BARCLAY AND ANDREW SHIELDS were the team of football experts at our Question Time in March 1994.

ALEX FYNN has been described as a "football strategist and iconoclast", which is a posh way of saying he's one of the few people who has thought about the future of football. Alex has supported Newcastle since the days of Jackie Milburn, whose picture stands in his office.

GARY MABBUTT began his career with Bristol Rovers before moving to Tottenham Hotspur. There he collected 16 England caps and an FA Cup Winners' medal, along with the respect of footballers and fans alike.

TOM WATT has been an Arsenal fan for 30 years. Best known as an actor, particularly Lofty in BBC TV's *EastEnders*, he writes on football to compensate for the cruciate ligament injury that stopped him playing – badly!

PATRICK BARCLAY supports Dundee and is chief football correspondent of the *Observer*, where his incisive views have become required reading every Sunday.

ANDREW SHIELDS, our panel's chairman, is sports editor of *Time Out*, and last year co-wrote *Soccer City: The Future of Football in London*. He supports Leyton Orient, although he'd rather pass over that.

ALEX FYNN, GARY MABBUTT, TOM WATT, PATRICK BARCLAY AND ANDREW SHIELDS

Welcome to "*So What's Wrong with Football?*" A debate on the current plight of the beautiful game.

Andrew To a Leyton Orient fan who has just watched his team concede two goals in six minutes to Barnet, the answer to the question is pretty straightforward – everything. Sack the manager! Sell the players! Storm the boardroom! But these are parochial concerns. What we're here to talk about tonight is the broader picture – a catalogue of petty squabbles, empire-building and general incompetence, which led to the manager of our national team being portrayed as a turnip in a tabloid newspaper, and England, of course, failing to qualify for the World Cup Finals.

How has all of this been allowed to happen? Where's the leadership? Where's the hope of inspiring a future generation when most of our top league matches are shown on a satellite TV system to which only ten per cent of households subscribe? Where is the coherent vision for the 21st century, the structure for the game at all its levels? Or maybe Terry Venables will wave his magic wand and everything will be all right again.

We'll keep going for about 90 minutes, but it won't be a game of two halves. Any misbehaviour in the crowd and we'll have the stewards eject you. After I've set the scene with a general question, it's non-stop questions-and-answers from the floor. When you're asking a question, please identify which team you support – so we can all have a good laugh.

First, I'd like to ask each of the panellists to tell us what they've most enjoyed and what they've least enjoyed about the present season.

Gary I think this has been a great season. I feel that a lot of things have happened this year that many people have been very pleased about. I think Terry Venables is the best person for the job of England manager and under his instruction, hopefully, we will see a new England side of the future. I also feel that Manchester United have been tremendous. I've been playing in the First Division and Premier League now for the last 12 years, and United today remind me of what it was like in the early Eighties with Liverpool. I think United will easily dominate our game for the next four or five years. What's been so great about them is that they didn't rest on their laurels after winning the championship last year, but were even more hungry to get success.

And, of course, we've got to take our hats off to Arsenal. If I were an armchair supporter I would support Arsenal. I've got friends who go week in, week out, and they've been saying to me they don't particularly enjoy it all the time, but... Arsenal have success that anyone would be pleased to have – the championships they've won, the cups they've won; and, really, it's due very much to George Graham. I feel the game's in a very go-ahead phase and things are looking good for the future.

Andrew So, Tom, do we enjoy Arsenal?

Tom Yes, we do, as it happens. Do you want me to explain?

Andrew Well, I think we're a little bit tight for time...

Tom It won't take long at all. To pick out the cup defeat by Bolton Wanderers at Highbury as one of the high points of the season will give you some insight into what it is like to support Arsenal. All right, we got played out of sight in extra time by a team who, in all honesty, aren't very good. And we left Highbury ashamed and distraught, promising ourselves that we'd take more interest in the garden or walking the dog, get into computer games, anything but football. Then we opened the papers the next morning and the glee with which the rest of the country greeted that result was one of those fantastic back-handed compliments which makes you feel very, very good about supporting Arsenal. The Cup-Winners' Cup run was no accident. I don't think it would have happened without that Bolton Wanderers defeat, to be honest. It's the game I will probably remember as the highlight of the season.

The Taylor Report was, potentially at least, the most profound change to hit the game in this country since the abolition of the maximum wage for players in the early Sixties. But this season the only change I see is that people are having to sit down rather than stand up, and the sea change in the culture of football that Taylor recommended – and that the fans deserve and have been owed for at least half a century – shows no sign whatsoever of taking place. Fans are still a threat, they're untidy, they're inconvenient, they don't do what you want them to do. We've lost the North Bank, we've lost the Stretford End, we've lost the Kop, but the authorities have got the same attitude to fans in every other way that they have always had. Anybody who's been to watch their team away from home this season will have that same sense of disappointment – that you're just being asked to pay more to be treated in exactly the same way. And that's profoundly depressing.

Patrick The thing I enjoyed most was England getting knocked out of the World Cup. Are there any Scotsmen in the audience? How many? Oh, not enough to carry on in that vein…

There have been a lot of good things. Gary talked about Terry Venables and the fact that we're getting back to playing football a foreigner would recognise – I think that's definitely a good thing. I think it's particularly good to see young players coming through, especially defenders like Stubbs of Bolton and Howey of Newcastle. I also thought Norwich's performances against Inter Milan, even though they lost, were an absolute definition of how English football could, in Utopia, be played.

> **Q** I'm a Tottenham supporter. The question is this: is one of the things that is wrong with football as a professional game the fact that it needs professional referees? Or does the inconsistency of refereeing come over only to the spectator, and not to those involved?

Gary Even if you did have professional referees, there would still be inconsistency. Personally, I don't feel that professional referees would particularly enhance the game. As a player I've never been one to rant and rave at referees because I honestly believe that, through the season, it's swings and roundabouts: in one game you could get a bad call against you, and in another game something could go for you. Over a season it evens itself out.

Patrick I think the key to it, actually, is something the question itself raises in a very moderate way. What fans need to do – and in a way it is the behaviour of fans rather than the behaviour of referees that depresses me – is to say: "That's the way it goes." It does equal out over a season. Referees are going to make mistakes, and ranting on about it all the time isn't going to make a blind bit of difference. The problem is that saying that referees are inconsistent offers an opportunity for fans, for managers, for players, to blame somebody other than themselves or their favourites. Nobody ever gets beaten fair and square any more. That is a far more serious problem, in my opinion, than the inconsistency of referees.

Q Do you think football should be more politically correct and appeal to female fans as well as male?

Alex I think that if you treated fans as customers then you would behave very differently to them. Clubs look at fans in an entirely different way to the way in which, for example, a supermarket looks at its customers. If I don't like the offers at Sainsbury this week I can pop round the corner to Tesco. But if I don't like what's on offer at Highbury, I can hardly go down the road to Spurs. And clubs know that, and therefore exploit the fans for all they are worth. They only know, basically, two ways of making money – because you lot out there are going to stump up whatever the case – so they play more games and they charge higher prices. Now if they treated fans as customers they would have to think about women, and about the facilities in the stadium.

Tom To be honest, I think football itself attracts women to the game. During the Seventies there was a move away from football by women and by children, but in the last nine or ten years women have been coming back in their thousands. I think Italia '90 had a lot to do with bringing women back into the game: it was a heroic business, and perhaps women who, for a generation or two, hadn't thought of football as a way of spending their time suddenly thought: "God, this is good, this stuff," and started going along. And of course there's a knock-on effect – if you get more women coming to football grounds, then football grounds become more enjoyable places to be, and that in turn attracts more women and children.

Gary At Tottenham, and at most top clubs now, they're encouraging women's football teams. We've got a side now that are moving up through the league, and it's a very popular sport. In Norway there are nearly as

many women participating as men – this has to be encouraged from grass-roots level. Why shouldn't all children be involved in football? It's a game that they *can* all be involved in – they can play or they can go and watch.

Andrew I think a lot of women who play for teams which are attached to professional clubs would say that the key battle is being allowed to play at their main stadium. At Millwall, for example, their women's team is excellent, but they have to play at Fisher Athletic's Ground. It would be nice to see them playing at the Den.

Gary That's true, but some clubs in this country don't even let their reserve sides play on their own grounds.

Andrew Patrick, one of the ways of encouraging more women into football would perhaps be through more women writing about football. Is there a traditional male bias in the press box?

Patrick Maybe, but there's not a great surge of female football writers coming through (or male writers for that matter), and it's not because they're being stopped by commissionaires on the way in. But I think it will happen eventually, just as it's happened in the grounds. I have made quite a study of women over the years, and one thing I've noticed is that they are, on average, several inches shorter than men, and so it's natural that they would have been less likely to stand in the heaving terraces of Tom's fame, because they wouldn't have been able to see the match. So I really do think, because of the change to all-seater stadia, and for many other reasons, that we are getting towards the situation that pertains in many European countries where the sight of females going to a football match doesn't raise anybody's eyebrows. In fact, I was told that in America the proportion of male to female players is something like 48 to 52. So it's something that's happening even as we speak.

Andrew I wonder if the final comment on this point should be the Arsenal mural which, when it was originally designed, had no black people and no women in it. The average football fan, according to the designers of the Arsenal mural, was male and white.

Q I'd be very interested to hear the panel's views as to whether they think the FA has a role to play in combating racism in football.

Patrick At the *Observer*, a sports reporter who happens to be black decided he would go to a Chelsea match as a fan. He expected to hear all kinds of abuse, not only directed towards him but also towards black players on the field. He came back and said there was no problem at all, it was lovely. I simply pass that on for what it's worth.

Gary I think that in the PFA we feel that the problem is always going to be among a minority of people. Over the last decade I think the improvements made have been excellent. Paul Ince was abused when West Ham played Manchester United, but if you've got a crowd of 32,000 and you get five people chucking things onto the pitch it becomes a big thing. You can do everything possible, but you can never stop the mindless idiot who's going to want to do things like that. Also, football supporters are always going to be looking for something different to wind somebody up about, whether it be his colour, the fact that he wears a toupée, maybe the fact that he's a diabetic. Whatever you do, there are all sorts of different things that they will shout and I think you will never stop that senseless minority. The best thing is that it's a very small minority.

Tom Well, at Arsenal we've got a funny situation. We've got a very multi-racial team and very multi-racial support these days. But we do have this incredible tradition of anti-Semitism that relates directly to the rivalry with Tottenham, and has done since the Forties at least. When teams come down and their supporters boo our black players, you can sit there and think: "You ignorant pigs," but when Tottenham come down and you listen to people everywhere in the ground singing songs about gassing Yiddos, it just chills you to the bone. Anti-Semitism is our brand of racism. We say we're not racist, but of course we are – twice a season when we play Tottenham. I've talked to a lot of supporters, particularly Jewish supporters, about how they feel about that, and how they think the situation had developed, and you are left with an impression very close to what Gary was saying, that racism is rather like hooliganism – you know who the hard lads are, they're 100 to 200 people who are there for the ruck, not there for the football.

Football hooliganism became what seemed like a mass problem because there were an enormous number of impressionable adolescent males in the company of those 100 or 200 committed violent, unpleasant people. There's a huge mass that will follow along in the wake of a committed minority. That minority is where attention has to be focused. Other fans, and players in particular, are in a unique position to influence the hangers-on. In the same way that closed-circuit television cameras and better relationships between clubs and police enabled the hard core of football hooligans to be moved out of the stadia, the same thing has to be done with the committed minority of racists, of anti-Semites, of whoever it is, whose behaviour is unacceptable to the vast majority of people who want to watch football. That minority has to be identified by the police and by clubs and be got rid of. And the hangers-on then either find something else to hang on to, or can be educated by the efforts of the other fans who are standing around them, and by the players who, after all, are the reason those people are there in the stadium in the first place.

Andrew Well, it's been a great match but time's running out – the ref's looking at his watch so we'd better round up for the evening. One final question?

> **Q** What is so special about football; what makes it so compelling for all of you?

Patrick It's going to an immense stadium like the San Siro or the Nou Camp, sitting in the press box but getting a real shiver of excitement and thinking how wonderful, how thrilling, it would be to be down there on the pitch.

Gary As a player, it has to be the fact that you are going out there week after week and hopefully giving pleasure to so many people.

Alex Jackie Milburn, Rodney Marsh, Frank Worthington, Gazza... and Gus Caesar.

Tom It would be that, even after 30 years of watching the same club, next Saturday brings the possibility of the team being more exciting (or more awful) than you can ever remember.

Andrew It's a wet Tuesday night in November, watching Leyton Orient play Bournemouth in the preliminary round of the Autoglass Trophy along with 700 other diehards – and seeing them win one-nil.

Patrick Oh, you old romantic, you.

CHAPTER 31 **An Evil Cradling**

BRIAN KEENAN was born in Belfast, reading English at Coleraine University and then working in Brussels and Spain. On his return to Ireland he taught at his former school and worked in community development centres across Belfast before taking an MA in Anglo-Irish literature. Seeking to satisfy an inner hunger and wanting a change from Belfast, Brian took up a position at Beirut University in 1985, becoming headline news when he was kidnapped by fundamentalist Shi'ite militiamen and held hostage for four-and-a-half years.

Brian's incarceration, his incredible bond with fellow-prisoner John McCarthy and his eventual release, made spellbinding reading in his book, *An Evil Cradling*. When we invited Brian to give a seminar, we told him he was not obliged to talk about his time as a hostage, but could choose any subject he wished. Brian developed a talk on the theme of "Peace". It was a visionary choice as, when he gave his talk at Newell and Sorrell in May 1994, it was just a few weeks before the IRA declared a cease-fire in Northern Ireland.

Brian's talk drew our biggest audience ever. He began by telling us he would rather have been locked up with Arab terrorists than have to speak under the glare of our spotlights. There was no evidence of nerves, however, in the composed, eloquent and moving speech he gave.

Peace.

It seems for weeks now, perhaps months, that the papers have been full of it. Insightful analysts have dissected it. Albert Reynolds and John Major have pledged themselves on paper to it. Scurrilous hacks have condemned it or dismissed it and, more depressingly, television screens have been glaring with the rage of those who will not tolerate it. David Owen labours like Hercules in Bosnia. John Hume and Gerry Adams have met and continue in a kind of secret conclave. There's some talk of American peace envoys. Nelson Mandela and the white protagonists of apartheid have somehow reached a questionable accommodation. Johan Holst, Norway's foreign minister, has apparently, we are told, brought together the Semitic cousins of the Middle East to declare enough is enough. Peace, it seems, is breaking out all over. Or is it?

The desire for peace is laudable and certainly highly commendable, but it is only a beginning – and a very small and fragile beginning. So often in the past I have heard the peacemongers chant their war cry and, ideally, I would have joined their chorus. But always one thought held me hesitant. No single, issue-based, popular peace movement either here or abroad has ever been successful in brokering the peace.

The question that such naive idealism leaves half-unanswered remains: "What is this peace?" Surely, unless people have a vision of what the peace might be – something *active*, something *habitable*, a peace that has a meaning beyond a cessation of violence – it is like no more than an exquisite painting which hangs in a darkened room. We have no engagement with it; we are hardly aware of its presence; it neither touches us nor influences us; we pass it by unknowing and ignorant.

Peace must be fleshy and whole. People must be able to smell it, people must be able to see it, to taste it, to touch it. Only then will they really want possession of it and only then will an insatiable desire demand absolute satisfaction.

So it is precisely this vacuum about what peace means that allows, in my own country, internecine feuding to continue. But, more importantly, this vacuum does not provide the challenge that present redundant political thinking requires to revitalise itself, to remake itself and to make itself effective and creative in a peace ethos. And I take the view that to shape, to colour and to give texture to a meaningful vision of the peace, we must first come to an understanding of what it is in us that imprisons us, that blurs and limits the vision.

About six months ago I was asked to speak at a conference in Derry City, and to address the theme "Beyond Hate". I thought, my God, where do you begin? And my only beginning was in the affirmation that hate exists. The history of humankind and, I suppose, part of each of our personal histories, is marked and scarred by its fearful presence. What is it that exists at the other end of hate? And is it necessary to drink from that hellish cauldron the better to purge ourselves of it? In order to overcome it and to redirect ourselves from it we must first understand our point of departure.

In looking for a starting point I ran out to the shop, bought a copy of *Roget's Thesaurus* and leafed through it. I got very tired after finding approximately 87 definitions of "hate". And each of them and all of them collectively seemed to me unsatisfactory. But they were signals, signposts along the way. What was that experience of hate, how did hate become part of what we call the human condition? Conceived with its roots and feelings of alienation, despondence, confusion, frustration and ultimately disassociation, hate is an outward and collective expression of an isolating, emotional turmoil. And in such conditions we are exposed to our faults, our fears and our desires, and these are accompanied by shame and guilt. We want no-one to see us as we see ourselves. We hide behind all kinds of recriminations and despise those who have what we cannot have: acceptance, companionship, fellowship. We become shadow creatures, baying and barking out our own irresolution. The world that we inhabit is negative and we can create nothing in it.

What, then, is the antidote to this raging poison? How can we find that quality within us that reunites us with the world and places us in creative empathy with our fellow man? I cannot and would not dare to pose a solution, nor can I give ready-made answers, beyond suggesting that it is only by first asking the right questions.

And in asking the right questions, we might hint or taste or view that antidote. We might be able to break out from what, I fear, has become a restrictive and culturally determined world view. To release us from the prison of fear, we must seek out that which creates and sustains the desire to live without dependence or submission to any authority. There can be no limited perspectives nor any particular exemptions. Liberation must be total and there must be nothing partial in its resolution. As such, it cannot be simply a passive reconciliation. It must be active, dynamic, always seeking interaction with another to make itself complete and consequently expand its own potential.

Too often we see the struggle around us as destructive interchanges which bring no good to any of the contestants. And all too often we then believe that peace means an absence of this conflict. But the peace I envisage is ultimately about conflict. It seems to me that most conflicts that we engage in are attempts to avoid real and meaningful conflict. They are, if you like, cover-ups. Real conflicts do not seek to cover up. They are experiences on the deep, existential level of our being and they are not destructive. They lead to clarification and to a catharsis from which both parties emerge with more knowledge and more strength. Wholeness and unity are only possible if people engage in this rich and meaningful conflict, communicating from the very centre of their existence and not from peripheral things.

Geographical borders and political rhetoric are not, and never can be, the full measure of our experience. How can we exercise such a passionate force? As in any creative enterprise, I'm sure that discipline and objectivity are the essentials. Discipline prevents us from being redirected into things that are not the expression of our own will. And when we think objectively we employ the facility of reason, and the emotional attitude that activates that reason is always, for me, one of a proud humanity. It ensures balance and communicable understanding. It allows me to see the difference between my picture of a person and that person's reality, independent of *my* needs, *my* fears, *my* preoccupations. Ultimately, it means thinking in a renewing way.

To be so actively self-challenging requires a special kind of faith, I think. And I will be quick and careful here to explain that I don't speak in terms of religious doctrine. I think this is a submission to an irrational authority that is divisive, as marked by the religious wars of history. But a secular and a rational faith, rooted in one's own experience and thought and in feeling, produces above all a certainty and self-confidence. And this carries with it a rich and intellectual emotional activity. The rational and scientific founders of the world as we understand it, Copernicus, Galileo, Newton and many more, were all dreamers and visionaries who each had this passionate, rational faith in the ultimate correctness of their vision. And, furthermore, set out to make it so.

Some philosophy, the school of which I can't recall (because I have a terrible habit of reading things and only remembering half of them), defined man by his ability to promise. Having a rational faith enables us to project ourselves into that promise and to make it more than a promise, to make it a reality. Without doubt, this is risk-taking and it is also courageous. It does not hide behind defensive systems or become the prisoner of its own insecurity. The man who has moved beyond hate commits himself absolutely and without guarantee. His outstretched hand bears no deceit and hides nothing, for it cannot.

But, as we all know, peace is not achieved in the twinkling of an eye, but is rather – and hopefully – in a continual state of becoming. The revolutionary peacemaker is energised and activated for the object of his concern; and that is the whole and total social realm. However, in this modern age of ours, the language of such compassionate commitment is too often met by fear, with its catcalls, or by the cynicism of silence. Such nihilism is trapped in a kind of unresolved despair and a fatal resignation from which, and I'm sure we have all seen it, the poisonous flower of hatred will spread its ugly seed. And I'm sure, like myself, we have all heard its hissing echo too much of late.

A commitment, then, to a meaningful peace means putting mankind in the supreme place. The economic machine and the political structure must serve him, rather than he serve it. Society must be organised in such a way that man's social and loving nature is not separate from his social existence. If the problem of human existence is, and I believe it is, somehow eased and even enriched by the fullest expression of love in all its diverse forms, then any community which *excludes* such an application is in contradiction with basic and essential human necessity. Such a society or such a community will inevitably and awfully self-destruct. For peace to be more than an eloquent echo, for peace to be a vision, coloured with a palpable and potential reality, I borrow words from a finer man than me and quote: "Let us only believe. May we believe the harder and the more despairingly as reality seems more threatening and irreducible, and then little by little we shall see the universal horror relax and smile at us and enfold us in more than human arms." Thus wrote a better thinker than I could ever be.

To kind of conclude, I think before people sign documents and structure peace, we must begin to examine things that have occurred, that have formed us and shaped us and scarred and marked us. And peace has to be total, it has to take hold of everybody and every part of everyone. And it can't be a peace given by politicians, it cannot be a peace given by paramilitaries, but it can be a peace which each of us can claim, because the capacity to live richly and in peace – whatever that means – is a part, and a very singular part, of each one of us. I have a calm but stubborn hope that the word "peace" can be made real and given an act of meaningfulness by all of us, not just those who wear the labels of the crown or of leadership, or those who tote the guns of liberation.

After Brian's talk he answered questions from the audience, some of which are reproduced here.

Question If you had not been abducted in Beirut, where do you think you would be today, and what sort of person would we now see in front of us?

Answer Oh dear. What would I be today? When I went to Lebanon I went for two reasons: because I was really sick and tired of Belfast and its irresolution... and because somebody told me the women were good-looking there. My intention was only to stay for a year, then I wanted to go further east. So I wouldn't be living in Ireland or England, I would probably be somewhere further east of the Middle East. I would probably still be teaching. But I would have a different set of values. Because that's what I came home with, a different set of values, a different world perspective that I wouldn't have acquired if I had not gone on my holidays for four-and-a-half years.

Q A question about hatred – how do you teach people not to hate? Northern Ireland, Palestine, Israel – how do you get rid of the hate?

A That's difficult, because it's very hard for people collectively to pinpoint what their hatred is, because it's an awful word to come to terms with. I visit Derry City a lot when I'm home. According to news reporters, our troubles first began in 1968. But the people there in Derry City – not by the leadership of politicians, but of themselves – have created another Derry in which the paramilitaries and the politicians have no place. They've created their own, new, tiny piece of civilisation. I'm quite amazed by the transformation that's occurred, to the extent that I think possibly what is happening in Derry City will be the blueprint for what can possibly happen in Bosnia or Eastern Europe. I think something vital is happening there. Maybe Derry City drank from that hellish cauldron and choked it all back up again. I see it happening and I see it working in a place where nobody would ever expect it to work. And I'm quite confident that in ten years' time, whatever happens in the Middle East, they'll see delegations of people coming from that beleaguered city to talk to people in Derry, and they'll be asking how it happened.

Q The Home Secretary claims that prison works in certain terms. I just wondered how your experiences had shaped your views of imprisonment within criminal justice?

A I can't find anything in me that tells me with any sort of affirmation that locking people up is going to cure whatever the problem is. I do sometimes have the sense that, although the crime might be committed by person A, the motivation and the reason for it comes from a more collective and a more communal source, and in that sense we're all guilty for perpetrating, or for living in and supporting, a type of society that almost implicitly encourages people to break the law.

The other thing, the lesson that I brought home with me from Lebanon, was one that was burnt into me for a long time. A man can take my liberty, he can chain me to a wall or chain me to a radiator, he can beat the living daylights out of me if he wants, but what he can never, ever, do in a hundred thousand million years, is take my freedom. Because I alone possess that. I alone give that meaning. I alone give that shape and force and direction. If only those who are quick to condemn and quick to lock up would grasp, just for a minute, that thought and say: "Well, if that is the case with each person who is in prison, then why can't we build on that?" Can you imagine how dangerous it is to lock people up for whatever length of time if they have a firm belief in personal freedom? Prison's not going to do anything at all. Locking away for years somebody who has the potential to be rich, creative, valuable, meaningful, ultimately won't do anything.

Q The last question is in two parts. The first part is serious – what are your plans for the future? And the second part is a bit less serious – where do you go on your holidays these days?

A When I was locked up, there were these people who used to come and visit me. Not real people, just in the air. They occupied me for hours and hours and weeks and weeks and we'd sit and talk, finding out about them and who they were. And one of these strange characters that came walking, stumbling, into my cell was a blind harper, straight out of 16th century Ireland, and we had a real hammer and tongs together for, I remember, three months. When I came home, he came home with me. He's been pestering me ever since. So I spend what time I can at Trinity College in Dublin researching into this man. His music is superb and quite unique. We shouldn't really call it Irish, it's something very different and very special, but nobody knows the man. Everybody knows the music and the myth, but not the man. And the more I read into it, the more complex I find him.

And as for my holidays, I'd really love to go, or did want to go, to Peru, but somebody threatened me that I'd end up in *The Guinness Book of Records,* so I decided not to bother.

CHAPTER 32 **2020 Vision**

GEOFFREY LAMB was born in South Africa, where he was a journalist and political prisoner; he is now an Irish citizen. He took postgraduate studies at the University of Sussex, and was later fellow and deputy director of the Institute of Development Studies there.

Geoffrey joined the World Bank in 1980 and worked all over the world – including Africa, Asia, Russia and Palestine – before heading a group working on the transition countries of the former Soviet Union, Eastern Europe and the Middle East. He is now the head of the Bank's office in London.

What will the world be like in 2020? Given the pace of social, political and economic change over the last 25 years, it's a brave man who will even attempt an answer. Geoffrey was that brave man and, in September 1994, he gave us an informed, global analysis of how population growth and economic change would alter our world beyond all expectations.

What will the world look like in 20 or 30 years time? And how will we get there in a way that delivers most welfare to as many people as possible?

I'll start off with the World Bank, which was started 50 years ago by John Maynard Keynes (among others) and is based in Washington. It's an institution that's owned by about 180 member governments, which means most governments in the world. We raise money from investors in the world's bond markets and lend it to developing countries – countries which most investors wouldn't dream of lending to directly. And it works pretty well, because we can borrow money in the world's capital markets on pretty much the same terms as, say, the US Treasury or the UK Government, and then lend it on to poor countries which would otherwise have a great deal of difficulty in getting money for their development needs.

We've lent about 300 billion in historic dollars – about 650 billion in today's dollars – since the World Bank was set up. We lend for things like dams and bridges and irrigation schemes and roads and power plants in third world countries. We also lend for education, for the fight against river blindness in Africa, for the fight against glaucoma in India; we lend for maternal health programmes, welfare programmes, nutrition programmes – social stuff, and also the hardware and infrastructure of economic growth.

Now, the irony is that what we do seems to me to be a fairly incontrovertibly good thing – it's broadly on the side of the angels. But the problem is that many of our natural allies – non-government organisations, the liberal media and so on – are pretty much turning against us. They think we're not helping the poorest of the poor very effectively. They think that in order to make sure our loans are paid back we impose economic provisions which make the poorest people in the world suffer. And some would also claim that we help finance the wrecking of the world's environment.

One striking fact is that our critics think we're much more powerful than we are. In 1994 the World Bank lent or disbursed about $20 billion to developing countries. It sounds like a lot of money. But private capital flows to developing countries were more than seven times higher, at about $150 billion. What we do, generally, is to come in where the market fails. The environment and education are examples of areas that we are especially concerned with because the private sector is not going to finance them on a grand scale. And we need to make sure that governments have sensible economic policies and responsible economic management – otherwise the best investments in rural health or clean water will be largely wasted. No government likes that sort of external discipline and, frankly, we often carry the can.

We're in what we think of as a sort of global mission to do good. But to do good on sound economic principles is an enormous challenge, and we're having to re-think what we do, what our priorities are, what the world is going to look like, what the big needs are going to be, and whether we really can deliver what is expected from us by sensible people who are interested in welfare, economic growth and development.

There are roughly five-and-a-half billion people on the planet now. In 2020 there'll be about eight-and-a-half billion. That's actually good news, because it's about a billion less than we thought it was going to be. So, relatively speaking, we're doing pretty well. But of the three billion extra human beings that are going to be here in 2020, about 90 per cent will be in developing countries. And two-thirds of those, say two billion, will be in the very poorest countries where, in today's terms, most people have an income of less than two dollars a day.

So we're talking about huge increments of people – less than we thought, but still huge increments of people – in countries which are going to have a very difficult time absorbing them, feeding them, providing jobs, providing transport infrastructures, providing education and so on. So that is a constraining and overwhelming fact about the world of 2020.

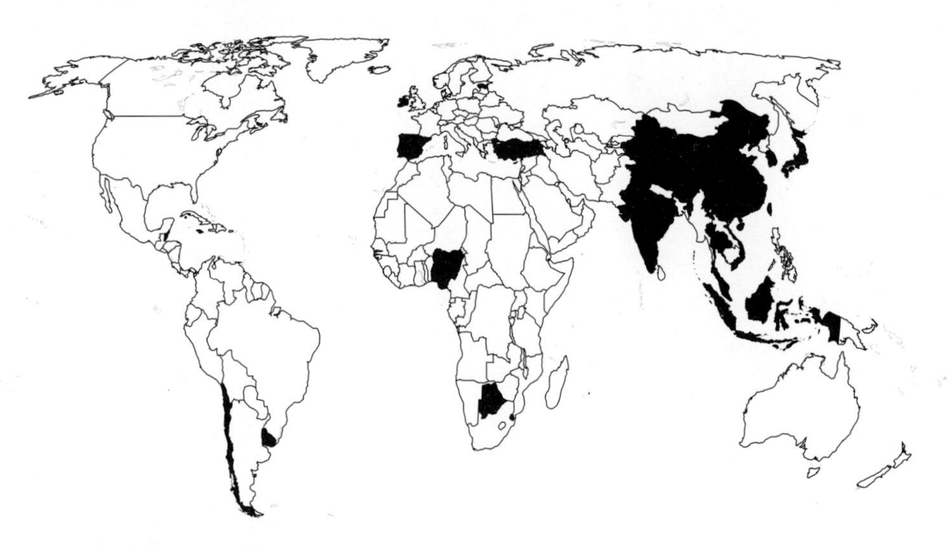

Population growth rate, 1985-93
Areas shown indicate average annual change of more than 2.2%

People are the first factor. Second are resources. Are there going to be enough to go around? If developing countries are really going to grow, an awful lot, by 2020, what's going to happen? Well, most of these new people are going to live in cities, coastal plains and river basins. In all the places where the world is most fragile. The fastest area of population growth is going to be in Africa (take a look at the map above), which is both the poorest region and the region where the natural ecology of the countryside, the soil, the trees, the water, is at its most fragile. At the same time, more Chinese are going to get cars and air conditioning. Indians are going to get fridges. More people will be working in factories, more people will demand food, which means more fertilizer and pesticides. There will be more polyfluorocarbons in the atmosphere, unless new technologies for refrigeration, air conditioners and the rest are universally adopted. So the growth area for pollution is going to be in the developing countries.

But although it's easy to imagine a scenario where there are going to be all these people cutting down rainforests, chopping down trees and polluting water, it's worth remembering that in the next 30 years *most* environmental degradation and pollution in the world will happen in countries like ours. Quantitatively, most pollution that's spewed out into the air, into the oceans, into the rivers, and most chemicals which poison us or our children in ways that we don't even know yet, will continue to be produced in Europe, North America and Japan. It's not the developing countries that are the biggest problem about the world environment. It's us.

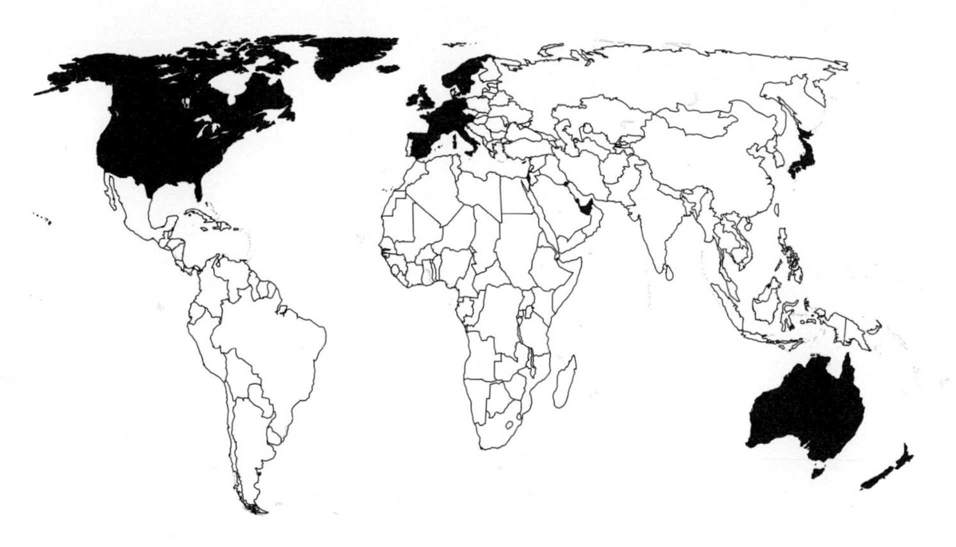

GNP per capita, 1993
Areas shown indicate income of US$8,626 or more

Here's a map showing wealth distribution around the world. To give you a notion of wealth, the world's GNP is around $22 trillion a year in 1992 prices. The areas that I've marked have about $18 trillion dollars of that production. There are three-and-a-half billion people in the world and the people within the marked areas account for less than a billion of them. So we currently have a situation in which countries such as Canada, the US, Japan and the European Union are living at a level which is commanding more than three-quarters of the world's annual production, yet accounting for only a quarter to a third of the world population. In rough terms, the shaded countries have average incomes of about $17,600 per head per year, compared to $70 in Mozambique or $2,000 in Poland.

Where are we going? Will this imbalance continue, or will economic growth in less well-off parts of the world affect wealth distribution by 2020? The answer is (as the map below shows) that China, India, South East Asia, Thailand, Malaysia and Indonesia are growing rapidly, and if you were to project that pattern of growth forward you would see some big changes in the balance of the world's production and wealth. The good news about the next 30 years is that the big, poor countries – China, India, Indonesia, maybe Brazil, maybe some other Latin American countries such as Chile and, conceivably, Argentina – have economies that are growing fast, and look set to continue with that pattern of economic growth. But they are not among the countries where there are very high and continuing rates of population growth.

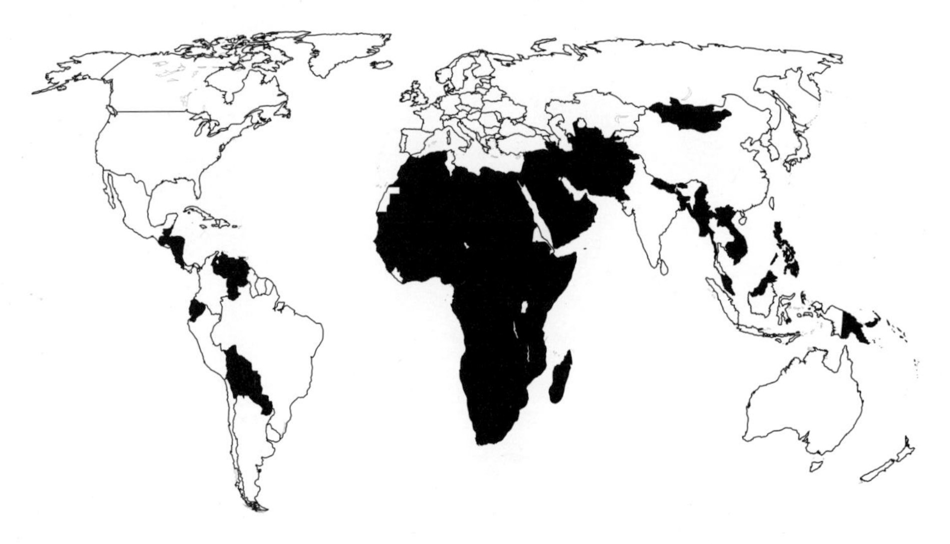

GNP per capita growth rate, 1985-93
Areas shown indicate average annual change of more than 3.0%

Africa, by comparison, is in agony. At present one in every nine people in the world, roughly speaking, is an African. In 2020, on current trends, one in six people will be an African and, by the end of the next century, one in four people in the world will be an African. The problem with such rapid population growth is that, any way you cut it, over the next 30 years Africa is going to grow economically really slowly, if at all. So there are going to be few African countries, unless there's a huge change for the better, that will consistently become more wealthy in terms of income per head.

So if you're trying to figure out the major trends for 2020, you'd be thinking along the following lines:

Population on a global basis looks okay, despite big regional variations, the most important one of which is the potential disaster of Africa.

Employment also looks okay because the places where you need the most jobs – India, China and Indonesia – are where you're going to get the most jobs, because they're going to be growing fastest. In the rest of the world jobs are going to depend a great deal on the flexibility of companies, economies and workers. In most industrial countries you can bet that the decline in jobs in manufacturing is going to continue, because the countries that are growing fastest are going to take them. And that's fine, as long as everybody else moves to do things that they can do better; as long as there is that flexibility in the world economy.

Resources – and therefore living standards – are probably okay, always remembering the African question mark, with two provisos. One is that when people first start getting richer, they consume a lot more of everything and waste a lot of resources. When you get richer still, you start to buy relatively less, it's of higher quality and your country has the money to have environmental standards, so you use fewer resources per unit of output than you used to. The other proviso is that, comparing current production with that of, say, 1960, the world now uses about 25 per cent less resources to make the same output. In other words, you use less copper tubing, less steel, less petroleum; you use less of everything because technology is becoming more efficient. So, overall, the use of resources for people to live well is going down.

As another thought, what do you think are our priorities when the World Bank tries to determine its role over the next 30 years?

Number one: we think it's pretty important that governments continue to have flexible, open economies, to be oriented towards trade and not to be protectionist.

Number two: we think we have to help countries invest in people. If you look at the Asian tigers whose growth is going off the map, the biggest thing that they did was to invest in education, basic health care and primary access to human services. And they made sure that when opportunities came along, people were flexible, educated, ready to grab. So we think empowerment of people is central.

Number three: we think investing in the environment is pretty important. The biggest single growth area by about the second or third decade of the next century is going to be environmental investment, especially at a very basic level. And if rich countries want to protect the environment, they are going to have to pay poor countries for it. If I was a decision-maker in China or India I'd say: "I don't give a damn that you don't want me spewing dirty brown coal into the atmosphere, I can't afford to invest in coal scrubbers. You've mucked up the world's atmosphere for 150 years, now you want us to pay for every marginal bit of muck that goes into the atmosphere. That's not fair. You pay for it; we can't afford to." So some mechanism is going to have to be found to do that.

Of course, one problem about all of this is that it assumes that the world will be governed in a more or less orderly fashion. But what we've seen in recent years is the emergence of social breakdown and failure at the level of whole nations. Yugoslavia, Afghanistan, Rwanda, Somalia, Sudan, Mozambique, Algeria teetering on the edge. There is a sense in which the old sureties of government, nation states and orderly control are breaking down in big areas of the world.

Another problem is human rights. The era is passing in which any international body can be only concerned with economic questions, and contend that human rights are essentially a political question for individual governments to deal with. The whole inter-relationship between human rights, social breakdown, migration, who ends up in your airports, who lands up in the refugee camps, is becoming interlocked with every other question, including economic questions, and somehow it's got to be dealt with.

It's a tough one. Some, in the name of our common humanity, would press the international community not to extend a single dollar to some countries until they stop the outrageous treatment of girls in terms of access to education, or not to allow them to trade internationally until they stop child labour in the carpet industry, and so on. But what do you do about the fact that carpets represent a sizable slice not only of exports, but also of the incomes of whole communities? We need some sort of umbrella agreement on such economic and social human rights between governments – to get more serious about making human rights economically possible over a reasonable time trajectory. We've got to be realistic about time. There is not going to be an end to child brick-making labour in India this century, no matter what the international community says. These things always move more slowly than one would like.

We've got to see that preventable poverty is as bad a transgression against human rights as torture or denial of political freedom. And we have to see, too, that they're all connected.

The final question is this: who, actually, will have the power in 2020 to make effective decisions on all these matters? What we've been witnessing over the last ten or 15 years is the declining power of governments to control economic or political events. We are seeing the explosion in communications technology begin to change our world fundamentally, in ways which governments and individuals can only dimly comprehend. We've seen a rise in the power and economic influence of international corporations – which have a big interest in stability, but are not equipped (and I think few of us would want them to be equipped) to enforce a global social compact. And we've seen the emergence of a different, and profoundly negative, kind of multi-national power (which even fewer of us would want) – an international mafia profiting from drugs, from arms, and from the interregnum between the command economy and the market in parts of the post-socialist world.

If one has a decline in the power of governments to exercise power, and at the same time a huge rise in poverty and social breakdown combined with very rapid social changes, that whole nexus of drugs, crime, mafias, trans-border flows, it's going to be a big headache – which I doubt will be solved by 2020.

REBECCA MEITLIS was co-director of English National Opera's Baylis Programme, which aims to introduce people of all ages to the enjoyment of opera. From a kernel of an idea that she had on a train, Rebecca commissioned, produced and directed the Baylis Programme's *Arion and the Dolphin*, one of the most ambitious creative events of 1994.

ALEC ROTH AND VIKRAM SETH were the other key figures in the production. Alec, a distinguished composer, devised the music, while Vikram, a best-selling author, wrote the libretto. The opera was performed by four professional singers, the Bournemouth Sinfonietta and over 400 local people from Devon and Cornwall. It was a triumph of teamwork, mixing artistic virtuosity with entrepreneurial skills, laughter with logistics and music with poetry.

Our evening at Newell and Sorrell in November 1994 was a similar triumph of teamwork, with Rebecca, Alec and Vikram taking turns to recount their story of the making of an opera. It was a remarkable and enchanting tale, which began with a quotation from Douglas Adam's *The Hitch-hiker's Guide to the Galaxy...*

"It's an important and popular fact that things are not always what they seem. For instance, on the planet Earth, man had always assumed that he was more intelligent than dolphins because he had achieved so much – the wheel, New York, wars and so on – whilst all the dolphins had ever done was muck about in the water having a good time. But conversely, the dolphins had always believed that they were far more intelligent than man – for precisely the same reason."

Rebecca That appears in the introduction to *Falling for a Dolphin*, a wonderful poem by Heathcote Williams. This mad idea for a community opera about dolphins began when I was sitting on a train outside Victoria Station. I was reading *Falling for a Dolphin*, and as I reached the end of the poem I was so moved that I burst into tears.

The Baylis Programme has commissioned three operas before. This time we wanted to involve not only children (we've done a lot of work with children), but also adults, people who just sing in the bath, people who were told as children that they couldn't sing – we wanted to give them all a chance to be in an opera. We were also very interested in working with people who have hearing problems. What's amazing about dolphins is that they live in a world where they feel sound, their whole body vibrates with sound, and they communicate through vibrations. This was a theme throughout.

So, having decided to do an opera about dolphins that involved adults, children, and people with hearing difficulties, I had to think of a composer. Right from the very beginning I wanted Alec Roth. Alec is the country's leading expert on gamelan, a type of Javanese orchestral music, and he has pioneered its use in schools, where everyone can make music together.

Alec agreed to write the music, so our next step was to find someone to write the words. I gave Alec a copy of Vikram Seth's *The Golden Gate*, because when I read it I thought not only could this amazing writer tell an entertaining story in verse, he could also make you laugh – maybe he could write a libretto.

Alec I read *The Golden Gate* and, like so many people, I found it absolutely wonderful. I rushed out to buy everything else by Vikram as well – that wonderful travel book *From Heaven Lake* and a book of poems called *The Humble Administrator's Garden*. And as I looked through those poems I felt I just had to set some of them to music. So I wrote to Vikram, not knowing him at all. He very generously gave me permission to set his poems to music, with one condition: when he was next in London he would like to hear what the results were. So we met, and I very nervously played through some of the settings of his poems, and he said: "Yes, that's fine, now why don't we do some Schubert?" So we got out the Schubert and Vikram sang while I played. To discover Vikram's love of music confirmed something that I'd felt intuitively. As Rebecca said, his writing makes you laugh, it makes you cry – and it also makes me hear music, all the time.

But Vikram wasn't interested in opera at all, so I asked him if he would write a song cycle with me instead.

Vikram What happened next was very odd. Quite apart from not liking opera, I was working on a long novel which was occupying most of my energies, and the idea that I should be diverted, golden apple-like, from my course didn't appeal to me at all. On the other hand, having heard Alec's settings of my poems, one of the things that struck me most about his music was how very verbal it was. Writers are used to being entirely ignored, your verse used as a sort of trampoline for the musician's inspiration. Not so in Alec's case. There was a true wedding of the words and the music.

So I was in two minds about the idea of writing the libretto. But after seeing two very odd operas when I was travelling around Europe, I suddenly felt that this project might be fun. When I got back to England Alec said: "Have you thought about my song cycle?" And I said: "I'll write an opera." Before I could say any more he dragged me to the ENO and sat me down with Rebecca.

Now until that evening I had no idea that what Rebecca had in mind was a dolphin opera. I said: "How interesting, Rebecca," Alec and I looked at each other across the table and I thought: "I'm as 'green' as the next man; I like dolphins, nice animals. But an opera about dolphins?"

Anyway, I got to thinking about it and a few days later the Greek story of Arion, who was saved from drowning by a dolphin, came to my mind. There, it struck me, was a theme – a human story – I could work with. When I suggested this to Alec, he came up with the fact that Arion had been a musician at the court of Periander, the tyrant of Corinth, and that this would play into our operatic hands. Since I had to leave London the next day and had a number of visits to make, we discussed our ideas on the upper decks of several red buses.

Alec What appealed to me about Vikram's suggestion was that Arion was a musician – a composer and a singer. The idea of an opera about a singer was very interesting, and this piece ended up being all about the power of music and song. The music comes from the words. Often Vikram's words strike a deep chord in me and I can almost hear the melodies come out of them from the start. The libretto is amazing, very rhythmical, and contains almost every verse form as well as prose.

Rebecca Having persuaded Vikram to take part, we developed the storyline. Arion goes to Sicily to a song festival, but on the way back the ship's crew mutiny and threaten to kill him. He leaps overboard singing a wonderful song, which attracts the dolphins. Act One finale.

In Act Two, we planned that Arion would go into the dolphin world and experience what it's like to be a dolphin. But we couldn't write this part, because we really didn't know much about dolphins. We looked at all the books, and then Alec decided he should go to the top. He wrote to Dr Horace Dobbs, one of the world's leading experts on dolphins, who invited us to go to Dingle with him.

In Dingle, on the south-west coast of Ireland, there is a wild hermit dolphin known as Funghie. The plan was that we would swim with this dolphin in the mornings, then Horace would educate us each afternoon, then we'd swim again, then go and have a Guinness. Which we certainly did.

We were incredibly lucky, because every day we went out, in the freezing cold, and every day we saw Funghie. We had the most amazing time. Dolphins are so playful, and have so much energy. When this beast rises out of the water you feel its exhilaration, its joy and curiosity. It was as though he was saying: "Who are these people who want to write an opera about me? I'd better give them a good show!"

Alec We got such a thrill from being with the dolphin that it gave us a lot of ideas about developing the libretto. In fact, going to Dingle completely changed how we thought about the opera, and the dolphins took on a more important role. We felt we just had to give more time to the scene where Arion meets the dolphin, and try to get some of its playfulness

across. Especially since we were going to be working with a lot of children, who were going to be the dolphins.

Vikram The strength of the opera for me was Alec's rendering of the human element – the captain of the ship who befriends Arion on the way out and is forced to betray him on the way back because of his crew's lust for the prizes that Arion has won. This is what gave me the spine of the opera. I couldn't have written a libretto solely about playful dolphins frolicking around and being wise.

So I agreed to go to Ireland, but I did not expect that Funghie the dolphin would have anything like such a profound effect on me. There was something about that particular dolphin which inspired everything that came after. When I reworked the part where Arion hears the news of the dolphin's death, it was informed by my sense of this wonderful animal.

We would never have got the kind of response we did, particularly from the children, if the opera hadn't been infused by that spirit in the writing of the words and, even more, in the writing of the music.

Alec I'll just give you a concrete example of how Funghie influenced the development of the opera. The first evening we arrived in Dingle I went down to the shore to look for the dolphin. The sea was very still and I was sure that it wouldn't come. Suddenly, the most extraordinary thing happened: I heard a sound as if someone were blowing in my ear. I turned to see who was there, just in time to catch sight of a dolphin disappearing under the surface again. So my first contact with the dolphin was hearing it breathe, with such a human sound. And for me that solved the problem of how we first meet the dolphins in the opera. I did exactly what Funghie had done for me, so in the opera you hear the dolphins breathing together before you see them. Watching the dolphin from a boat, too, I was exhilarated by its acrobatic displays, leaping into the air and diving under the boat. I tried to convey through my music something of its movement and sheer joy of life.

Rebecca When we got back from Dingle we needed to start getting an idea of who was going to perform this opera. We knew it was to be a community, we knew we wanted the involvement of schools, we thought it might be a good project to do outside London, preferably by the seaside, and we were looking for a place that was not a standard theatrical space.

We wrote to all the regional arts boards with a project proposal, and it was Keith Nimmo from South West Arts who picked it up. He put us in touch with the Theatre Royal in Plymouth, which has a wonderful tradition in community theatre, and with the Bournemouth Orchestras, who are of international standing and are based down in the South West.

South West Arts applied to a Marks & Spencer scheme on our behalf and Helen Corbishley, a personnel manager, was seconded by them to be our project manager. Helen had the impossible task of walking into English National Opera to do a project that had never been done before. One of her first tasks was to find a wonderful venue. And she found a drill shed at HMS Drake, one of the active naval bases in Plymouth; an amazing space.

We had months of fund-raising activities, and began to collaborate with schools, students and teachers. The brief to Alec, Vikram and Henk Schut (the designer) was that they should leave gaps in the structures where students could have their own creative input. That is incredibly difficult to do, because it's very hard handing your vision over to somebody else.

Alec There had to be something for everyone. I also hoped it would appeal to a wide audience, many coming to opera for the first time. We wanted to give all the participants the chance to use both their skill and their creativity and, though carefully structured, the opera is written so that some opportunities for improvisation by performers are built into it. Opera is a collaborative activity – we were not just interested in the sounds of music, but also in the process that makes people make those sounds. So I provided the score as if it were a recipe and the people of Plymouth were cooking a meal with it; we were all in the kitchen making that meal; we all had a hand in creating the opera.

Rebecca Throughout the project, creative partnerships of many different people worked towards the final production. Henk worked on the design with students of jewellery, metalwork, fashion technology and fine art;

Denni Sayers collaborated with students from the sign choir of Eggbuckland Community College to integrate sign language into the choreography; Seona Pritchard liaised between primary schools and the Bournemouth Sinfonietta so that the children's musical ideas could be developed and performed by professional musicians. And for months we worked with primary schoolchildren who, through movement, painting, acting, singing, composition and story-telling, devised their contributions to the opera. The most exciting thing was that we really felt like we were opening imaginations.

The world premiere of *Arion and the Dolphin* took place on June 14 1994, in the drill shed at HMS Drake. We did five performances, and it was absolutely wonderful. So many people got so much out of it in so many different ways.

I think one of the really important reasons why the opera worked so well was because of dolphins. Quite simple really. When I met Dr Horace Dobbs, I said: "It's absolutely extraordinary the synchronicities that are happening with this project." And he replied: "We don't call it synchronicity any more, we call it dolphinicity."

"Irish dolphin, swift and single
Dwelling off the coast of Dingle,
Choosing now and then to mingle
With the flipperless and glum;
Bringing wonder and elation
To our jaded human nation,
I present you this creation
Of my fingers and my thumb."

Vikram Seth

Vikram (left) and Alec (right) in Dingle ➤

CHAPTER 34 **Confessions of a Spin Doctor**

HARVEY THOMAS, CBE, is an international public relations consultant and former Director of Presentation for the Conservative Party. He became interested in communications when he heard Billy Graham preach at Haringey Arena in 1954, and six years later he joined the Billy Graham Evangelistic Association – for whom he directed many international crusades and conferences around the world. Recruited as a public relations consultant to the Conservative Party in 1978, he soon became a central figure, masterminding conferences, rallies and election events. He has helped Margaret Thatcher, FW de Klerk, George Bush and Helmut Kohl with speeches and personal presentation, and has coached government ministers, public figures and countless business executives on the art of public speaking and how to present themselves on TV and radio.

For anyone who has ever wanted to get a message across, Harvey's talk in March 1995 was illuminating and instructive, peppered with jokes, insights and anecdotes gathered from his 30 years of making an impact.

I was recently told a story about someone who was a brilliant spin doctor:

A customs officer stopped a young boy who was cycling from Mexico into California. Across the handlebars of his bicycle he had two great big sacks. And of course the customs officer threw his arms up – drugs being taken blatantly across the border! "What's in the bags?" "Sand." "Oh yeah?" "Yeah." "All right, let's empty the bags out here onto this platform." So he emptied the bags out and it *was* sand.

The customs officer couldn't see anything wrong, so he let the boy put the sand back in, searched him to see if he was carrying anything illegal, and watched him pedal into California.

This happened every week. Every Monday at noon along came this guy on his bicycle, and the customs officer examined the bags and found nothing wrong. Finally, the customs officer became so frustrated he said: "Look, I know you're putting something across me here. We examine these bags and search you every time you cross, now what are you taking across the border?" And the boy thought for a moment, then said: "New bicycles."

Now that was a brilliant piece of spin doctoring. All the attention was directed onto something else. But how do you put a "spin" on something? Mike Atherton does it with a little bit of earth in his pocket. Max Clifford does it with toes. How do you put an angle on something?

Some of the best examples come in speeches. When Martin Luther King said: "I have a dream, my friends," it was a piece of spin doctoring. It was putting the right words in the right place to the right audience.

But sometimes spin doctoring can go wrong. Do you remember the Labour Party's Sheffield rally in 1992? It went drastically wrong – because of the spin doctors.

They failed in two areas. The first was that they made Neil Kinnock walk through 10,000 screaming people up to the platform, thinking it would be like a hero coming to save Britain. What actually happened was that he was unable to put across his serious political message.

The second mistake was that they forgot to tell him that his microphone was live. And on every television set in the country we heard him say: "We're all right, we're all right, we're all right." It destroyed his reputation of having any gravitas. John Major was very pleased. But it wasn't really Kinnock's fault; that's what spin doctors are supposed to do, to look after things and make sure they communicate thoroughly, effectively.

Another example of spin doctoring gone wrong was when Richard Nixon was advised to go on television and say: "I am not a crook." Well, one American said: "Sincerity is everything. If you can fake that, you've got it made." But, of course, the fact is that Nixon *was* a crook and he looked like one. And everybody could see that. It was bad advice.

Last year I had the enormous privilege of working with FW de Klerk on his election campaign. He was due to have a televised debate with Nelson Mandela, and we discussed it at great length, because it's the spin doctor's job to work out what questions are going to come, how things are going to go and the kind of replies that you need to make. I said: "What I would like you to do when you get onto the stage is to go straight over, shake Mr Mandela's hand and say: 'Well, Nelson, here we are again, we're finally going to debate face-to-face and the world can watch and hear what we have to say.' " FW said: "It isn't me, I can't do it." And that meant I couldn't push it. You need sincerity to be an effective communicator.

So we left it, and halfway through the debate Nelson Mandela said: "And I hold out my hand to the man who's made this possible, FW de Klerk," and it made him look as if he was the man with all the initiative.

But spin doctoring has to be genuine. I have been accused many times of being the person who made Mrs Thatcher lower her voice. Can you see it? "Now Margaret, get it down here, Margaret. Lower, lower, lower, Margaret."

What we actually did was to encourage her to go slower, and to speak more slowly, more distinctly. The effect of that was to lower the tone with it.

Spin has been around a long time. Goebbels said: "Tell a lie often enough and everyone will believe it." That's not true any more. Sooner or later people are going to start asking: "Is that right? Has the Emperor got clothes on?" People are more sophisticated today and it doesn't work.

I was in South Africa about a year ago. I had a fairly rough time there; I'd smashed my leg on a steel girder backstage for a rally we were doing for de Klerk. The good news was that I didn't set off the ten-pound Semtex bomb that was behind the girder when I bashed into it. It would have blown us to pieces, and I've been blown up in my life once already.

I was sitting on the Brighton Grand Hotel bomb. It was six feet under my bed, in the room underneath me; I went up through the roof, down three floors, a girder caught my body, ten tons of rubble fell down on top of me. It took 16 firemen two-and-a-half hours to dig me from under the rubble. I was fine, I didn't break a bone.

All of which has nothing to do with the bomb in South Africa. I'll get back to the point. You may remember a picture that appeared in all the newspapers a year or so ago of three white men hanging out of a car, one of them begging for his life, and a black man shooting them. The following week I was in Mmbatho, setting up a meeting for FW, and I got lost. I was chatting to people and asking the way, when one of them said: "Hey man, you don't know who we are, do you?" I said: "No." They said: "Do you remember that picture last week of those three white guys hanging out of a car, and a black man standing there with a gun shooting? That's my friend here. He shot 'em." There was no menace in his voice; I had no concerns for my own safety, the threat just wasn't there. You can tell when you've got

genuine communication. So I said: "Why did you do it?" And he replied: "Well, they killed 50 of our people the night before, although that wasn't reported." I told him: "You needed a spin doctor. You needed someone to put the news out for you, because you don't have the expertise to do it."

So what is spin? It comes down to the title of my next book: *If They Haven't Heard It, You Haven't Said It*. Spin is taking the facts and the reality. Spin cannot change the facts, only the way in which they are presented to somebody. It's putting across the emphasis that *you* want, preempting everything else so that the people who receive the message understand what you're saying.

Let me give an example. In the mid Eighties Reagan gave a speech about tax reforms. He had 15 minutes on prime time television. He spent 12 or 13 minutes saying: "My fellow Americans, you've been having a tough time on taxes." And everyone's sitting at home, thinking: "Boy, have we ever." "I want to make that easier for you." "Great." "We've thought of a number of different ways." "Oh good, you've been considering it." By the time he got to the last three minutes everyone was totally convinced that this tax package was going to be absolutely brilliant for them. And only then did he bring in the details. He put three steps together that feature in every kind of effective communication. Who do you want to influence? How do you put them in the right mood? What information do you want to get through?

There are three tools of "spinning" – the secrets behind what we do in this business.

The first is organisation. There is an enormous lack of crisis-preparation in companies in this country. I meet senior managers all the time and no-one is ever prepared for a crisis; no-one is prepared for the difficult moment. If nobody is prepared then when something untoward happens you can't put the aspect on it that you want to communicate to other people. I used to prepare for five speeches every time a politician made one speech. The first plan was for the reaction to what we or they had written for the speech. The second was to react to what they actually said when they stood up and opened their mouths. The third was to be able to deal with what they wished they had said when they realised afterwards what they had actually said. The fourth was to react to what they would be quoted as having said the next day in all the newspapers. And the fifth was what they would claim they had meant when they said something entirely different.

Second thought. Use the press and the media, that's what they're there for. It's a battle of wits. I'm not suggesting anything dishonest or untruthful, merely that we should emphasise the points that we want to put across. The way to use the media is to get ahead of them, which is something we don't see in politics these days because everyone's too busy trying to catch up and to react to something that happened last night.

The third secret is using public events. When I came into politics I changed the way things were presented by teaching people how to speak in public. There was a French politician who said: "Speech was given to man to disguise his thoughts." But the truth is, as Lord Thorneycroft said, that in the end image is what you are.

There are six points I want to cover very briefly that are characteristic, in my mind, of successful spin doctoring.

The first one is, be genuine. It's got to be real. If it isn't real then you will never succeed for very long. You can't fake sincerity. I couldn't persuade FW to shake Mandela's hand because it wasn't him. Genuine simplicity of communication, absolute straight-up integrity and honesty, breaks through and is *the* most effective spin you can have on anything.

Number two. It has to be a presentation, not a show. You can't put on the falsity of a show. If an actor doesn't know his words absolutely perfectly, then he's in trouble. But with spin you don't have to be word-perfect, you just have to be well prepared. Abraham Lincoln said: "I couldn't be two-faced, because if I had two faces I sure wouldn't wear this one." And there's a lot of truth in that. If you're straight up, you can get through it. If you're putting on a performance, you'll never succeed for long.

Thirdly, you have to understand what your message is. Many people don't. This government doesn't know what its message is, and I say that as a Conservative. It's going to have to get it together, and the other parties are going to have to do the same thing; they're going to have to know what their message is.

There was a Baptist preacher who wanted to preach on the evils of gambling, and he decided to go and have a look to see what it was all about. So he went down to the racecourse and watched every race. Each time a Catholic priest came out of the pavilion, went over to one of the horses, made some signs over it, spoke to it and went back to the pavilion again. And every race it was that horse which won! So the Baptist said to himself: "Boy, this isn't gambling, that priest is putting a blessing on those horses." So in the next race the minister put all his Sunday school money on the horse the priest had spoken to. It went out and fell down dead halfway round. The Baptist went round to see the Catholic priest and said: "Father, have you been putting a blessing on some of these horses today?" He said: "Yes I have, my son, why?" He said: "Well, what happened to your blessing on the last race? I lost all my money on that horse." And he said: "Ah, my son, you're not a Catholic, are you?" And he said: "No, I'm a Baptist, why?" And he replied: "Because, my son, if you were a Catholic you would know the difference between a blessing and the last rites."

To be a spin doctor, a communicator, you've got to know what you stand for, in detail, and why it is different from something else.

Fourthly, you have to understand the context. The full situation, the broader picture.

I was in Thailand quite recently, and I went to the canals behind Bangkok. The disgusting condition of those canals has to be seen and smelt to be believed. I was going through the canals on a little boat with a colleague and we saw people using the canal as a toilet, to wash clothes in, to wash themselves in, to get water from to cook with. It was absolutely disgusting. And at the end of a row of wooden huts was a woman sitting with her feet in the water, cleaning her teeth. And my colleague said: "I certainly wish we could teach these people personal hygiene." I nodded my head. "You take that woman, for example. Somebody ought to teach her to clean her teeth up and down."

In the spin doctor business, in the communications business, you have to be able to put things in the context of where they are, to understand the broader picture.

Fifthly, you have to be able to see yourself as other people see you and to be prepared to laugh at yourself. Sometimes that's very difficult. I was in Bolivia a week or so ago and there was a dinner being given. The host thought he would be nice to me and give me a British toast, so everyone took up their glasses and said: "Up your bottom." So what could I say? I took my glass and replied: "Up yours."

And lastly, good spin doctoring, good communications, commercial or otherwise, is nearly always 85 per cent positive, rather than 85 per cent negative. It's going wrong when everybody is criticising everything. Mrs Thatcher taught me a great lesson when we were working on a speech back in 1980. I said: "I don't like that bit." "Don't you, Harvey? What would you put in its place?" "Well..." "Don't waste my time. I've got a country to run. If you've got something better to suggest, fine, let's have it. Otherwise, shut up." Knocking all the time doesn't attract people to you, doesn't attract the attention that you're looking for, doesn't give the image that you want.

So be positive, get the format right, keep it simple, and see yourself as other people see you. Finally, remember motive. Motive is very, very powerful. Motive is what should drive those of us who work in the communications business. And we shouldn't be ashamed of it.

PAUL SMITH Enquiries *Tel* 0171 379 7133.
ERIK REES 55 Whitton Avenue East, Greenford, Middlesex UB6 0QB. *Tel* 0181 902 4183.
VICTORIA THORNTON Architectural Dialogue, West Hill House, 6 Swains Lane, London N6 6QU. *Tel* 0181 341 1371. *A Guide to London's Contemporary Architecture 1994* (Butterworth, £9.95).
IAIN JOHNSTONE *Cannes: The Novel* (Chatto & Windus, £13.95); *Man with No Name: Clint Eastwood* (Plexus, £7.95); *Wimbledon 2000* (Heinemann, £15.99). The film *Fierce Creatures*, co-written with John Cleese, will be out next summer.
ROBERT SWAN The Robert Swan Foundation, 50 Sulivan Road, London SW6 3DX. *Tel* 0171 371 5922; *fax* 0171 371 0496.
MALCOLM POYNTER Studio 65a, Rear of 65 Alvington Crescent, London E8 2NN.
JOHN HEGARTY Bartle Bogle Hegarty, 24 Great Pulteney Street, London W1R 3DB. *Tel* 0171 734 1677.
TOM LLOYD *The 'Nice' Company* (£16.99), *Managing Knowhow* (£9.99), *Entrepreneur!* (£9.99), all Bloomsbury; *The Charity Business* (John Murray, £19.99).
TIM HUNKIN Created *The Secret Life of the Home*, a new gallery at the Science Museum. *Almost Everything There is to Know* (Hamlyn, £7.99). For commissions contact AP Watt, *tel* 0171 405 6774.
SEBASTIAN COE *Running for Fitness*, *The Olympians*, *More than a Game* (out of print but available in libraries).
WENDY COPE *Making Cocoa for Kingsley Amis* (£6.99), *Serious Concerns* (£5.99), *The River Girl* (£3.99), *Twiddling Your Thumbs* (£3.99), *Two Cures for Love* (audiocassette, £7.99), all Faber & Faber.
CHRIS WOODHAMS Greig Middleton, 66 Wilson Street, London EC2A 2BL. *Tel* 0171 392 4000.
JOHN STEPHENSON Jim Henson's Creature Shop, 30 Oval Rd, London NW1 7DR. *Tel* 0171 428 4000.
MARK BOYLE Boyle Family represent themselves in this country and are their own dealers. To make an arrangement to view their work write to: Hillside, Crooms Hill, Greenwich, London SE10 or *tel* 0181 858 4094.

ALAN EREIRA *The Heart of the World* (Jonathan Cape, £6.99). For more information about the Tairona Heritage Trust, please write to Chisholme House, Roberton, Nr Hawick, Rox., Scotland TD9 7PH.
BERNARD INGHAM *Kill the Messenger* (HarperCollins, £7.99).
JONATHON PORRITT *Captain Eco* (£6.99), *Save the Earth* (£12.99), both Dorling Kindersley; *Lifelines: Letters to Change the World* (Red Fox, £3.99).
FRANK DICK *Winning: Motivation for Business, Sport and Life* (Abingdon, £16.99); *Sports Training Principles* (A&C Black, £11.99); *Training Theory, But First, Sprints and Relays, High Jump, Strength Training* (all British Amateur Athletics Board, £5 each).
BRIAN BLESSED *The Dynamite Kid* (£5.99), *The Turquoise Mountain* (£4.99), *Nothing's Impossible* (£5.99), all Simon & Schuster; *Blessed Everest* (Salamander, £16.99).
LIVE WIRES For more information about Live Wires, English National Opera and the Baylis Programme, *tel* 0171 836 0111.
OLIVER POSTGATE AND PETER FIRMIN Six *Ivor the Engine* titles are available from Diamond Books at £1.99 each; six *Clangers* titles are available from Little, Brown at £3.99 and £4.99 each; *The Saga of Noggin the Nog* (Collins, £12.99); *The Very Best of the Clangers* (£9.99), *Pogle's Wood* (£6.99), *Ivor the Engine and the Elephants* (£6.99), all BBC Videos; *Bagpuss* (Pocket Money Videos, £4.99).
DAVID BELLAMY © Botanical Enterprises (Publications) Ltd 1993, 1994. The Conservation Foundation, 1 Kensington Gore, London SW7 2AR.
NIGEL REES *Epitaphs* (£6.99), *Phrases and Sayings* (£20), *The Politically Correct Phrasebook* (£4.99), all Bloomsbury; *The Guinness Dictionary of Jokes* (Guinness, £6.99).
HELEN SHARMAN c/o Fox Ltd, Concorde House, 101 Shepherds Bush Road, London W6 7LP. *Tel* 0171 602 8822; *Seize the Moment* (Victor Gollancz, £4.99).
HELENA KENNEDY *Eve was Framed* (Vintage, £7.99).
ALAN DAVIES *Alan Davies Live at the Lyric* (Polygram Videos, £12.99).

ANDY SHEPPARD Andy Sheppard and Steve Lodder can be heard on CD with Nana Vasconcelos on *Inclassifiable* (Label Bleu). Other Sheppard recordings include *Rhythm Method, Delivery Suite* (Blue Note); *Soft on the Inside, In Co-Motion, Introductions in the Dark* (Antilles); with Carla Bley and Steve Swallow, *Songs with Legs* (Watt/ECM).
DONATIONS would be gratefully accepted by the Cancer Relief Macmillan Fund at Anchor House, 15-19 Britten Street, London SW3 3TZ. *Tel* 0171 351 7811.
DORIS LESSING © Doris Lessing 1995. Extracts from *African Laughter* courtesy of HarperCollins Publishers Ltd (£16.99). A wide range of Doris Lessing's books is available from Flamingo and HarperCollins.
ALEX FYNN *Heroes and Villains* (Penguin, £5.99); *The Secret Life of Football* (Queen Anne Press, £11.95); *Out of Time: Why Football isn't Working* (Pocket Books, £5.99).
TOM WATT *The End* (£9.99), *A Passion for the Game: Real Lives in Football* (£14.99), both Mainstream.
ANDREW SHIELDS *Soccer City* (Mandarin, £5.99); *The Lad Done Bad* (Penguin, £8.99, from May 1996).
BRIAN KEENAN *An Evil Cradling* (Hutchinson, £6.99).
GEOFFREY LAMB The World Bank, New Zealand House, Haymarket, London SW1Y 4TE. *Tel* 0171 930 8511.
ARION AND THE DOLPHIN Information about *Arion and the Dolphin*, Alec Roth and Vikram Seth's opera, is available from Alec on 0171 497 3754.
VIKRAM SETH *A Suitable Boy* (£9.99), *Arion and the Dolphin* (£4.99), *From Heaven Lake* (£6.99), *Beastly Tales* (£4.99) all Orion; *The Golden Gate* (Faber & Faber, £5.99); *The Humble Administrator's Garden* (Carcanet, £6.95).
HARVEY THOMAS *If They Haven't Heard It, You Haven't Said It* (LGC Communications, £12.95).

PAUL SMITH Paul on bike: Harold Smith; photographs in main text courtesy of Paul Smith Ltd; Q&A shots: Michael Fair.
ERIK REES Portrait and handwriting samples courtesy of Erik Rees.
VICTORIA THORNTON Portrait courtesy of Architectural Dialogue; Sackler Gallery: Dennis Gilbert; Sainsbury Wing courtesy of the Trustees, National Gallery London; Clore Gallery: Victoria Thornton.
IAIN JOHNSTONE Portrait courtesy of *The Sunday Times*; *Casablanca*: Warner Bros (courtesy Kobal).
ROBERT SWAN Pictures courtesy of the Robert Swan Foundation.
ALAN WHERRY Portrait: Brian Aris; "Enthusiastic terrier": Tim Sambrook/RSPCA.
MALCOLM POYNTER Pictures: Roland Kemp, courtesy of Malcolm Poynter.
JOHN HEGARTY Portrait and "Creek" Levis advert courtesy of BBH; Gibbs advert: The Advertising Archive; Heineken advert courtesy of Lowe Howard Spink.
FRED ATKINSON AND BRYAN QUILTER Portraits courtesy of Sir Fred Atkinson and Diana Quilter; cartoon: Henry Martin.
TOM LLOYD Portrait courtesy of Tom Lloyd.
TIM HUNKIN Portrait and illustrations ("Inside a Supermarket" reproduced from *Almost Everything There is to Know*) courtesy of Tim Hunkin.
SEBASTIAN COE Portrait: AllSport/Tony Duffy.
WENDY COPE Portrait: Mark Chichester-Clark, courtesy of Faber & Faber.
CHRIS WOODHAMS Portrait: Glyn Williams.
JOHN STEPHENSON Portrait © Jim Henson Productions Inc; Turtles picture courtesy of STAR TV; Dinosaurs picture: © Disney.
MARK BOYLE Pictures courtesy of Boyle Family.
ALAN EREIRA Portrait: BBC, courtesy of Jonathan Cape; Kogi shots: F. Nock/ The Hutchison Library.
BERNARD INGHAM Portrait courtesy of *The Daily Express*.
JONATHON PORRITT Portrait: Philip Carr; "Tree of Life": Mark Edwards/ Still Pictures.
FRANK DICK Portrait: Simon Cook; Linford Christie: Empics/Hulton Deutsch.
BRIAN BLESSED Portrait: Andrew Scaysbrook; Bruce Woodcock and 1924 Everest expedition: Hulton Deutsch; Brian on Everest: Steve Bell.
LIVE WIRES Pictures: Marksteen Adamson; music kindly supplied by Sean Gregory.
OLIVER POSTGATE AND PETER FIRMIN Portrait: Ian Coates; Clangers illustrations taken from *Iron Chicken* (Little, Brown at £3.99); all other illustrations courtesy of Peter Firmin.
DAVID BELLAMY Portrait courtesy of The Conservation Foundation; cartoon: Steve Way.
NIGEL REES Pictures courtesy of Nigel Rees.
HELEN SHARMAN Pictures courtesy of Helen Sharman.
HELENA KENNEDY Portrait: Alan Robinson; Scales of Justice: Michael Fair.
ALAN DAVIES AND ANDY SHEPPARD Portraits: Fritz Curzon.
DORIS LESSING Portrait: Ingrid von Kruse; Zimbabwe shot: Tony Stone.
ALEX FYNN, GARY MABBUTT, TOM WATT, PATRICK BARCLAY AND ANDREW SHIELDS Portrait of Patrick courtesy of *The Observer*; of Andrew courtesy of *Time Out*; of Tom: Robin (Foto Plus); of Gary courtesy of Tottenham Hotspur FC; of Alex: Michael Fair. Crowd shot: Jessie Simmons.
BRIAN KEENAN Portrait courtesy of Hutchinson Books.
GEOFFREY LAMB Portrait: Fritz Curzon.
REBECCA MEITLIS, ALEC ROTH AND VIKRAM SETH Portrait of Rebecca: Sue Adler; rehearsal shot: Timothy Craddock; picture of Alec and Vikram: Dr Horace Dobbs; all courtesy of Rebecca Meitlis.
HARVEY THOMAS Pictures courtesy of Harvey Thomas.